Podcasting for Profit

Other Titles of Interest From Maximum Press

Top e-business Books

- *101 Ways to Promote Your Web Site*

- *3G Marketing on the Internet*

- *Protecting Your Great Ideas for FREE*

- *101 Internet Businesses You Can Start From Home*

- and many more...

For more information go to *www.maxpress.com/ibmpromo1*
or e-mail us at *info@maxpress.com*

Podcasting for Profit

*A Proven 7-step Plan to Help Individuals and Businesses
Generate Income Through Audio and Video Podcasting*

Leesa Barnes

MAXIMUM PRESS
605 Silverthorn Road
Gulf Breeze, FL 32561
(850) 934-0819
maxpress.com

Publisher: Jim Hoskins

Production Manager: Gina Cooke

Cover Designer: Lauren Smith

Copyeditor: Mary Miller

Proofreader: Jacquie Wallace

Indexer: Susan Olason

Printer: P.A. Hutchison

This publication is designed to provide accurate and authoritative information in regard to the subject matter covered. It is sold with the understanding that the publisher is not engaged in rendering professional services. If legal, accounting, medical, psychological, or any other expert assistance is required, the services of a competent professional person should be sought. ADAPTED FROM A DECLARATION OF PRINCIPLES OF A JOINT COMMITTEE OF THE AMERICAN BAR ASSOCIATION AND PUBLISHERS.

Recognizing the importance of preserving what has been written, it is a policy of Maximum Press to have books of enduring value published in the United States printed on acid-free paper, and we exert our best efforts to that end.

Library of Congress Cataloging-in-Publication Data

Barnes, Leesa.
  Podcasting for profit / Leesa Barnes.
    p. cm.
  Includes bibliographical references and index.
  ISBN 978-1-931644-57-0 (alk. paper)
  1. Webcasting. 2. Podcasting. 3. Marketing. I. Title.
TK5105.887.B37 2008
006.7'876—dc22
                          2007034682

Acknowledgments

I'm grateful to the following people for their unconditional love and support:

- My mother, for being my biggest cheerleader.

- My father, who still doesn't understand what I do, but supports me anyway.

- My sisters Simone and Tiffany, who laughed with me, listened to me, and provided the moral support that only sisters can provide.

- To Marvin, for helping me to stay calm every time my clunky computer decided to quit.

- And to Sean, for being a technical genius and keeping all my business plans a secret.

I'm thankful to those who influenced me to start podcasting in the first place:

- Penny Haynes (*http://www.1stpod.com*), for introducing me to this mad, mad world called podcasting.

- Adam Curry (*http://curry.com*), for helping to start it all.

- Dawn and Drew (*http://dawnanddrew.podshow.com*), the very first podcast I listened to.

- Leo Laporte (*http://www.twit.tv*), for proving that one can take over the digital world with just one podcast.

- Andrew Michael Baron (*http://www.rocketboom.com*), for telling me just to do it.

And to the many people who have taken my podcasting courses, signed up for my ezine list, read my blog, and listen to my podcast. I'm honored that you allowed me to be a part of your podcasting journey.

Disclaimer

The purchase of computer hardware, software, or services is an important and costly business decision. While the author and publisher of this book have made reasonable efforts to ensure the accuracy and timeliness of the information contained herein, the author and publisher assume no liability with respect to loss or damage caused or alleged to be caused by reliance on any information contained herein and disclaim any and all warranties, expressed or implied, as to the accuracy or reliability of said information.

This book is not intended to replace the manufacturer's product documentation or personnel in determining the specifications and capabilities of the products mentioned in this book. The manufacturer's product documentation should always be consulted, as the specifications and capabilities of computer hardware and software products are subject to frequent modification. The reader is solely responsible for the choice of computer hardware and software. All configurations and applications of computer hardware and software should be reviewed with the manufacturer's representatives prior to choosing or using any computer hardware and software.

Trademarks

The words contained in this text which are believed to be trademarked, service marked, or otherwise to hold proprietary rights have been designated as such by use of initial capitalization. No attempt has been made to designate as trademarked or service marked any personal computer words or terms in which proprietary rights might exist. Inclusion, exclusion, or definition of a word or term is not intended to affect, or to express judgment upon, the validity of legal status of any proprietary right which may be claimed for a specific word or term.

Foreword

In my book, *The Business Podcasting Bible*, I made the bold claim that the podcast will be as important to communication as was the printing press. I also claimed that the social revolution brought about by the printing of the Gutenberg Bible (which moved this important piece of media from the hands of the elite to the hands of the people) is a great reminder of the power we now have at our disposal.

Little has changed my mind since then. The industry has advanced as quickly as I had hoped. Reasons why are perhaps a topic for another book.

Nevertheless, the truth remains that the automation of time shifted and portable media changed all the rules. Moreover, when the rules are changed, there is good money to be made. Podcasting is not as much a technology as it is a massive shift in the focus of media's power: You don't have to be "big" to broadcast anymore. You don't have to be attached to anything (antennas, cables, computers, and so forth) to receive your content anymore. You don't need to have an audience in the hundreds of thousands to be profitable anymore. You don't need to have a license anymore. You don't need to make your content fit into traditional formats anymore. The list of changes could take up an entire book.

These changes have resulted in a new relationship with media. The world of "Must See TV" has quickly been replaced with "My Life, My Media, My Choice." That change must be understood and embraced before you read the first chapter of this book.

Again, the automation of time shifted and portable media is the strength of podcasting. Podcasting's relationships with blogs, RSS, Apple, and anything else you might want to associate the concept with are the markings of podcasting right now. There were times not long ago when you couldn't talk of sitcoms without mentioning Lucy or the evening news without discussing Dan Rather. Times have changed, and will continue to do so. However, just as we can't deny the impact of the idiot box in our living rooms, this massive disruptive change brought about by podcasting needs to be examined and understood, before it is taken advantage of.

What you have in this book is the most advanced examination of the money to be made that I've seen yet. It differs considerably from any other book out there, including mine, because it covers many of the options—but wraps them in a shell that most of us can wrap our arms around. This is extremely important.

One popular debate point among podcasters, at the time of this writing, is the ideal ad insertion model. Do we copy what we've seen in radio and television and insert spots of 15/30/60 seconds? Do we go back to the old days and have the host read the commercial—or better yet have the sponsor put its name on the entire event? What about the infomercial or product-insertion formula? Does it work? Is it ethical? These topics are covered, but I'd dare suggest the conversation should, and needs to be, bigger than that.

This book is much bigger than that.

Leesa writes of the indirect, direct, and integrated models of podcast monetization in this book. I first used those terms back in 2005 to direct the dialogue about the opportunities in front of us and couldn't be more thrilled that she's made reference to this term in her tome. Whereas I predict the user-generated content of Amazon Reviews and the like will complain of her lack of focus on the 87 different ways you can insert a 15-second advertisement into your podcast, I'd dare suggest that *such isn't the point.*

As you read this book (possibly multiple times), you'll see that the integrated model of podcast monetization not only offers the most potential for revenue but also piggybacks on the opportunities we already have in front of us.

To put things simply, anyone, anywhere, can now deliver the very media that we once could only receive from the high priests of content distribution. Limiting that power to merely imitate the models they once forced on us makes no sense at all. Once your communication with your audience respects their call of "My Life, My Media, My Choice," you will find that they will, in fact, not only choose you but also pay the premium you are worth for making such a choice.

This book has bigger ideas than anything I've seen to date on this topic. I hope that you will not only embrace these ideas but make them your own as well.

—Paul Colligan
PaulColligan.com

Table of Contents

Part I: Getting Started   1

Chapter 1:
Self-Assessment   3

Chapter 2:
Plan Your Podcast for Profits   22

Chapter 3:
Creating and Launching Your Podcast   56

Chapter 4:
Grow Your Audience
87

Part II: Generating Profit 115

Chapter 5:
Selling Products and Services 117

Chapter 6:
Podcast Consulting and Teaching 140

Chapter 7:
Advertising and Sponsorship   157

Chapter 10:
Measure   224

Chapter 11:
Optimize Your Results   256

Chapter 12:
Outro   267

Introduction

Your "Members Only" Companion Web Site

The world of audio and video podcasting changes every day. That's why there is a companion Web site associated with this book. On this site you will find the latest news, expanded information, and other podcasting resources of interest.

To get into the Web site, go to *podcasting.maxpress.com*.

You will be asked for a password. Type in:

starfish

and you will then be granted access.

Visit the site often and enjoy the updates and resources with our compliments—and thanks again for buying the book. We ask that you not share the user ID and password for this site with anyone else.

"So, how can you earn money through podcasting?"

This is the first question that I'm always asked. Whether I'm presenting in front of a group of business owners or talking to someone over coffee, after I tell the person why podcasting is so great, he or she always wants to know where the money is.

When I launched my first audio podcast called *Cubicle Divas* in October 2005, I didn't think there was any money to be made. *Cubicle Divas* was my passion, my outlet to connect with my clients and to attract prospects. I couldn't get a radio show because I lacked a huge following at that time, so podcasting became my broadcast to the virtual airwaves. I loved conveying my ideas without having anyone edit or censor me. I enjoyed reading the comments that came from listeners who either patted me on the back or told me what needed to be improved.

Imagine my surprise when in January 2006, after podcasting for only four months, I saw money rolling in. There were other benefits as well, but the biggest was seeing my business revenue increase because of my podcast. It wasn't a huge amount of money at first, but just enough to convince me that given the right strategy, I could actually generate revenue and profit from podcasting.

Not only was I making money from podcasting but so too were others. With every podcasting conference and expo I attended, I met more and more podcasters who were no longer podcasting as a hobby but were now podcasting as a business or to help their business. Independent podcasters were now showing skeptics, enthusiasts, and mainstream business people that you really could derive an income from podcasting. In addition, the more I looked the more diversity in successful strategies I saw. It became increasingly clear that there were, in fact, many ways podcasting could generate income or help a business increase revenue. Whether you are an individual with a passion to share with the world or a businessperson looking to increase profits, podcasting can help. The rest of this book will show you how. First, let's pause for some basic training.

What Is Podcasting?

According to Wikipedia.org, a podcast is a digital media file that is distributed by subscription (paid or unpaid) over the Internet using syndication feeds for playback on mobile devices and personal computers.[1] The term *podcast* was first coined by a technology writer named Ben Hammersley who used the term in a February 2004 article in a U.K.-based newspaper called *The Guardian*.[2] Podcast is a hybrid between the "pod" in iPod and the "cast" in broadcast. In just 12 short months, the word podcast went from being just a word in a newspaper article to being selected by the *New Oxford American Dictionary* as the 2005 Word of the Year because of its rising popularity.[3]

Many people have tried to get away from explaining a podcast in these terms because it gives the impression that you can only listen to a podcast with an iPod. Because podcasts can be listened to or viewed on anything that can play audio or video files, many podcasters feel that using the word "pod" in podcast is presenting another hurdle to jump over in its attempt to make podcasting more mainstream. In a keynote address at the 2006 Podcast and New Media Expo, Leo Laporte, who operates one of the biggest podcasting portals on the Internet called *This Week in Tech* (TwiT), suggested that the industry refer to podcasts as **netcasts**.[4]

Although most people are lukewarm to the idea of changing the name, many have chosen other ways to explain what a podcast is without mentioning the connection to iPod. In particular, many people will say that podcasting is:

- An audio blog or an audio newsletter; instead of reading it, you listen to it

- Similar to Internet radio as you can listen or view podcasts online

- It's like TIVO; you can listen or view a podcast whenever you want

- It's similar to a magazine, you subscribe and get new issues (or episodes) when a new one is published.

In many of my presentations, someone will say, "Leesa, this sounds like nothing more than audio or video on a Web site. There's nothing new about that." It's true. Audio or video on a Web site is nothing new. However, what makes podcasting so unique and different is that it's syndicated. Syndicated content appears in media all the time. Everything from television shows to newspaper columns to comic strips are syndicated. The content creator writes the column or draws the comic strip once and through the power of syndication, the content appears hundreds, thousands, even millions of times on various channels and in various media.

Although it's important to understand what podcasting is, it's equally important to understand what podcasting is not. A podcast is not:

- An infomercial. It's not an opportunity to peddle your wares. Take this approach and the only person consuming your podcast will be you.

- A radio or TV program. Although some of the rules that make radio and TV successful also apply to podcasts, you're not bound by them. Podcasts are best used to convey information in small bite-size chunks, rather than the whole bulky chocolate bar. According to many surveys, most people want to consume their audio podcasts in 20 minutes or less, while video podcasts need to be five minutes or under to be watchable.

- A talking-headcast. No one wants to view or listen to a lecture. When consuming a podcast, people are looking for **infotainment**—a combination between information and entertainment. An infotaining podcast is one that's interactive and adds a sprinkling of fun.

- A static medium. In other words, people will least likely be sitting at their computers consuming your podcast. Podcasts are portable, and according to the 2007 survey conducted by Edison Research, 54 percent of podcast consumers listen to podcasts while they're in motion,[5] so keep that in mind when producing your content.

• A scripted, well-greased machine. What make podcasts so appealing are their amateur qualities and appearance of spontaneity. If a podcast looks too scripted and if the characters are unbelievable, no one will consume it. If you even try to pass it off as an amateur production, podcast consumers will see right through it. This was the case with lonelygirl15, a very popular video podcast that saw its popularity and audience spiral downward after it was revealed that the main character, a 16-year-old girl, was actually a 19-year-old actress. Questions about the video's authenticity began after viewers noticed holes in the storyline.[6]

Why Individuals and Businesses Should Care About Podcasting

Time magazine selected *You* as its Person of the Year in 2006.[7] In April 2007, Apple reported selling 100 million units of its popular iPod.[8] **Blogosphere,** the name that describes the collection of personal journal Web pages, doubles in size every 200 days.[9] **Wikipedia,** the online encyclopedia that can be updated by anyone, doubles every 160 days and has over two million entries in a dozen languages.[10] Launched in 2003, MySpace is the fifth-ranked destination on the Internet, which trails Yahoo, MSN, and Google, all launched a few years before MySpace.[11] YouTube, the video file-sharing Web site, was bought by Google in 2006 for $1.65 billion USD and is used by millions of people daily to upload and share videos.[12]

Collaborative tools have changed the way consumers shop, buy, and even complain about a product or service. The marketplace now has more control over what they want to hear and see. Instead of calling an 800 number to ask for a refund, consumers are turning to blogs, podcasts, and wikis to voice their concerns and dissatisfaction with a merchant. Instead of filling out a survey or speaking to a manager at a restaurant about poor service, consumers turn to the Internet, create a quick video or audio file and share their grievances with a mass of thousands quicker than most stores can offer a refund. In their book *Wikinomics*, authors Don Tapscott and Anthony D. Williams describe this phenomenon in one of their chapters. Sony-BMG had installed crippling digital rights software on tons of personal computers. This might have gone unnoticed if it weren't for the actions of one man—Cory Doctorow. Not only is Doctorow a science fiction writer, but he's also:

"A coeditor of Boing Boing: A Directory of Wonderful Things, *one of the most popular and influential organs on the Web. With an audience*

of 750,000 readers daily and growing, Boing Boing's readership now eclipses most mainstream media outlets (the Wall Street Journal *is at 2.5 million and falling), and the self-described 'activist, blogger, public speaker, and technology person' has no qualms about using the well-trafficked Weblog as an outlet to raise hell. Sony's DRM missteps might have been overlooked as a poorly judged technical debacle. But with Doctorow fanning the flames, it burst into a worldwide public relations firestorm that has cost the company dearly."*[13]

The power to make change and start a digital protest is easier than ever with online collaborative tools. From a business standpoint, you can either continue to ignore what your target market is doing online or join them. In their book *Naked Conversations,* Robert Scoble and Shel Israel talk about the power of blogs. Everywhere you see the word "blogs" in the quote below, insert the word "podcast." The authors stress that businesses need to "join the conversation" because:

> *"Blogs build trust. Most companies know the value in that. Blogs also humanize companies, or at least the people who work inside them. Your blog lets potential customers see who the person on the other side of the desk is before they engage you in potential business. The more you talk with someone, the better you understand who he or she is, and you are most prone to conduct transactions with people you know well enough to trust."*[14]

Not only are businesses who join the conversations online positioned to do better, they are also on their way to tapping into profitable markets that other companies ignore. Podcasting allows you to capture an audience that the big players are ignoring. In his book *The Long Tail*, Chris Anderson writes that niche markets are ignored by companies with million-dollar budgets. They ignore these small audiences because to them, they're segmented and, thus, are unprofitable. Instead, they pay for the eyeballs and have the money to target a mass market.[15]

However, many podcasters have filled the hungry appetites of these segmented markets with niche content. With a podcast, you can target the audience that is being ignored and still be profitable or raise your profile to new heights. Imagine finally finding a knitting podcast hosted by a person who gives you advice on which yarn to buy for your next project or a podcast where the topic is all things Marilyn Monroe.[16] On the other hand, a grammar podcast that teaches you how to use the right words in the right context is becoming so popular that the producer of that podcast appeared on the *Oprah Winfrey Show*.[17]

While making money with a podcast is very attractive, what gives podcasting its longevity is that it zeros in on some of humanity's basic needs. In psychologist Abraham Maslow's Hierarchy of Needs, self-actualization is the one thing that many humans rarely achieve. Belonging to a group and feeling that they are connected to others is one thing that humans crave. Podcasting has helped to foster a community that isn't based on your ethnicity, gender, or nationality. This brings to mind the Loyal Order of the Water Buffaloes on the cartoon called *The Flintstones*. Fred Flintstone and his neighbor, Barney Rubble, were members of this blue-collar fraternity. The group was homogenous in its makeup—male, white, and working class—but it was all too easy for Flintstone to have his membership revoked due to his loud mouth.

If the Water Buffaloes launched a podcast to help recruit new members, they would be surprised by the types of people who would show up at their next recruitment drive. It wouldn't just be the citizens of Bedrock, the city where Flintstone and Rubble lived. People would've come from everywhere. It wouldn't just be men. Women would show up for membership as well. The Water Buffaloes would be shocked to see executives wanting to be members along with truck drivers and factory workers. The reality is that the podcast audience is not homogenous. Podcasts are connecting people according to their interests and hobbies, not their gender, race, nationality, or culture. Because podcasts are niche-focused and tap into humanity's basic need of belonging, podcasts are:

- *Intimate.* The Water Buffaloes met in a large auditorium with hundreds of other men. Unless you were the grand Poobah, you were a voice that was lost in the crowd. Podcasting is different. Paul Colligan and Alex Mandossian talk about the role of intimacy in podcasting at length in their book, *The Business Podcasting Bible*.[18] A relationship is created between the person's earbuds and your voice. For just a few minutes each week, you have formed a one-to-one relationship with a customer, prospect, or fan. The relationship you create with that person through your podcast even lasts longer than sex. According to the Kinsey Institute, only 7 percent of married couples in the United States report having sex four times or more a week.[19] Compare this to the number of Americans who report downloading a podcast each week (13 percent)[20] and you can conclude that perhaps podcasting is more important than sex.

- *Inclusive.* To be a member of the Water Buffaloes, you had to be a man. In one episode, Wilma and Betty, the wives of Fred and Barney, disguise themselves as men and attend a Water Buffalo meeting when their quest to change the bylaws to permit women is defeated. With podcasting, it's your interests and hobbies that connect you with a podcast, not your gender. Even if the podcast is targeted to a specific nationality or a specific race, you're still welcomed into this community by the mere fact that you're interested in it. One of my past clients, Barbara Bradbury, a U.K.-based relationship coach who produces a podcast called *Relationship Matters*, was surprised when she looked at her statistics and saw that she had people listening from countries she never knew existed before. You can now belong to a community of podcasters no matter your race, class, gender, sexual orientation, nationality, ethnicity, or language. That no matter how ugly or how bizarre or how odd your interests are, a podcast will help you find a community of others who are just as ugly and as bizarre and as odd as you are and who will embrace you with open arms.

- *Informal.* The Water Buffaloes stood on ceremony. Members had to wear their large Water Buffalo hats when they attended meetings, pay dues, and go through a process to elect new members. Meetings were held monthly and only on that day could the Water Buffaloes discuss specific Water Buffalo matters. Podcasting, on the other hand, fosters a warm, friendly, and relaxed environment. When consuming a podcast, it can feel as if you've entered someone's living room. The conversation is light and casual. In his keynote address at the 2006 Podcast and New Media Expo, Ron Moore, executive producer of *Battlestar Galactica*, spoke about how he uses his podcast to promote his television show. Moore said that while recording his podcast, he grabs a smoke because he's in his living room and no one can hear him anyway.[21] For Moore, a podcast gives him a direct line to the core audience who love the show. In a figurative way, Moore gets to invite them over to his house, where they sit next to him in a chair and listen to him talk for hours. Although there is a good way to produce a podcast so that you can obtain optimal sound and video quality, the format and style of podcasting is casual and doesn't follow prescribed regulations. Quite simply, regulations don't exist.

Is Making Money Evil?

I've attended many podcasting conferences since 2005 and whenever someone mentions "podcasting" and "money" in the same breath, it spawns a heated discussion. One camp, whom I'll call the **moneyists**, want to make money with their podcasts and turn a profit. These people are in the entrepreneurial, small business, and corporate settings where achieving a return on investment is their sole focus. The other camp, whom I'll call the **hobbyists,** believe that podcasts are the Holy Grail of new media and should never be tarnished by money. Hobbyists believe that you should be driven by your passion and not by profits. This may sound familiar as it is the same cry we heard when the World Wide Web was first catching on. Although there is plenty of room for both the moneyists and the hobbyists (as there still is today on the Web), anyone who wishes to make money can do so using the powerful tool of podcasting.

For this book, I conducted more than 100 hours of interviews asking individuals and businesses about their podcast monetization strategies. Although many were eager to talk to me, I was surprised to come across a few who refused my request for an interview. Some feared that their audience would see them as money-grubbing fiends whose only reason for starting a podcast was to siphon them of their hard-earned cash. Others didn't think they were making money because they didn't have advertisements running in their podcasts.

How sad. What's even sadder are the complaints I hear from the hobbyists who are disappointed about not putting out a new episode in weeks because of podfading. The term **podfading** was coined in 2005 by Scott Fletcher who gave up on publishing two of his own podcasts due to fatigue.[22] Podfading is where one will stop producing any new podcast episodes simply because he or she is burnt out. If you look at *Cubicle Divas*, somewhere after my seventh or eighth episode, I stopped publishing my episodes weekly. I grew tired of having to do everything on my own. I not only planned the episodes but I also recorded the interviews, edited the files, mixed in the music, uploaded the podcast to my server, published it to my blog, and then promoted the new episode to my e-mail list.

Although I enjoyed planning the content and recording the interviews for my podcast, I no longer felt any passion about doing the post-production work. I found the editing, mixing, and publishing of my podcast files to be tedious and boring. So, with the extra income coming in, I was able to hire others to do the stuff I no longer liked to do. Furthermore, making money through your podcast is definitely a great motivator and confidence booster. Not only was I seeing an increase in sales for some of my products, but there was also an increase in subscribers to my e-mail list, as well as some money coming in from placing ads in my syndicated feed. All these activities convinced me that I had an audience and knowing that there was someone other than my mother listening helped me to stay committed to publishing on a regular schedule.

Making money from your podcast is also important to helping you understand how many sales you're generating in return for all the money you're spending on developing, creating, and producing a podcast. Doing this will help you to compare your podcasting efforts to other promotional efforts and decide which ones are worth keeping and which ones you should stop doing. In summary, making money from your podcast is not evil, just like making money from a Web site is not evil. In fact, podcasting for profit will help you:

- Achieve financial goals for individuals and businesses

- Delegate the podcasting tasks you no longer want to do

- Stick to a regular schedule and produce excellent content

- See if podcasting might replace other less profitable promotional tools you may currently be using.

Profit Methodology

In their book, authors Colligan and Mandossian point out that podcast monetization falls into two distinct categories: direct and indirect.[23] In the direct model, you derive money directly from your podcast. In the indirect model, you make money because you're saving in other areas. Although the definitions provided by Colligan and Mandossian are good, here's how I'm defining the terms for this book:

- **Direct Method.** The tools you use to monetize your podcast content. You would be paid for playing an audio advertisement, for mentioning a product, for selling your premium content, or by asking your audience for a donation. Although having an audience is a key ingredient to how much you can charge, you're making money from directly selling your content to others or asking others to subsidize the cost of producing your podcast content.

- **Indirect Method.** The opportunities that arise that help you to monetize your podcast skills and expertise. In other words, you make money by being hired to speak or teach others about podcasting. Whether you get a book deal or sign a TV contract, whether you lead a workshop or speak in front of an audience, you are making money indirectly from podcasting simply because your skills and expertise are in hot demand.

Along with these two methods to making money podcasting, I'd like to add one more. The integrated method is one of my favorite methods and I first heard the term while listening to a teleclass conducted by Colligan. He and I chatted at length about this method and I'm finally convinced that it deserves its own category. Colligan calls this **funnelcasting**,[24] while I prefer to call it **breadcrumb podcasting** (see Chapter 5: Selling Products and Services). No matter what it's called, here's how I interpret the third method:

- **Integrated Method.** The techniques used to monetize your audience by turning them into customers. In essence, you use your podcast to generate leads and turn your audience into paying customers. This is especially effective for those who sell products and services and need a way to turn that valuable podcast audience into clients.

In summary, the three methods podcasters are using to make money podcasting are:

- **Direct**—monetizing their podcast content

- **Indirect**—selling their podcasting skills and expertise

- **Integrated**—turning listeners into customers for existing products and services

In this book, you will learn how to use all three of these methods to generate profits through podcasting. You will likely find some of the chapters more applicable than others—and that's a good thing. Some of the strategies will make sense for your situation and you'll choose to implement them right away. However, not every strategy is right for every reader. Don't discard any idea too quickly because this world of new media is a fast-changing one and there are no rules. Keep your mind open when it comes to podcast monetization because you never know where it may lead you.

Each chapter contains case studies of real podcasters who are deriving an income stream from their podcast. Some of the names you might recognize, others you won't. The goal is to provide a wide range of audio and video podcasters, most of which are independently produced. This means that they didn't start with a huge budget or with a huge company financially backing their efforts. Instead, many financed their podcasts using their own cash earned through other ventures.

Figure I.1. Podcasting for profit wheel.

The Seven Steps to Podcasting for Profit

In this book, you are presented with a proven seven-step plan for podcasting profits. This plan embodies the sum total of knowledge and experiences gained by creating my own profitable podcasts and by helping hundreds of other individuals and businesses worldwide profit from their podcasts. I also conducted more than 100 hours of interviews with podcasters who are making five- and six-figure incomes from podcasting alone. Figure I.1 shows you the seven steps to podcasting for profit. Now let's take a quick glance at each step, which will be the basis for the rest of this book:

Step 1: Assess

Not every individual or business should be podcasting and not everyone is ready to podcast for profit. In Chapter 1, you will find a self-assessment that will help you determine whether or not you should be podcasting and whether you're ready to make money podcasting. There are five key areas that you need to consider before you decide whether to take the plunge.

Step 2: Plan

If you're still reading this book after the self-assessment in Step 1, you need to put together a well-considered plan to help guide your efforts. What is your purpose? Who is the intended audience? How should you craft your podcast? Should you do an audio or video podcast? How will you measure success? These are just a few of the questions you must ask during the planning phase. Chapter 2 will help you sort out this and many other things related to your podcasting effort and help you leverage your time instead of wasting it reinventing the wheel.

Step 3: Launch

After assessing your goals and making your plan, the next step is to record, edit, and publish your podcast. Unlike other books on podcasting, you won't find screenshots of software programs taking you step by step through the recording and editing process. Instead, Chapter 3 will give you a nonprofessional's view of the recording and editing techniques that help me get a studio sound without stepping into one. In addition, you'll learn many other things including the differences between using a hosted solution versus an independent one when deciding where to publish your podcast.

Step 4: Grow

No matter what your podcasting goals, the larger your audience the better. In addition, just because you launch your podcast doesn't mean anyone will find it. Chapter 4 gives you tips on how to use both online and off-line promotional tactics to build audience numbers. Not only will you get tips on how to grow your audience but you'll also learn which tools you must use to garner a legion of fans and create a community around your brand.

Step 5: Profit

Chapters 5 to 9 cover the various monetization strategies that many podcasters are using today. None of these is based on theories or "What if's?" Instead, you'll find practical examples of real-life people just like you using a podcast in extraordinary ways to generate a new income stream or enhance an existing business.

Step 6: Measure

The tricky question of how to track your success is addressed in Chapter 10. Although there is no silver bullet, we will explore the best statistics to use when evaluating your success and how to put it all together so you know how to interpret the numbers.

Step 7: Optimize

No matter what level of success you achieve with your first effort, things don't stop there. Your goal should be to constantly evaluate and improve your podcasting effort. When you find that something is working, do more of it. When you find that something is not working, make a change. No one has all the answers, but in this book you have a proven methodology that will lead you to them.

With this introduction, we are now ready to delve into the details of these seven steps. Then you will be on your way to podcasting for profit.

Part I

Getting Started

Even though this is a book about podcasting for profit, jumping right into the money parts of the book is a recipe for failure. Whether you're new to podcasting or have been podcasting for quite some time, before you can make money podcasting, you have to assess your goals, plan the components of your podcast, launch it using the solution that best fits your budget and needs, then grow your audience. These steps allow you to put together a podcast that will help you to become financially successful.

1

Self-Assessment

Although anyone can podcast, not everyone should. Assessing your goals and understanding your own comfort with making money will help you discover what you should work on. In this chapter, you will take a self-assessment to determine whether you should continue reading this book (see Figure 1.1).

The 7 Steps to Podcasting for Profit

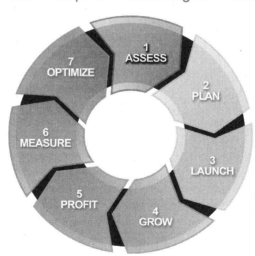

Figure 1.1. Podcasting for profit steps—assess.

Setting Goals

I wanted to play for the national women's basketball team badly. I had that goal from the time I started bouncing a basketball in elementary school. I would dream about traveling all over the world while representing my country. I saw myself hoisting my country's flag over my head as I celebrated winning the gold medal with my team. I envisioned myself on the front cover of every newspaper, frozen in time as I bit down on the gold medal. I visualized myself being interviewed by journalists as I said, "Hi Mom," into the camera in three different languages.

That was my ultimate goal—to play in the Olympics—however, that dream nearly went up in smoke. I was in my senior year of high school and I was a cocky, eager, and young basketball player. Everything was going well for me at that point. I was the captain of my high school basketball team, I was selected the Most Valuable Player by my peers, and I was trying to choose between two basketball scholarships to the United States and my reputation as a fearless player made my opponents afraid to face me. While practicing with an elite basketball team in February 1993, I jumped for a rebound, but came down awkwardly on my left leg. I immediately went crashing to the ground in pain. I spent the rest of the practice on the sideline with an ice pack on my knee.

Two days later, after going to the hospital and visiting a sports doctor, I found out that I had completely ruptured a ligament in my knee that would require surgery. I remember being in tears as I saw not just one, but two goals go up in smoke. Not only was I going to lose out on the scholarships, but my dreams of making the Olympic team would never happen. At 19 years old, I couldn't see beyond tomorrow and I wept thinking about the end of my basketball dreams.

A week after tearing a ligament in my knee, I had surgery. The recovery was painful. I went through six months of rehab to build strength in my knee. The exercises were tedious, the progress was slow, and I was in a horrible mood. I was depressed and angry that I had to do those dumb exercises. I couldn't watch any games on television because doing so made me even more depressed. However, while recuperating during this time, a friend gave me a get-well gift. It was a book, the biography of Michael Jordan to be exact. I eagerly opened the book and started reading. After a few chapters, I reached the part where he suffered through a painful foot injury that got worse with every game. Because he was such a competitor, Jordan was reluctant to miss any games, however, the pain only got worst. Soon, Jordan made the painful decision to have surgery. Although he was upset that he would have to miss most of the season to recover, it was his positive attitude that helped put him back on the court. While going through rehabilitation, he visualized himself taking jump shots, making passes, and eventually winning a championship. He kept those goals in his mind while he went through the painful recovery process.

After reading Jordan's experience, I now approached my rehab differently. When I sat on the stationary bike pedaling, I envisioned myself running back and forth on the court. When I finally put weight on my injured leg for the first time, I looked ahead at the next step, which was dribbling a ball on to the basketball court. I celebrated each time I could lift my leg with weights attached or each time I could jump higher. I started to envision my goal once again of playing on the Olympic team. If Jordan could return to basketball and win all those championships after an injury, then I, Leesa Barnes, could return to basketball and play for the Olympic team.

Eighteen months after my injury, my university coach told me about an open tryout for the Olympic team. Although there were only two spots open and the national team was making stops in about four more cities, I made the 45-minute trip on the subway to the gym where the tryouts were being held. Despite the fact that the odds looked slim that I would make the team, I was still determined to meet one of my goals. Two hours later, one of the coaches thanked me for my time and said I was too small at 5 ft 9 in to play for the national team. As I walked off the basketball court, I smiled the entire way home, knowing I had overcome what was one of the biggest challenges I would face. You see, even though I failed to make the Olympic team, I was happy that I had the chance to try out. The biggest accomplishment was knowing that my injury didn't stop me from pursuing my dream.

Many people fail in their attempts to reach a goal. The founder of Taco Bell, Glen Bell, failed at two restaurant chains before selling Taco Bell to Pepsico in 1978 for millions of dollars. Donald Trump went bankrupt before becoming a billionaire. Oprah failed as a television news anchor before going on to host a show seen by millions worldwide. John F. Kennedy lost the nomination for vice president of the United States in 1956, but went on to become president of the United States four years later. Stories of triumph are evident throughout history from both famous and ordinary people who never lost sight of their goals.

If you're reading this book, your goal is to make money through podcasting as an individual or as a business. The good news is that you don't have to fail at podcasting before you succeed. Using the seven steps to podcasting for profit will ensure that you launch a podcast and make money without making costly and embarrassing mistakes. Yet, some of you may be looking at your own podcast strategy and wondering whether you can make money. Maybe you have spent the past few months planning to launch, but your podcast still isn't published. On the other hand, maybe you haven't released a new episode in several weeks. Alternatively, maybe you're afraid of annoying your audience if you decide to sell any products. Or, maybe you just can't wrap your head around all the techno mumbo jumbo. No matter what your situation is, it's time to do some self-reflection to figure out what's holding you back and how you can overcome this stumbling block to achieve financial success.

How Do You Define Success?

I interviewed quite a number of podcasters both informally and formally. Going to many podcasting conferences helped me to discover the challenges and successes that podcasters have been experiencing. I also interviewed many podcasters for this book. On top of that, I have been a podcaster since 2005, having produced several podcasts for myself, my business, and for others. No matter whom I talk to, each podcaster defines success in different ways. The diversity was fascinating and demonstrated the rich opportunity podcasting presents. Some individual podcasters have achieved a six-figure income because of their podcasts. Others have left full-time jobs to work full-time on their podcasts. Many businesses have been able to increase sales and brand recognition. One podcaster appeared on *Oprah* because of her podcast. You can replicate these achievements for yourself or your business. Whether you're new to podcasting or have been podcasting for a while, the time is right. In order to experience your own success in podcasting, you need to begin by looking in the mirror and doing a self-assessment. First, you need to identify and write down your goals. This is the first step to helping you define your success.

Setting Profitable Goals

Since this is a book about podcasting for profit, then of course, your main goal is to generate income using the direct, indirect, or integrated methods described earlier. But how much? By when? Using which method(s)? Just saying that you want to create a profitable podcast is not enough. Rather than being vague, it is more productive to write down your goals using the S.M.A.R.T. formula,[1] which stands for:

- S—**Specific.** Gives you a sense of purpose. Your goal is specific if you answer yes to the question, "Is it clear and well-defined?"

- M—**Measurable.** Benchmarks to set along the way. Your goal is measurable if you can answer the question, "How much or how many?"

- **A—Agreeable.** Consensus among stakeholders, peers, and anyone who has an interest in the success of the project. Your goal is agreeable if you can say yes to the question, "Is everyone on board?"

- **R—Realistic.** The skills, resources, and time you already possess that enable you to make your objectives a reality. Your goal is realistic if you can answer yes to the question, "Is it doable given what I already have?"

- **T—Time Sensitive.** Gives you a deadline or target date with fixed dates or with a start time and end time. Your goal is time sensitive if you can answer the question, "By when?"

Setting S.M.A.R.T. goals not only helps you to understand where you're going but it also helps you to get others to buy into your ideas. If you are trying to convince your boss or another business unit to join you on your podcasting for profit journey, agreeing to the same goals means that you will have less disagreement when you measure your return on investment (ROI). Let me illustrate this with an example from my days of playing basketball. I remember one game in particular, an exhibition game where my university team flew out to Winnipeg to play the number one ranked women's basketball team in the country. The Winnipeg Wesmen women's basketball team, otherwise known as the Lady Wesmen, was just a few games away from tying the longest winning streak set in the 1970s by the University of California at Los Angeles men's basketball team, which won 88 straight games over a three-year period.[2] When my team walked into the gym, the stands were packed with fans. Cheerleaders lined the sidelines, a makeshift band was playing music, and a few journalists from local papers had their cameras ready to take photos. Every game the Lady Wesmen played between 1992 and 1994, whether it was a regular season or exhibition game, was big news as it meant there was a strong possibility that they could break the 23-year record.

Sadly, my team only added to the Lady Wesmen's winning streak as we were clearly out muscled and ill prepared to play against the top-ranked team in the country. At half time, we were down by 40 points, the worst point spread I experienced in all the basketball games I have ever played. As we huddled with our coach at the bench, we knew we weren't going to win the game. Instead, we set a goal to hold our opponent to just 20 points in the second half. As we walked back out on the court and started the second half, we worked together as a team on just that one goal. When the final buzzer blew, I looked up at the scoreboard to see that we lost the game by a whopping 60 points. Despite the large point spread, my teammates and I celebrated the fact that we accomplished our goal because we held our opponent to just 20 points in the second half. If we had simply said that we wanted to lose gracefully, that would've been a poor goal because all 12 of us on the team would've interpreted this differently. Some would've resorted to scoring more baskets while others would've dragged their feet on the court since we were going to lose anyway. However, by saying that we wanted the other team to score less than 20 points in the second half, this gave us a goal that was:

- **Specific**—We set a goal to play better defense.

- **Measurable**—Twenty was the magic number.

- **Agreeable**—The entire team agreed to focus on this goal.

- **Realistic**—Given that we had the skills and knowledge to play better defense, we knew that we could prevent the other team from scoring more than 20 points.

- **Time Sensitive**—We were limited by the amount of time left in the second half of the game.

Now, let's apply this methodology to podcasting for profit. You want to generate revenue with your podcast. You may be setting this goal for yourself or to get agreement from your team, business unit, or department. No matter whom the goal is for, you need to make it. Using the S.M.A.R.T. methodology, you can set just one goal or many. I would suggest that you set one goal for each of the three methods—direct, indirect, and integrated. Let's just say that you're an individual and you've been podcasting for six months. You decide that you want to make some money with your knitting podcast using the direct method. There is a wrong way, a good way, a better way, and a S.M.A.R.T. way you can write down your goal:

The Wrong Way:

- "I want to make money with my podcast."

- "I want to increase product sales with my podcast."

- "I want to generate sales leads with my podcast."

Although these are specific, they are too general.

A Good Way:

- "I want to make $500 with my podcast."

- "I want to increase product sales by 10 percent using my podcast."

- "I want to generate 50 sales leads with my podcast."

These are good because they are specific and measurable.

A Better Way

- "I want to make $500 in 30 days with my podcast."

- "I want to increase product sales by 10 percent within three months with my podcast."

- "I want to generate 50 sales leads next month with my podcast."

These goals are better because they are specific, measurable, and time sensitive. It still needs just one more adjustment.

The S.M.A.R.T. Way

- "I want to make $500 in 30 days with my podcast using sponsorship, text ads, and tip jars."

- "I want to increase product sales by 10 percent within three months by offering listeners a 20 percent discount coupon."

- "I want to generate 50 sales leads next month with my podcast by offering listeners a free telephone consultation if they register on my Web site."

Bingo! This is a S.M.A.R.T. goal because it's specific, measurable, realistic, and time sensitive. In addition, you probably received agreement from other stakeholders due to how unambiguous the goal sounds.

To craft your own profitable podcasting S.M.A.R.T. goal, you need to ask yourself the following questions:

- How much revenue, how many sales leads, etc. do I want to generate with my podcast? This means identifying a **specific** amount.

- Which method can help me **measure** my goal—direct, indirect, or integrated?

- Which **specific** tool within each method will help me achieve my goal?

- Is this goal **realistic**? Can I generate that much revenue or increase sales by that amount with my podcast given my skills, resources, and time?

- What dates or timeline can I associate with my financial goal? How can I make this more **time-sensitive**?

- How can I ensure that I get **agreement** from those whom this goal will affect?

Take some time right now to write down your S.M.A.R.T. goals. If you're unsure of the direct, indirect, and integrated methods to podcasting for profit, review the Introduction. Then, sit down or call a meeting with your stakeholders and hammer out some podcasting for profit goals. Remember these tips:

- Keep your goal to just one sentence. This helps you and your stakeholders to focus.

- Your goals will change. You will discover a new profiting strategy or your podcast may become wildly successful. Anticipate that something will come along in your podcasting strategy and knock your assumptions out the window. If this happens, modify your goals to reflect these changes.

Podcasting for Profit Self-Assessment Questionnaire

Denise Wakeman and Patsi Krakoff, the two women who form The Blog Squad, put together a list of 20 questions to help people determine whether or not they're ready to add a blog to their marketing mix.[3] Many of the questions in their assessment apply to podcasting, so I've edited a few of their questions and added a few of my own for an assessment called the *Podcasting for Profit Self-Assessment Questionnaire*. These are 20 questions that will help you assess your own readiness to not only improve your podcast but also use the skills you already possess to create a profitable podcast. Let's explore these questions one by one to help you assess whether you or your company should be podcasting.

Your Skills and Expertise

Understanding what you already possess will enable you to create a podcast that highlights your talents.

1. Do you enjoy communicating your ideas and opinions through speaking?

Answer *yes* if...

I typically tell prospects that if you don't like writing, try marketing yourself and your business through speaking. If you find that you shine whenever you speak, meaning that you love speaking in front of groups or you rely on your voice to inspire change, you're well suited for podcasting.

Answer *no* if...

On the other hand, if you panic whenever you're in front of crowds or if you become shy and withdrawn when a microphone is thrust in your face, you may not want to venture into podcasting.

[ ] Yes
[ ] No

2. Do you think you have a pleasing voice?

I question whether you really need a great "radio" voice to be a successful podcaster, so I am thinking you don't. Also, this is a self-assessment, so in my mind what others tell you is not relevant.

Answer *yes* if...

You are comfortable hearing your own voice, chances are others will be too. You don't have to sound like a radio DJ, after all this is a new media. A sincere voice is what is valued in podcasting.

Answer *no* if...

In general, if you are unable to speak clearly due to a heavy accent, a speech impediment, or for whatever reason, that is a problem. If people cannot clearly understand your spoken word, they will not remain listeners. Also, except in special circumstances, you should have conversational knowledge of the language you'll be podcasting in. For example, English is my mother tongue and French is my second language. However, despite how much fun it would be to podcast in French, I have spoken so little of it over the past 10 years, I have forgotten most of what I learned and could only hold a very basic conversation in French. Another thing, if you're not comfortable hearing recordings of your own voice, answer no to this one.

[ ] Yes
[ ] No

3. Do you consider yourself animated and charismatic?

Answer *yes* if...

Some people have a natural way of expressing themselves. If throughout your life, people have told you that you're an entertainer, or if you like being center stage, a video podcast would be right up your alley.

Answer *no* if...

On the other hand, if you're afraid of criticism, don't want to be visible online, or freeze in front of a camera, forget podcasting, especially video podcasting.

[ ] Yes
[ ] No

4. Do you want to raise your profile in your field using a new technique?

Answer *yes* if...

To be recognized for being an expert, you need to do things to be seen and heard. While speaking engagements, media interviews, and networking events are great ways to market yourself, your interests, and your business, a podcast is a tool that will help you to reach more people quicker. Your voice becomes the authority, plus you'll look current since you're using new technology to raise your profile.

Answer *no* if...

Your profile may already be elevated to a rock star status, or you're not interested in raising your own profile, or you're just not ready to use yet another technology tool to promote yourself. If this is you, answer no to this question.

[ ] Yes
[ ] No

5. Do you have an inquisitive mind? Are you naturally curious?

Answer *yes* if...

You enjoy finding out about new techniques, researching new information, and reading books that your friends or colleagues aren't reading—then podcasting is perfect for you. Successful podcasters tend to seek out the angles on a story that others ignore or don't have time to explore. This means they present information to their audience that's different and unique, rather than reiterating what already appears elsewhere.

Answer *no* if...

However, if you're a person who feels you know everything and has a difficult time keeping an open mind when you discover something new, answer no to this question.

[ ] Yes
[ ] No

Your Online Marketing Experience

Your experience marketing online can help you to understand how comfortable you are using new and innovative tools to communicate your message. You don't have to be an Internet marketing expert; however, knowing your own comfort with technology will help you decide how easy it will be for you to embrace podcasting.

    6. Do you listen to podcasts regularly?

Answer *yes* if...

Obvious question, but yes, I had to ask. Before producing their own podcasts, successful podcasters typically found out about podcasting by listening to a few themselves. I subscribe to over 100 podcasts through iTunes and I listen to them on a regular basis. The very first podcast I ever listened to was *Dawn and Drew*, a couple who record their daily lives, as well as Adam Curry's *The Daily Source Code*. Consuming a variety of audio and video podcasts gives you access to a variety of topics, production qualities, and content.

Answer *no* if...

If you're not interested in listening to a few podcasts before producing your own, answer no to this question.

[ ] Yes
[ ] No

    7. Are you reasonably tech-savvy and not intimidated by the Internet?

Answer *yes* if...

You don't have to know how to develop Web pages or type in commands into your computer. If you are comfortable opening up a browser and navigating to various Web pages, answer yes to this question.

Answer *no* if...

You panic every time you sit in front of the computer or claim to be all thumbs when you operate the mouse. If you identify yourself as tech-phobic, answer no to this question.

[ ] Yes
[ ] No

8. Are you frustrated with spam and e-mail filters and want a different way to get your message delivered online to your prospects and clients?

Answer *yes* if...

You want a more direct way to reach new and current customers. With only a small percentage of e-mail messages getting through spam filters, answer yes to this question if you're looking for a new way to deliver your message without using e-mail.

Answer *no* if...

If you're not frustrated with spam or e-mail filters and you're satisfied with your e-mail marketing campaign, answer no to this question.

[ ] Yes
[ ] No
[ ] Not applicable

9. Do you want to cut through all the online marketing hype with an authentic voice?

Answer *yes* if...

We are bombarded with advertising and marketing messages all the time. Also, experts and consumers are questioning the use of pop-ups, long sales letters, and other marketing ploys to grab people's attention. If you want to use an online marketing tool that conveys your voice and style in a way that no press release can, answer yes to this question.

Answer *no* if...

On the other hand, if you feel that your press release or Web site already conveys your authentic voice, or if you strongly believe that long sales letters, pop-ups, and pop-unders are effective marketing tools in your strategy, answer no to this question.

[ ] Yes
[ ] No
[ ] Not applicable

10. Do you want to have more control over your online presence without having to go through a webmaster?

Answer *yes* if...

This is one of the biggest problems that many people have with their Web sites. Whether they need to change a misspelled word or add a sentence, they have to send the changes to their webmaster and wait until he or she has the time to update the Web page. If you or your company is looking for more control over your online presence, answer yes to this question.

Answer *no* if...

You're satisfied with your online presence and don't mind waiting a few days for your webmaster to change items on your Web site. If you like the way things are with your Web site, answer no to this question.

[ ] Yes
[ ] No
[ ] Not applicable

11.   Are you eager to learn and apply new marketing strategies?

Answer *yes* if...

You're tired of using yellow page ads, flyers, business cards, brochures, e-mail newsletters, and a Web site to market yourself or your business—then answer yes to this question.

Answer *no* if...

You feel that you know everything there is to know about online marketing and you're not willing to learn anything new—then answer no.

[ ] Yes
[ ] No
[ ] Not applicable

Your Business

Recognizing what you're in business for helps you to know how a podcast can help you grow. Even if you're podcasting as a hobby, you should assess yourself based on these questions to understand what goals you have for yourself. Here are some questions to help you assess whether your business goals can justify you producing a podcast.

12. Do you want to expand the reach of your business to a national or even a global audience?

Answer *yes* if...

You're looking for an inexpensive way to expand your brand beyond the city you operate your business in—then answer yes.
Answer *no* if...
You don't want to expand your business nationally or even globally.
[ ] Yes
[ ] No
[ ] Not applicable

13. Have you written down non-podcasting goals for your business?

Answer *yes* if...
You have clearly written down your goals and you know exactly what you want to accomplish in this fiscal year. Answer yes if you have goals written down.
Answer *no* if...
You don't have goals written down. If this is the case, you can easily turn this *no* into a *yes* by reviewing the section on establishing S.M.A.R.T. goals.
[ ] Yes
[ ] No

14. Do you want to create a leveraged income stream?

Answer *yes* if...
Leveraged income refers to trading your knowledge for money, instead of trading time for money. If you want to develop an additional income stream that requires little maintenance after the initial setup, answer yes to this question.
Answer *no* if...
You're not looking for a way to stop trading every hour in the day for money. If you don't want an additional income stream, choose no.
[ ] Yes
[ ] No
[ ] Not applicable

15. Are you looking for a hassle-free way to attract new prospects and clients?

Answer *yes* if...
Not many of us enjoy sales, nor do we want to come across as being too pushy. If you want to use a stress-free way to attract new people to your business, answer yes to this question.
Answer *no* if...

You're satisfied with cold calling, attending networking events, and using a used car salesperson technique to finding new prospects. Select no if you don't mind using these techniques.
[ ] Yes
[ ] No
[ ] Not applicable

Your Target Market

Having a handle on what problems your target market faces in their lives, careers, or businesses means that it will be easier for you to develop a podcast to help them solve their pain points. Here are some questions to help you assess if a podcast will help you connect with your target market easier, cheaper, and with less hassle.

16. Do you understand what keeps your target market up at night?

Answer *yes* if...
Knowing what your target market's pain points are can help you create episodes easily. If you know exactly whom you're targeting and what problems they're experiencing in their lives, careers, and businesses, select yes to this question.
Answer *no* if...
You don't have a clue whom you're targeting or what keeps them up at night.
[ ] Yes
[ ] No

17. Do you get feedback from your target market and use it to improve yourself or your business?

Answer *yes* if...
Your target market is in regular communication with you, either by e-mail or by phone, on the ways you can improve your business.
Answer *no* if...
You're not in the habit of accepting feedback from your target market, whether good or bad. Select no for this question if you infrequently get feedback from your target market.
[ ] Yes
[ ] No
[ ] Not applicable

18. Can you easily reach your target market through your ezine, Web site, or other online marketing tools?

Answer *yes* if...

Your target market is using the Internet and you can connect with them easily using a variety of online marketing tools.

Answer *no* if...

You have a difficult time connecting with your audience online. According to many surveys, the majority of podcast consumers are between 25 and 50 years old, with the fastest-growing group being baby boomers.[4] If your target market falls outside of this group, it doesn't mean they're not online, nor does it mean they're unreachable. It may mean that they're not ready for your podcast. Select no if you currently find it difficult to reach them using the Internet.

[ ] Yes
[ ] No

19. Do you enjoy sharing resources with your target market?

Answer *yes* if...

You're used to sending information about a new widget in your e-mail newsletter, or posting tips on your blog, or offering complimentary strategy sessions. Because most podcasts are available at no charge, you can use it as another tool to share resources with your target market.

Answer *no* if...

You're adamant against offering anything for free online. You'll soon become irritated with podcasting as most of them are offered at no cost.

[ ] Yes
[ ] No

Your Attitude Toward Money

Well, this *is* a book about making money, so I had to ask. Many people see money as evil, dirty, and something that should never be talked about. If that's you, pick up a copy of T. Harv Eker's book called *Secrets of the Millionaire Mind: Mastering the Inner Game of Wealth*. In his book, Eker states that our past conditioning, our experiences, and even the way our parents viewed money affects our money blueprint.[5] The good news is that with the right training, your money blueprint can change so you can start thinking rich. Take a moment to answer the final question in this self-assessment.

20. Are you ready to turn your passion or hobby into podcasting profits?

Answer *yes* if...

You're ready to learn how to launch a profitable podcast. If you want to make money podcasting, say yes to this question.

Answer *no* if...

You believe that podcasting and money should never be said in the same breath, put this book down. You first need to change your money blueprint, so get Harv's book instead. If you don't want to make money podcasting, select no to this question.

[ ] Yes

[ ] No

Evaluating Your Answers

The more often you answered yes to the questions in the *Podcasting for Profit Self-Assessment Questionnaire*, the better equipped you will be at becoming a successful podcaster. Let's look at each in more detail so you can understand which areas you need to focus on as you continue moving forward.

Scoring Key

Give yourself one point for *yes* and zero for all other answers. Add these up to find out what type of star you receive.

15 to 20 (Podcasting for Profit Gold Star)—You're on your way to becoming a profitable podcaster. You have the tools, the content, and the attitude to meet your podcasting for profit goals.

9 to 14 (Podcasting for Profit Silver Star)—You're close to becoming a profitable podcaster. You'll need to brush up on a few areas, however, you have some of the basics and after you read this book, you will achieve your podcasting for profit goals.

8 or less (Podcasting for Profit Bronze Star)—You've got some things to work on, but hey, that's why you're reading this book, right? You'll get all the tools and techniques for producing a profitable podcast that'll bring you fame, money, and the pursuit of happiness (not in that order).

How You Stack Up

Now that you understand how you score overall, let's look at how you can improve in the areas where you didn't score very high. The questions in the *Podcasting for Profit Self-Assessment Questionnaire* are categorized into five key areas. In Table 1.1, circle the numbers you answered with a yes.

- If you circle three or more *yes* answers in any one category, you're strong in this area.

- If you circle two or fewer *yes* answers in any one category, read the suggestions for improving your chances at podcasting.

Even after assessing your skills, your online marketing experience, your business, your target market, and your own attitude toward money, the following chapters will guide you through the steps on how to create a profitable podcast.

Category	Circle the Yes	Ways to Improve
Your Skills and Expertise	1, 2, 3, 4, 5	Your role may be best suited behind the scenes as a producer or limited to being a host.
Your Online Marketing Experience	6, 7, 8, 9, 10, 11	Collaborate with or hire someone who has the technical skills that you lack.
Your Business	12, 13, 14, 15, 16	Spend some time with a business coach, your business partner, your employees, or even your spouse to create goals for your business.
Your Target Market	17, 18, 19	Survey your customers to find out what their pain points are.
Your Attitude Toward Money	20	For this one, if you don't circle it, identify why you're not ready to make money podcasting. Then, write down all the good things that can happen if you launch a profitable podcast.

Table 1.1. Podcasting for Profit Self-Assessment.

Taking Action

In this chapter, you learned how to assess your skills, expertise, online marketing experience, business, target market, and comfort with money to determine if you're ready to podcast for profit. Here are some steps you should complete before going on to the next chapter.

1. Create S.M.A.R.T. goals for your podcast.

2. Complete the self-assessment and see where you stack up.

2

Plan Your Podcast for Profits

Once you define your goals, it's time to plan your next steps. This is the part of a podcast that is often overlooked; however, it's critical to plan in order to achieve success. In this chapter, you will discover the ingredients you need to organize and plan your strategy (see Figure 2.1).

Introduction

In September 2006, I took a road trip to the very first Podcamp held in Boston, Massachusetts. I shared the trip with half the band from Uncle Seth, namely the lead singer, Tara Thompson, and the bassist, Jay Moonah.[1] A drive from Toronto to Boston should take only about 10 hours, depending on how much of a lead foot you have. We left Toronto on Friday afternoon around 3:00 P.M. and drove an hour and a half east to Kingston, then crossed the border into the northern part of New York State. We drove another hour and a half south along the I-81 into Syracuse, New York. Once we hit Syracuse, we were clueless as to where to go next. None of us had a road map. Instead, we were relying on a bulleted list of driving instructions that Jay printed off his computer that very morning. According to the written instructions, we needed to get on the I-90 East and take that another six to seven hours straight into Boston. Yet, the labyrinth of bridges, roads, and exit signs left us very confused. We never found the I-90 and, instead, stayed on the I-81 south.

The 7 Steps to Podcasting for Profit

Figure 2.1. Podcasting for profit steps—plan.

When we hit Binghamton, New York, I had a funny feeling in the pit of my stomach. I could sense that something wasn't right. Since we didn't have a road map, I couldn't confirm that we were going the wrong way, but my intuition was telling me we were. It wasn't until we passed the WELCOME TO PENNSYLVANIA sign that my worst fears were confirmed. We had driven for five hours and were now too far south and too far west of our destination.

We stopped at a gas station in Scranton, Pennsylvania, grabbed a map, plotted our path, and hit the road once more. It was now after midnight and we had been on the road for nine hours. It took another four hours to drive east through Pennsylvania, then Connecticut, and finally into the state of Massachusetts. When we finally reached Boston, it took yet another 45 minutes to find the hotel. Fourteen hours after leaving Toronto, I climbed into my hotel bed, exhausted, tired, and kicking myself over and over for not bringing the $15 road map that was sitting on my bookshelf at my home in Toronto.

There's a saying that I hear a lot of people use: If you fail to plan, you plan to fail. Obviously, this is exactly what happened on my drive to Boston. Because we didn't plot our trip using a trusty road map, we ended up taking the wrong road to the wrong state. This experience reminded me of the value of planning. Seasoned entrepreneurs will tell new entrepreneurs to write a business plan before starting a new business. Professional speakers know the value of crafting their speech days before delivering it in front of a group. Project managers spend weeks understanding the tasks and deadlines on even the shortest projects. Whether you've been podcasting for years or you haven't even released your first episode, planning is the key to creating a profitable podcast.

Often, the hardest part of planning is getting started—so let's just jump into it right now. If you are able, I suggest you open a new word processing document or grab a sheet of paper and I will help guide you through the first pass of your plan in this chapter.

Although each unique situation requires some unique planning elements, we will start with the basics and you can add whatever you see fit to meet your special needs. Start by typing these headings into your document:

- **Topic**—How should you choose one that will keep you interested, but also bring you profits?

- **Competitors**—What other podcasts already exist that are similar to your own?

- **Concept**—The angle, approach, format, frequency, profit strategy, promotion strategy, and so forth of your podcast

- **Name**—What will you call your podcast?

- **Content**—Where will it come from? How will you collect it?

Now let's take a closer look at each section.

Your Podcast Topic

Whether you are podcasting to promote an existing business or as an individual, the topic you choose is important. You may say, "Well I already know my topic" and you may be right. However, keep in mind that for every topic there are endless subtopics and angles you can use to reach and satisfy a specific audience in creative ways. Some subtopics/angles will work better than others will so it's worth some thought. Here is some help in exploring your podcasting topic.

Topics for a Business Podcast

You probably already have at least a general topic in mind for your podcast. For example, if you sell car care products and want to promote that business with a podcast, your topic would be something related to car care. But what exactly? Should you simply tell listeners what's on sale at your business each week? Probably not. That would meet your needs, but not your audience's needs. To refine your topic, you need to think about your intended audience. In fact, your audience *is* your entire focus. In the end, meeting the needs of your audience is the only way to achieve any of your profitable podcasting goals. Be loyal to your audience's needs and they will reward you. So, in our car care example, perhaps you could define your audience as people who like to take good care of their cars. Rather, these people have an emotional attachment to their cars and the way they look. So, here are some topic ideas:

- Car care myths debunked

- 30-second car care tricks

- Time-saving products for car care

- Parking lot survival tips

- Preventing car theft

- Car care products to avoid.

Any of these could be the topic for a niche podcast. Coming up with your podcasting topic is a great opportunity to let your creative juices flow. Here are some questions to help jump-start your thinking about your podcast:

- What is the core competency of your business (valued by your clients)?

  _____

  _____

  _____

- What problem is your company good at solving?

_____

_____

_____

- What are the top three things your customers expect from your business?

_____

_____

_____

- What are the top three interests of your customers related to your business area?

_____

_____

_____

- What does your company have firsthand knowledge about that puts you head and shoulders above the competition?

_____

_____

_____

- What information could you provide that your customers would value and trust coming from you?

_____

_____

_____

Topics for a Non-business Podcast

If you are not a business owner but are looking to profit from your podcast through the direct or indirect methods, what you need to start with is a passion for your topic. And everyone has passions (the more the better). When you have passion and knowledge (or the willingness to become knowledgeable through ongoing research), others with similar interests will be drawn to you like bees to honey.

All the podcasters I interviewed for this book—and those I've met at conferences since 2006—agree that being passionate about your podcast topic is critical. Your passion is what will help you to build your audience and help you continue podcasting over the long haul. You've got to love your topic because there will be some weeks when you don't feel like writing those show notes or cleaning up an audio segment or editing those seven video segments. If you're passionate about your topic, the technical details will only appear as a minor annoyance instead of a full-blown migraine.

During this phase of planning, it's time to be creative. Remember, even if you are already sure about your topic, you still have many different subtopics and angles within that topic area to consider. One way to begin is by asking yourself a series of questions. Now, I'm not talking about packing a bag, leaving your family, and hiking into the woods to reflect in the quiet of nature. Instead, a few questions will reveal your passion so you can launch a podcast with a fixed topic in mind. This reminds me of an advertisement I recently saw in a magazine. It features a celebrity who fills out a form with his answers to a few questions about his childhood ambition, last purchase, favorite movie, among other questions. One question asks who his inspiration is. The celebrity writes in, "My parents." Another asks about his indulgence. "My boat," the celebrity writes. The ad clearly captures the celebrity's passions in life, including the name of his favorite credit card, which is the same card that appears in the ad.

Ask yourself the following questions, and then write down your responses:

• Do people regularly ask you for advice or help with a particular topic?

_____

_____

_____

• What problem are you really good at solving?

_____

_____

_____

- What software, tool, or device do you know how to operate, use, or install with ease?

_____

_____

_____

- What do you have firsthand knowledge of that is of interest to others?

_____

_____

_____

- What firsthand knowledge or information do you have that would appeal to others like you?

_____

_____

_____

- Do you have access to a person, business, natural resource, tourist destination, and so forth that is of interest to others?

_____

_____

_____

- If you were going to listen to a podcast on your topic, how would you want it structured?

_____

_____

_____

These are just some of the questions that can help you refine your podcasting topic. It also helps to discuss your ideas with friends and family. This is what I did in late 2005 when trying to decide my life purpose. At that point in my life, I had been unemployed for about a year and a half. I started a life-coaching business in September 2005 to help women find their mission in life. After three months, I felt unfulfilled and restless. Although I had helped many women in that time frame identify their core strengths, I was confused about my own. It was helpful to talk about the future with my peers, colleagues. and friends. Much soul searching along with their input led me to close my life-coaching business, write a business plan, and open my podcasting consulting business in March 2006. I rediscovered my passion with the help of those in my trusted network. So, your friends and family are another resource that can help you refine your podcasting topic and direction.

Your Topic and Niche Markets

When you are trying to build a profitable podcast, you must remember that your audience is also your market. The bigger your audience, the bigger your market. However, the beauty of the podcasting medium is that you do *not* need a huge mainstream audience to succeed. In fact, most will do much better in "superserving" a small niche audience rather than trying to go head-to-head with CNN, NPR, CBC, or BBC. If you produce quality content and keep your focus on serving the needs of your audience, your audience will grow and you will have profit opportunity.

Darren Rowse, a six-figure blogger who blogs at *problogger.net*, offers a few more insights you should consider. Although he wrote these tips for bloggers, they are extremely relevant to podcasters as well. Rowse advises that bloggers need to ask themselves the following questions about the topic they chose before they even create a blog:[2]

1. **Are you interested in the topic?** Although it might be tempting to start blogs based on what *other* people are interested in or what makes *commercial sense,* there is little logic in starting a blog on a topic that you have no interest in. As a result, it's well worth asking yourself, "Can I see myself on this topic in 12 months' time?" If you can't, I'd suggest finding another topic.

2. **Is the topic popular?** Another crucial ingredient is that people *want* to read information on the topic you're writing on. Of course, keep in mind that you are writing in a medium with a global audience of many millions and, as a result, you don't need a topic that **everyone** is searching for, just one that **some people** are searching for because even if it's something that even a small percentage of people have an active interest in it can be a lucrative area.

3. **Is the topic one that is growing or shrinking?** Obviously, it's great to get on a topic before it becomes big rather than when it's on the decline. This is not easy to do, of course, but predict the next big thing that people will be searching for and you could be onto a winner.

4. **Will you have enough content?** One of the key features of successful blogs is the ability to continue to come up with fresh content on their topic for long periods of time. Conversely, one of the things that kills many blogs is that their authors run out of things to say. Answering the question regarding whether there is enough content can be done on two levels:

   – Do you have enough content within you as an author?

   – Do you have access to enough other sources of content and inspiration?

In the end, Rowse advises you to choose a niche audience or market:

> *"While it'd be great to find a topic that you're passionate about that just happens to have massive demand and no competition— the reality is that most topics that you come up with will have at least one weakness to them. Don't let this get you down—there comes a time when you just need to make a decision and start blogging. The key is being aware of what the weakness is so that you can work to overcome it."[3]*

Rowse's advice, while directed to bloggers, is pertinent to podcasters as well. I offer Rowse's tips not to discourage you but to help you see the bigger picture. If you can see 12 months from now that you will have the same passion for your topic as you do right now, then you're off to a great start. Just one word of caution: Don't be tempted to choose a topic just because it appears to be financially lucrative. You might want to podcast about the popular Web site Facebook because it's hot right now, however, if you don't like the impersonal nature of online communication tools, chances are that you will abandon your podcast about Facebook. Choosing a topic just because you think it will make you the most money will leave you feeling bored, burnt out, and even angry if the expected financial windfall is relegated to a small trickle. Plus, your audience will notice your lack of interest and slowly you'll lose them one by one.

Another piece of advice is to narrow down your topic as much as you can. Podcasters who are producing profitable podcasts focus on a niche or deliver a topic in a way that would be of interest to their niche. Tim Street, the producer behind *French Maid TV*, takes common problems and uses his French maids to teach viewers a solution. In one such episode, the French maids showed how easy it is to register a domain name through a company. I don't find that content particularly interesting, but Street doesn't care because I'm not his target market. Street clearly understands that men within a certain age range with a particular income will watch *French Maid TV*. This is an example of how to deliver a topic that will attract your target.

On the other hand, a topic such as mortgages is broad. You can create an audio podcast that focuses on mortgages; however, you will find that only a handful of listeners will listen. If you target everyone, you're speaking to no one. If you want to profit from your podcast, you'll need to have an audience listening and interacting with you. Instead of podcasting about mortgages, you can narrow the topic and focus on mortgage advice for first-time buyers. If you target baby boomers, chances are your podcast will struggle for listeners because most baby boomers are looking at purchasing another piece of property, either a cottage or vacation home, or downsizing now that the kids have left home. Instead, you should dole out mortgage advice to first-time homebuyers who have just graduated from college or just got married for the first time.

Planning Your Podcast Episodes

The biggest issue that pops up for new podcasters and for podcasters whose audience isn't growing is, "How can I create episodes my audience will value?"

Many see developing episodes as a daunting task, and it can be. However, planning where you get the content from will help you stay on track.

Where to Find Great Content

The easiest and quickest way to find great content for your podcast is to look on your bookshelf or search through your computer for recorded content. Now, I'm not talking about that Annie Lennox CD or Duran Duran MP3 that you own because these are copyrighted content that can't be redistributed or re-broadcasted without the copyrighter's expressed consent. In addition, you'll probably have to pay a huge fee just to play a 10-second clip in your podcast anyway. Instead, you should get your hands on any recorded content that features information that you or one of your employees delivered. This information should fit the topic of your podcast in order to be useful. In other words, a video recording of Sam's retirement party in the boardroom won't be useful if the topic of your podcast is going to be on negotiating tips.

If you're not already recording what you say and do, you need to start. Repurposing content for multiple uses is what I call **leverage**. When you leverage your time, leverage your content, and leverage your information, you then create leveraged income. Every time you (or someone else involved with your business or podcast) give a speech, presentation, workshop, teleclass, webinar, client session (with permission), and so on, find a way to record it so that you are building a library of content to be leveraged. Then you can use that content to create many weekly podcast episodes.

Here's an example of what I mean by leverage. A one-hour recorded speech by your CEO can be:

- Transcribed and turned into a white paper or compiled into a special report

- Burned to CD or DVD and be used at future speaking engagements to sell at the back of the room

- Sold as a digital download in an area of your Web site that's password protected

- Syndicated as a podcast to lead new prospects to your sales funnel

- Shared on your company intranet with employees who had to miss the quarterly town hall

- Downloaded by your sales representatives so they get up-to-date information on a new product while on the road.

Remember that leveraged content creates leveraged income.

Target a Problem

Very early in my podcasting adventures, I didn't have a plan. Like my road trip to Boston, I went wherever the wind was blowing. It didn't take long for me to run out of ideas. Each week became such a chore as I scrambled to find content to include in my podcast. Popular advice tells us that when creating a product, service, or business, we need to define our target market. However, I find this difficult to do. Saying that I'm targeting women between the ages of 25 and 50 who are working full-time doesn't help me narrow in on the issues that keep them up at night. Women in that age bracket have quite a number of issues that keep them up at night, such as children, careers, money, or even that time of month. Targeting a group of people based on age, income, and other demographics is not the best way to start generating content for your episodes.

Scott Bourne, the cofounder and principle of Podango Productions, spent over 25 years in the radio broadcast field. Radio broadcasters have used typical demographic information to demonstrate to companies that a particular market listened to their station. Today, as Bourne says, the rules are changing:

> *"If I want to reach young adult males, I would typically in the old days use a hard rock station since that used to have a very high young adult male audience. If I wanted to reach females in the middle age range and below, let's say 25 to 54, then I would use soft rock because all the studies show that. Only today, it's much more sophisticated. We no longer rely on simple age brackets and sex to determine who our audience is. For example, if I want to reach unmarried females of childbearing years in urban environments [where do I go]? Understanding who your audience is, where they are, and what they are working for is the key to being successful."*[4]

To be successful at creating a podcast that your target market will consume, you should instead target a problem, then use your podcast to offer solutions. It's easier to come up with episodes when you can identify the problems first. In the marketplace, there are many examples of companies that are growing rapidly because they created a product or service to target a problem rather than a demographic. The iPod is an excellent example of this. In 2001, when the iPod hit the market, it became popular so quickly not because the iPod was targeted to a particular demographic but because it was targeted at a particular problem.

What was the problem the iPod solved? It was twofold:

1. The iPod helped people to leave bulky CDs at home. Music lovers no longer had to lug around miniature suitcases to enjoy their favorite tunes.

2. The iPod helped people take their digital content on the go. Consumers were no longer chained to their computers after digitizing the content from their CDs and DVDs. Audio and video content was now portable.

The results? In 2004, three years after the iPod hit the market, Apple reported selling two million units.[5] Three years later, the number of iPods sold jumped to 100 million units.[6] Using the iPod as an example, what will help you develop episodes effortlessly is not to focus on who you want to target, but what are your target's pain points. In other words, knowing what keeps your target market up at night is the best way to develop episodes that will, in turn, build your audience. You should be able to come up with at least 10 different problems in order to make your podcast a success and then to be able to profit from it.

Mind Map Problems into Episodes

When coming up with episodes, I use a process called mind mapping to help me brainstorm and visualize ideas. I first came across this concept through Ramon Williamson, a business coach, who calls this "clustering." For the purpose of this book, I'll call this process a mind map where you're displaying visually the ideas that are stuck in your head. According to Wikipedia:

> "A **mind map** is a diagram used to represent words, ideas, tasks or other items linked to and arranged in a circular pattern around a central key word or idea. It is used to generate, visualize, structure, and classify ideas, and as an aid in study, organization, problem solving, and decision making."[7]

There are many software programs that help aid in the development of a mind map; however, I typically just use colored markers and a few sheets of blank paper. I start by drawing a circle in the center of a blank page. In the circle, I write one word that is usually the theme or topic of my podcast. Let's

Figure 2.2. Mind map step 1—the topic.

use the example of a university admissions office that wants to use a podcast to help students through the registration and application process.[8] The topic of the podcast is college admissions, so I'll write that word in the circle in the middle of my blank page (see Figure 2.2).

At this point, I now need to create other circles that each contain the problems and issues students face with the registration and application process. Some of those issues include:

- What grade point average do I need?

- What prerequisites do I need to get in?

- Where do I get money to finance my education?

- Is there kosher food on campus?

- Where can I find housing?

- What should I put in my portfolio?

- Who should I ask for reference letters?

- What's Canada like?

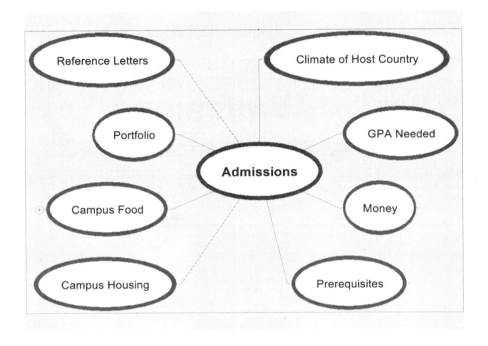

Figure 2.3. Mind map step 2—the problems.

I would now start drawing circles around the main circle using a different color. Choose just one or two words to write down as the problem in each circle. Figure 2.3 shows how the mind map would look with the problems circling the topic.

The last step is to take just one of the problems and write it in a circle in the middle of a new page. Let's work with *campus food* because this is one of the issues that students have when filling out the registration forms during the admissions process. The circles that surround the topic campus food won't be problems at this point. Instead, it will be the answers to those questions, or the solutions you provide when faced with your target's pain point. In this case, we'd look at everything from price, menu options, dietary concerns, and availability. Our mind map would look like the image in Figure 2.4.

Take a look at Figure 2.5 to see how the completed mind map would look if we kept it all on one sheet.

Remember:

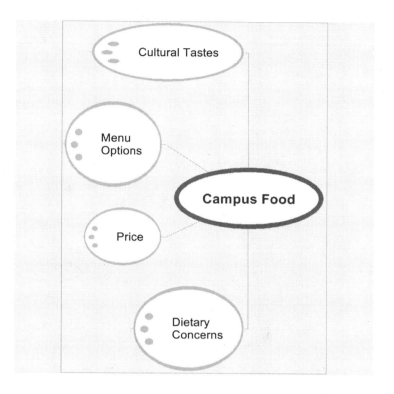

Figure 2.4. Mind map step 3—the solutions.

- The circle in the middle of the figure is the topic of your podcast and you can use it in the name of your podcast. For example, admissions would become *The Five-Minute College Admission* podcast.

- The circles surrounding the one in the middle are the problems or pain points of your target audience. You would include these words when you create episode titles. For example, the topic campus food would become an episode called *What to Eat on Campus*.

- The circles surrounding each problem are the solutions to the problem. These become the content for your episode. If you're interviewing someone in the college admissions office, you would ensure that he or she talks about whether there's kosher meat available on campus, how much

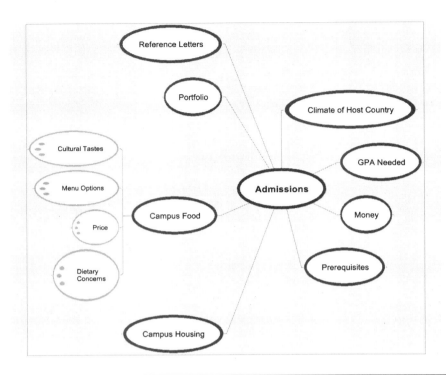

Figure 2.5. Episode mind map.

a student can expect to spend on meals per week, and whether there's a good mix of fast food and healthy meals.

Other Ways to Generate Episode Ideas

Sometimes, despite your best efforts, you can't think of your target audience's pain points. If you're stuck, there are various ways to find out what keeps your target market tossing and turning in bed:

1. **Develop an ask campaign.** There's no better way to know your target market's pain points than just to ask them. You can put together a survey, send an e-mail to your colleagues or list, and ask any of the following questions:

- What are the three biggest issues you're facing right now?

- What are the three skills you want to master in the next six months?

- If you could snap your fingers, what three problems would you hope would go away in your business?

Edit these questions according to the theme of your podcast. I'm just providing these as examples. Whatever you do, have no more than three questions on the survey, name, e-mail, and the previous question. If it's too long, people may become overwhelmed and abandon the survey altogether. The easiest way to track the responses is to use an online service such as *www.surveymonkey.com* to create your survey for free. This will be easier to track and manage than asking people to reply to your e-mail with their answers.

2. **Look at the referral keywords in your Web statistics.** The keywords that people are plugging into search engines give a great clue as to why they went to your Web site in the first place. Go to your Web site statistics and look at the keywords that are pulling people to your Web site. With *Cubicle Divas*, I was surprised to see that people were searching for information on how to sell better. I quickly found an expert to interview on that very topic. If you don't have Web statistics with your hosting package, use Google Analytics by registering for a free account at *http:// analytics.google.com*. Copy and paste the small bit of code into the homepage of your blog or Web site and very soon Google Analytics will display the results.

3. **Listen to what your clients are telling you in meetings.** When I was doing one-to-one coaching sessions, my clients would often ask me questions on how to do something better. Whether I could answer the question right away or not, I would write the question down and write up an article or design a workshop to address that problem. Once I launched my podcast, I would answer that question by interviewing an expert.

4. **Use frequently asked questions from speeches, presentations, and workshops.** If you speak to groups and you speak about the same topic, list the top 10 questions you always get asked. These questions can be viewed as the problem and the answers you provide are the solutions. Those solutions become content for your episodes. The best way to capture these commonly asked questions is to record your speeches. Use a digital recorder so you don't have to fuss with transferring data from a tape.

Also, make sure that it has a connection that plugs into your computer to make it easy to transfer files. The companion Web site lists a number of models you can purchase.

Who's Your Competition?

When writing a business plan, you have to research your competitors to understand how you can be different. In particular, knowing who your competitors are helps you determine how strong your idea is, what's missing, what opportunities exist, and what threats you can anticipate and plan for. Now that you've created goals, the next step in planning a profitable podcast is to discover what everyone else is doing. To be exact, you need to find podcasts that:

- Reflect the type of podcast you want to launch.

- Target the audience you plan to target with your podcast.

- Are using their podcast to make money.

Sounds like a tall order and you may be tempted at this point to skip this step because ignoring the competition is easier than understanding them. This is a ploy that's used in basketball all the time. Before a basketball game started, both teams would warm up on opposite ends of the court. Both teams would run drills and do non-exhaustive activities to loosen the muscles and get the body ready for the game. I often played for coaches who encouraged me to focus on the warm-up and less on the opposing team. That would mean practically ignoring who was on the opposite end of the court. Even if during the warm-up one of the basketballs from the opposing team bounced toward my end of the court, I'd pick it up and throw it back to them without even making any eye contact. It wasn't until the referees blew their whistles and called for the starting lineup that I would take a look at the opposing team.

There are many reasons we ignored the competition during the warm-up. If I peeked over at the opposing basket and saw a girl who's 6 ft. 4 in., I would worry during the warm-up about how I would score just one basket against her. Or, if the team looked focused and had their "game faces" on, I would worry that they would beat the shorts off my team. Ignoring the opposing team meant that instead of worrying that they would beat my team, I instead focused on perfecting my own skills. Although ignoring the competition works while preparing for a basketball game, you can't afford to ignore the competition in podcasting. Whether it's another company or another individual, it pays to understand what each podcaster who targets your audience is doing with his or her podcast. In her book *Devil with a Briefcase: 101 Success Secrets for the Spiritual Entrepreneur*, Jan Janzen says that knowing who your competition is can be a good thing because:

> *"It will help you to foresee trends, great ideas, possibly even enable joint business ventures or allow you to send business to each other if you can't handle the volume and build momentum overall in your industry."*[9]

Learning what competing podcasts are doing increases the likelihood that yours will be different and unique. When you're analyzing the competition, take note of the following:

- What is the name of the podcast? Does it grab you? Or, does it make you yawn?

- How often is it updated? Daily, weekly, monthly?

- How long is each episode? If most of your competitors have really long podcasts, you could be the first to produce a short one.

- How does the podcast bumper sound? Is the intro really long? Does the outro or call to action lead people to their Web site or to buy something? Is the music high energy or serene?

- Who are the hosts? Are they industry experts, hired voice talent, or employees?

- What is the Web site address of the podpage?

- How many episodes have been published to date?

- What is the date of the most recent episode?

Podcasting allows you to try a new format. Just because every podcast that targets your market is 20 minutes in length, is published weekly, and is an interview format, it doesn't mean you have to follow the beaten path. You can be the maverick and produce a podcast that is shorter, edgier, and more frequent. What will help you build subscribers and make money will be how much you stand out, not how much you appear like everyone else.

Noting the features of the podcast is just one aspect of your competitive analysis. You also want to take note of the **podcast equity**, in other words, the value that people put on the podcast. This can be measured based on how much awareness a podcast has gained. A good example of this is the type of coverage Dixie Cups received as a result of sponsoring *Mommycast*, an independent podcast hosted by two moms from the United States. Instead of producing their own podcast, Dixie Cups spent $100,000 sponsoring *Mommycast*. Because this was the first deal of its kind in podcasting, both Dixie Cups and *Mommycast* received a lot of media coverage.[10] There are a number of ways to measure your competitor's podcast equity:

- Plug in the name of the podcast in a search engine and take note of the number of search results that are returned. Also take note of:

    - The number of media mentions.

    - The places where the podcast producer is speaking (or has spoken).

    - The number of other podcasts and blogs that reference your competitor's podcast.

- Use a site such as *www.alexa.com* to see how much the traffic has increased to your competitor's podpage over a 3-, 6-, or 12-month period.

- Visit the podpage and see how many comments are left after each episode.

- If they're using social networking tools such as Facebook, Twitter, or a wiki, check to see how interactive your competitor's audience is.

- Use directories such as Technorati, Digg, YouTube, flickr, and de.li.cio.us to check out who else is capturing information about your competitor's podcast.

- Use podcast directories to search for competitors. Either type a keyword into their search box or just click on a category. You will get a list of podcasts that meet your criteria. One of the more popular podcast directories is iTunes, a program developed by Apple. Other Web-based podcatchers are Podcastalley.com, Podcast.net, Podcastpickle.com, and Odeo.com, just to name a few.

All these components will tell you about your competitor's podcast equity. This should be used to judge how influential your competitor's podcast is in your industry specifically and in podcasting in general. Analyzing your competitor's podcast equity, in addition to the features, helps you to "focus on the big picture, and not the numbers."[11] This 360-degree view helps you to understand how the podcast producer, the audience, the media, fans, and critics judge your competitor's podcast from their own unique perspectives, unburdened by jargon or filters. When this happens, you can use this collective information to design a podcast that meets your goals, offers something unique to your target audience, and helps you to differentiate your podcast from your competition.

Your Podcast Concept

So far we have considered goals, topics, audience, market, and competition. It's time to consider the concept you will use for your podcast. By this I mean the "personality" that makes your podcast unique. In the area of concept, you will have limitless opportunities to be creative. Although you can copy another podcaster's concept and personality, it's better for you to create your own personality, especially if you want to podcast for profit. Audiences are less fickle with podcasts compared with television or radio shows. In other words, podcast audiences are more willing to give a podcast a chance or two before unsubscribing. However, if audiences sense that you're trying to mimic or copy the identity of another podcast, you'll find that they won't stick around for too long. In this section, we will look at the things that define the concept or personality of your podcast.

Audio or Video?

I am often asked, "Should I choose audio or video podcasting to convey my message?" I can't tell you which one is better as both have benefits and drawbacks. However, here are some factors to consider when deciding whether you should go with audio or video.

- **What is your budget?** If you don't have a lot of money, an audio podcast will be cheaper to produce compared with a video podcast.

- **Is your content just talking heads?** If you plan on interviewing people, an audio podcast would be best suited for this. It's not to say that you can't use a video podcast for interviews; however, unless you add a lot of visual elements in postproduction, you'll find that your "talking head" video podcast will drive people away.

- **What is easier for your target audience to consume?** Video files tend to be large compared with audio files. If your audience is still using dial-up, this will be a deciding factor in whether you choose audio over video.

- **Is your information based on tutorials?** If you need to show screenshots to demonstrate your product or service, a video podcast will convey your information better than audio. On the flip side, you could produce an audio podcast, then encourage people to purchase a subscription to your video podcast to see the tutorial step by step (see Chapter 8).

Length

Very early in podcasting, many people were preaching that audio podcasts should be no longer than 20 minutes in length. For video podcasts, the length was much shorter, typically under five minutes. There were countless surveys released that showed that the majority of listeners wanted to consume their podcast in 20 minutes or less, equivalent to the length of time the average person commutes to work one way. However, the length of your podcast isn't determined by you. It's determined by your audience. You can easily guess what your audience wants and you can go ahead and present your desired length to them. Yet, don't be surprised if you get helpful comments from your listeners stating that they want your podcast to be longer or shorter.

I've spoken to many podcasters informally who tell me that they adjusted the length of their podcasts based on what their audience told them. One woman who produces a podcast for work-at-home moms shared with me that 20 minutes isn't enough for her audience. After the kids are sent off to school, work-at-home moms want to learn new skills as they work on their home-based businesses during the day. With broadband access and a bit of free time, work-at-home moms want a show that's almost an hour in length. Another podcaster I spoke to always produces an hour length audio podcast for his audience, mainly marketing professionals. He told me that once he produced a show that was only 30 minutes long and he received many e-mails from cranky listeners complaining that it was too short. Another podcaster shared with me that his audience loved his video podcast, but it needed to be shorter. He cut it down from 10 minutes to 7 minutes. Even my own podcast, *Cubicle Divas*, has gone through a number of changes. I used to do five segments in a 20-minute format. Now, I produce two segments that are 30 minutes in length. Again, this is a direct result of what my listeners wanted.

Frequency

Publishing your podcast on a regular schedule is good in the beginning. Some podcasters publish their podcast at the same time and around the same day each week. Others publish depending on which direction the wind blows, meaning very sporadically and on an unpredictable schedule. My recommendation is to choose a regular schedule in the first six months of podcasting. Sticking to a regular schedule when you first start out or after having re-branded your podcast helps you to build an audience, maintain expectations, and build rapport. After six months, survey your audience to find out what works for them and follow their feedback on what should be improved.

Segments

A segment is an individually recorded and produced section of your podcast. These individual segments are mixed together into the larger podcast. Music is also mixed in to signify the transition to the new segment. Most podcasters will have four segments in their podcast—the introduction, the welcome, the main interview, and then the outro (otherwise known as the extro). If you accept advertising or sponsorship in your podcast, this would count as an additional segment as well. For each of these segments, you may want to identify the timing. For example:

Introduction—00:00:00
Welcome—00:00:03
Sponsor Message—00:05:00
Main Interview—00:05:30
Outro—00:30:00

Although the intro starts at the zero time mark, it's only three seconds long in this podcast. At the three-second mark, the host begins his or her welcome message. This lasts about five minutes, at which time the sponsor's message is played. The sponsor's message lasts 30 seconds, which then transitioned into the main interview. After 25 minutes, the interview ends and then the outro is played. Between the segments, transitional music is played. This lets the audience know that you're moving from one segment to the other. A tip is to play the same clip of music for each segment, but make it different from the others. In other words, when you transition from the welcome to the sponsor's message, the music should be the same week to week. Yet, the music played when you transition between the sponsor's message and the main interview is different from the one you selected as the transition from the welcome to the sponsor's message. Use this template as a guide when planning your podcast, but just like with the format, length, and frequency, be prepared to adjust your segments depending on the feedback from your audience.

Profit and Promotional Strategy

It is vital that you define your profit-making strategy during this early planning phase of your podcast. Even if you don't intend to implement the profit element immediately upon launch of your podcast, you will be better positioned to execute a profit strategy if you have planned for it up front. Part II of this book takes a closer look at various profit strategies. Review Part II of this book as you develop this element of your plan.

Planning how you will promote your podcast needs to be considered early on as well. Take some time to put together a list of ways you will market the launch of your podcast. When you get to Chapter 4, you'll find additional ways to build your audience and develop a community around your podcast.

Naming Your Podcast

Many seem to worry about what to name their podcast and with good reason. Whatever you name your podcast will become part of your brand. It will define who you are or what your business is about. It's important that you spend some time planning the name of your podcast because it's the one thing that will remain constant no matter how many episodes you produce. If you decide on a name now and then try to change it later, you'll run into many problems:

- You'll have to spend time and money updating your logo, Web site address, podpage, and information in the podcast directories.

- You may lose some of your subscribers if they don't recognize that you changed to a new name.

- The buzz you built around your brand will have to be built around another one.

Before you think of that winning name, let's clear up one misconception about naming your podcast. Many get confused when I say that the name of your podcast will never change, but the name of your episodes will. A great example of this is television shows. For example, *Seinfeld*, a popular U.S. sitcom that aired for 10 seasons in the 1990s never changed the name of its show. Even though each episode is different from week to week, for example, week 10 is "The Soup Nazi" or Week 13 is "The Maid," fans knew they were watching *Seinfeld*. If the name of the show changed every week, fans would get confused and wouldn't know if they're watching the same show. Your podcast follows the same rules as a television show. You can change the name of each episode every time you publish a new one; however, the podcast name (similar to a television show name) must remain consistent.

Names that Stand Out

I went to Podcast Alley and pulled a few names from the business category. Here's a list of about 20 podcasts that jumped out at me:

- The Accidental Creative

- The Sales Roundup Podcast

- The Podcast Sisters

- Don the Window Cleaner

- Money Girl's Quick and Dirty Tips for a Richer Life

- Beginning SEO Podcast

- The Naked Career

- Cubicle Divas

- Middle Management Lobotomy Podcast

- Going Linux

- The Disciplined Investor

- Practical Preparedness

- Technology for Business Sake

- The M Show

- Experts on the Issues

- Bad Boss 911

- Thinking for Business Success

- Duct Tape Marketing

- Negotiating Tip of the Week

- Audio of a Freelance Publisher.

Which titles stand out so much that you are just dying to listen or view the podcast? If you sense a bit of anticipation to go to your nearest podcast directory to get a hold of one of the podcasts above, that's the emotion you want to evoke in others. The name of your podcast should make the people so curious that they do everything they can to listen or view your podcast.

This is similar to going into a bookstore. You have time to kill, money in your pocket, and a strong desire to find a gem. You walk through the doors and head to your favorite section: arts and crafts. Your particular interest is in basket weaving, so you peruse the shelves looking at all the books in the genre you're interested in. You pick up one book off the shelf, flip through the pages, then return it. You pass five others books until you spot another one. You slide it off the shelf, flip through, then return it to the shelf. What prompted you to take one book off the shelf and not the other? Probably the color, the size, or the title. Whatever it was, it caught your eye long enough for you to take action. In the podcasting world, size doesn't matter. For many, the title will be the very first thing that will encourage them to subscribe, listen, or ignore you and go to the next podcast.

Tips to Make It Memorable

In a presentation at Podcamp Toronto in February 2007, Bill Sweetman, host of *Marketing Martini* podcast, said that there are a few reasons why choosing a catchy name is very important to the lifeblood of your podcast.[12] In particular, a catchy, memorable podcast name helps you to:

- **Stand out and be remembered.** On November 24, 2004, there were only 484 podcasts listed in Podcast Alley. When I checked on June 10, 2007, there were 32,492 podcasts in Podcast Alley.[13] The competition is rising in the podcasting space, so a well-thought-out name can help you to rise above the pack.

- **Convey your personality.** Sweetman said that he loves marketing, yet he loves martinis even more. Hence, the reason he settled on *Marketing Martini* as his podcast name.

- **Avoid legal hang-ups.** You'll be able to double-check that you're not using a trademarked name. Do a search in Google to see who else is using your name and how they're using it.

For his podcast called *Marketing Martini*, Sweetman said that he selected that name for his podcast because his podcast is "short, concentrated, and a shot of a drink."[14] He then thought of the types of drinks that are concentrated and because he likes martinis, he figured that this would make sense. *Marketing Martini* is no longer than 10 minutes in length and is a weekly business podcast for busy professionals that serves up a condensed shot of practical Internet marketing advice. My own podcast, *Cubicle Divas*, always elicits the question, "Why Cubicle Divas?" I chose that name because I dole out advice to women on how they can launch a business on a shoestring budget. Typically, the women who listen to my podcast are those stuck in a cubicle; however, their quest to be self-employed makes them a shining star. Hence, *Cubicle Divas* has become a clever naming technique as I don't have to say it over and over. When creating a name for your podcast:

1. **Make sure your name is short.** Some directories will cut off your name after a certain number of characters. That means that if someone wants to see the full name of your podcast, they will have to click through to see your podcast's full profile. If someone is browsing, they will skip over your podcast in preference of one that shows the full name without having to go through any extra clicks.

2. **Make sure it passes the ear test.** Say your proposed name to a few people and listen to their reaction. If the person asks you to repeat the name a

few dozen times, you may want to reconsider. *Cubicle Divas* passed the ear test because whenever I say it, the person would repeat it, not for clarification, but because it was clever. My other podcast, *Podonomics*, fails the ear test because people often think I'm saying *Podanomics*, *Podinomics*, or *Podenomics*.

3. **Make sure it passes the "church lady" test.** Sweetman recommends checking your name so that it doesn't include erotic words that could trip up spam filters. For example, when I first launched my blog, it was called *podonomicsexplored.blogspot.com*. Whenever some of my readers received my e-mails through Feedburner telling them my blog had been updated, they told me it was dumped into their spam or bulk folders. Can you see why? If you look closely, you'll see s-e-x in my URL. That word alone triggered the spam filters.

4. **Don't include your name unless you're a celebrity.** Don't waste the precious real estate by adding your name to the podcast title. *Leesa Barnes's Cubicle Divas* makes little sense unless my name brings a lot of weight. At last check, my fan base can be counted on both hands and feet.

5. **Don't use your company name.** As you'll learn later on in this chapter, you'll be more successful in gaining an audience with a name that tells people the solution they will learn. For example, if Apple started a podcast and called it *Apple*, I wouldn't find that interesting because I don't know what part of Apple the *Apple* podcast will cover. However, *Learn to Podcast*, a podcast produced by Apple has more appeal since I know exactly what the podcast will teach me.

Other Factors to Plan For

Now that you've planned your topic, name, episodes, segments, and frequency, it's time to plan how you want others to use your podcast. Crafting up a set of guidelines will help others understand what they're allowed to do with the content they're listening to or viewing. At this stage, you will also want to take the time to plan how you will convince others to join you on your podcasting parade. Understanding how to sell the podcasting concept to those in your company or to your boss is yet another element you need to plan for.

Employee Podcasting Guidelines

Companies and corporations need to be proactive in how they deal with employees who podcast. Whether an employee chooses to podcast about tips and tricks she learns on the job as a sales representative or chooses to podcast about her hobby as a bottle cap collector, having guidelines will ensure that everyone on your staff is following the same rules. If we use blogging as an example, there are countless cases of people being fired or demoted due to opinions published on their blog. Many times, the employee and the company are caught up in litigation that is both lengthy and costly. IBM was one of the first corporations to publish podcasting guidelines for its employees and make it publicly available on the Internet.[15] In summary, the guidelines advise employees to:

1. Keep confidential IBM information confidential.

2. Be mindful of how you say things.

3. Make sure the audio quality is really good.

4. Protect your privacy and those whom you work with.

5. Do not give interviews with reporters or other podcasters who want IBM's official position on an issue.

6. Make sure you don't claim to be the official voice of IBM.

7. Ensure that using a podcast is the best way to communicate with your audience.

The IBM employee podcasting guidelines is an example, but you'll need to create your own based on your business needs. If you have a legal department, draft up your own and have them review it.

Disclaimers, Terms of Use, Copyrights

Planning a list of statements that helps your audience understand how they can use the information they hear in your podcast is important if you want to avoid litigation. For the podcasters who will be podcasting about a hobby, having disclaimers and terms of use may be overkill; however, for those who will be podcasting about creating wealth, spending money, or any health issues will need to plan what their disclaimer or terms of use will say. I'm not a lawyer, so I can't offer legal advice in this section; however, here are a few examples that you can use as an example as you craft your own.

British Airways published a series of sleep advice podcasts that featured sleep expert Dr. Chris Idzikowski. Known as the *Dr. Sleep* podcasts, British Airways provided information to travelers on everything from in-flight sleeping on long flights to how to overcome jet lag. On their podpage, there's a disclaimer that states:

> *"The opinions and ideas presented in these podcasts are those of the author alone and in no way represent the opinion of British Airways Plc. The information contained in the podcasts is not intended to be instructional for medical diagnosis or treatment and users should contact their doctor if they have any healthcare-related questions. You download this file at your own risk and British Airways Plc will not be liable for any loss or damage that you may suffer as a result of or connected with the download or use of this file."*[16]

Scotia Bank publishes a podcast called *The Money Clip*, a weekly podcast giving advice on how people can make the most out of their money. At the bottom of their podpage, you can click a link and review their terms of use. It covers how information is gathered and used from visitors, the accuracy of statements said in the podcast, how trademarks are used, and the risks associated with forward-looking statements.[17]

Other things you should consider:

1. Let visitors know that comments left in writing or played in your podcast belong to the person who left the comment and it doesn't reflect your opinions. This is especially important for business podcasts if you want to protect your brand from being associated with a negative comment left on your podpage by your audience member.

2. Also let visitors know that if they leave comments in writing or by other means, they are allowing you to use it in your podcast without compensation. Again, this is important as it gives your audience a chance to filter their own feedback since it could be played in a future episode.

3. Let your audience know that your podcast is copyrighted and can't be edited to be re-produced elsewhere. I remember a recent sales meeting where the prospect was concerned that someone would take the podcast that features their CEO and create a mash-up by editing and mixing his voice so that his speech sounded distorted. Having your copyright information listed on your podpage can help avoid this mess. For information on how to craft your own copyright, check out the *Podcasting Legal Guide*. As of 2007, two versions exist—the first version, authored by Colette Vogele and Mia Garlick in 2006, is based on United States laws[18] and a similar version, authored by Kathleen Simmons and Andy Kaplan-Myrth, was adapted for Canadian law in 2007.[19] Podcasters who live in other countries can use these guides for general ideas; however, you should seek legal counsel in your country for a more definitive answer.

Selling Podcasting to Your Boss

Every game has a champion, every story has a hero, and every workplace has an enthusiast. You are probably that person, someone who is convinced that podcasting will help your company raise its profile, increase sales, or gain valuable search engine traffic. Your boss, on the other hand, may not be as open to trying something new. He has budgets to maintain, staff to retain, and a boss to keep happy. How then do you convince your own boss to consider a podcast? You could invite a podcasting consultant to come in and convince your boss for you. However, the first step is for you to sell the idea to your boss. Doing so helps you to brush up on your selling and convincing skills. It also helps you to gauge your own excitement about podcasting. Chances are, if you're excited about podcasting, no matter how much you screw up the selling process, it will be your enthusiasm that will win your boss over.

Here are some tips on how to sell podcasting to your boss.

- **Be passionate.** If you approach your boss with a quiet, low key attitude, chances are that your boss will be wondering why you're wasting his or her time. Instead, show your enthusiasm and be excited about podcasting.

- **Be knowledgeable.** You don't have to know the technical pieces. Actually, if you talk about the technical aspects of launching a podcast, you will lose your boss due to boredom. Instead, explain why a podcast is rising in popularity. Grab statistics about the decline in the effectiveness of ads. Then show why a podcast is the next big thing (don't forget to mention the syndication part).

- **Use case studies and show results.** Look for companies like your own that have used podcasting. Then, instead of showing numbers, demonstrate the results. For example, if you're a training company, just showing that your competitor was able to get 5,000 subscribers to its podcast isn't enough. You need to demonstrate that your competitor's podcast helped your competitor save $1 million in training costs. Being able to show how companies similar to your own used a podcast to decrease costs, increase sales, and raise awareness of their brand will become a huge selling point in your presentation.

- **Show the return on investment.** Now it's time for you to identify a problem at your company. What problem will a podcast help your company to solve? Show how much you'll need to spend on launching a podcast, then show how that money spent will help you reach your goal.

- **Be persistent.** Your boss may not say yes after the meeting. If so, you can remind him or her about podcasting without becoming a pest. Send your boss articles from time to time of companies using a podcast. Offer to post a column in your company's newsletter or intranet about podcasting so that others learn about it. Request a budget to attend podcasting conferences so you can network with others and bring valuable information back to the company.

- **Show what others are saying.** Do a search for your company name in a search engine. You should also do a search on the keywords that your company wants to be ranked high for on page one in a search engine. Analyze the results. Take a screen shot of what you see, then show it to your boss. Let him or her know that podcasting can help increase your ranking. It helps if you can compare your rankings to those of your competitors, especially if they're listed higher than your company in search engines.

It's up to you whether you request a formal meeting, complete with presentation slides and a catered lunch, or if you just have an informal chat with your boss over coffee at a local coffee shop. Whichever method you select, follow the previous five steps. Become the champion of podcasting in your company.

Taking Action

Planning your podcast takes a lot of work; however, spending this time to craft your podcast will help you understand where you're going. Remember to follow these steps:

1. Select a topic for your podcast.

2. Plan your episodes using the mind map methodology.

3. Analyze who your competition is, then listen to or view your competitors' podcasts.

4. Develop the concept for your podcast.

5. Decide on what you'll name your podcast.

6. Don't forget to craft up a disclaimer, podcast guidelines, and a short presentation on how you'll sell podcasting to your boss.

3

Creating and Launching Your Podcast

After you have a well-thought-out plan, it's time to implement. Creating and launching your podcast may seem like a daunting task, but it can be easy if you focus less on the technology and more on the technique. In this chapter, you'll learn how to choose the right tools to create and launch your podcast (see Figure 3.1).

The 7 Steps to Podcasting for Profit

Figure 3.1. Podcasting for profit steps—launch.

Introduction

I had a conversation with a colleague of mine who excitedly told me about her new podcast. "Just go to my Web site and listen, Leesa. My podcast sounds great." I did just that. I plugged her Web site address into my browser and it took me to a Web site. I noticed an audio button and pressed *play*. It was a 15-minute recording of her talking about something she was peeved about. There was no intro music, no exit music. At one point, she coughed into the microphone and even answered her door when the doorbell went off. The recording captured all of that.

While the audio continued to play, I scrolled down the page looking for the one thing that would make her audio file a podcast. After scrolling down to the bottom of the page, I was perplexed as I couldn't find what I was looking for. I then scrolled back to the top, frantically searching for that one thing and again, nothing. I then had to break the news to my colleague—her podcast was simply an audio file on a Web site. Although she had placed an audio file on her Web page, it was missing a key ingredient that would make her podcast a true podcast. She was dismayed to hear my news since she paid her webmaster a lot of money to put the audio file on her Web page. Plus, she paid a lot of money to a recording studio to record the audio piece. I too was disappointed because what she asked for was not what she received.

There was one critical ingredient missing that she needed to turn her audio file into a podcast. What is that ingredient? Syndication—otherwise known as RSS. **RSS** is a short way of saying "real simply syndication" and it is usually represented on various Web pages by a small orange icon. Without the syndicated part, your podcast is quite simply just an audio or video file sitting on your Web page. Syndicating your audio or video files helps you to reach a much wider audience and it also allows your audience to consume your podcast without ever going to your Web site.

Syndication has existed in television and on radio for eons. Newspapers and magazines use syndication to publish the same column or comic strip in dozens or even thousands of outlets across the continent. The *New York Post* will publish the same *Dear Abby* column that also appears in the *Los Angeles Times*. People on the East Coast will see the very same episode of *Lost* as those on the West Coast will watch three hours later. Syndicating your podcast can be illustrated by two of my favorite daytime talk show divas: Marilyn Dennis and Oprah Winfrey. You might be wondering what these two women have to do with podcasting. The bigger mystery is who's Marilyn Dennis? Dennis is a Toronto-based celebrity who has a daily talk show on television. Winfrey is a Chicago-based celebrity who has a daily talk show on television.

Although both women share the same profession, what makes them different is that one woman is a household name, while the other is not known to anyone outside of Canada.

In Toronto, I see both Dennis and Winfrey on television. Dennis's show *Cityline* is shown at 10 A.M. on a station called City-TV. Oprah's show is shown at 4 P.M. on CBS. However, because of the nature of my job, I travel a lot. When I leave Toronto and fly to London or New York or San Francisco, I still see Oprah's show. Because of the power of syndication, all I need to do is check local listings to find out when Oprah's show will be on television. When I call my mother in Toronto from whatever hotel I'm staying in, we talk about Oprah's show. No matter where in the world I am, I can chat about the contents of the show, the same exact one that my mother watched two, three, or a dozen time zones away. As of January 2007, *The Oprah Winfrey Show* is seen in 126 markets around the world.[1] Unfortunately, once I cross the border or fly internationally, I leave my beloved Marilyn Dennis behind in Toronto because her show isn't syndicated worldwide.[2] That's the power of syndication. It allows you to reach a broader, global audience without having to extend yourself financially. Not only does syndicating your audio and video content online help you to reach a global market, but it maximizes your time because you use less time to create a bigger impact.

Understanding how to launch your podcast following the tips in this chapter will help you to launch an actual podcast using syndication. Not only do you need to record your content, but you'll need to edit it, mix in music and sound effects, and publish it to a blog or Web page that is RSS enabled. In this chapter, I won't spend time going through the nuts and the bolts on how to record, edit, and publish your podcast. You won't find screen captures of how to edit using a sound editing tool, nor will you find step-by-step tutorials on how to prepare your blog for a podcast. There's a plethora of books penned by other podcasting experts that already cover this area. Those authors have taken the painstaking task of doing all that work for you. You'll find a list of these books on the companion Web site that accompanies this book.

Since there are a lot of great books that show you step by step how to record, edit, mix, and produce your podcast, I will instead focus on helping you choose the right solution that will help you reach your podcasting for profit goals. I will show you the advantages and disadvantages of using certain tools based on my hit, miss, and stick method. In other words, it took me two years—and a lot of money—to figure out how to get a studio-sounding podcast without spending a ton of money. For example, you will learn how to get an RSS feed without doing anything technical. What you will learn in just this chapter will save you a bunch of money and time.

Developing Your Brand

Every company has a brand. Logos, colors, and slogan all tie in to create a company's identity. This process can also be applied to your podcast. Without it, you won't stand out. Podcast directories will ignore you and your audience may avoid your podcast because it may appear as if you're not serious about podcasting. Here are some of the creative aspects that you need to define as part of your brand.

Creative Elements

The design of your podcover and podpage require careful planning. These creative elements help to develop your brand and build your podcast equity.

Podcast Page

With a few exceptions, your podcast should be published on a blog with its own unique URL. The reasons?

- It's easier to find

- It's easier to promote

- It's easier to index by search engines

- It's easier to set up

- It's easier to add audio and video without doing anything technical.

Your podcast page, or **podpage**, becomes part of your branding. You need to think about colors, designs, logos, and your unique podcast message to build your podcast equity. Most people will visit your podpage week after week and never subscribe to your podcast. For this reason, your podpage needs to be easy to navigate and not confuse your audience.

Here are some elements you need to take note of with your podpage (see Figure 3.2 for a visual illustration of the points below):

1. **Offer a player on your podpage.** Some podcasters only offer a download link. This doesn't give your visitor a chance to sample your podcast. Also, due to the size of podcast files (e.g. a 15 minute podcast averages 12 MB in size, while a three minute video podcast averages between 50

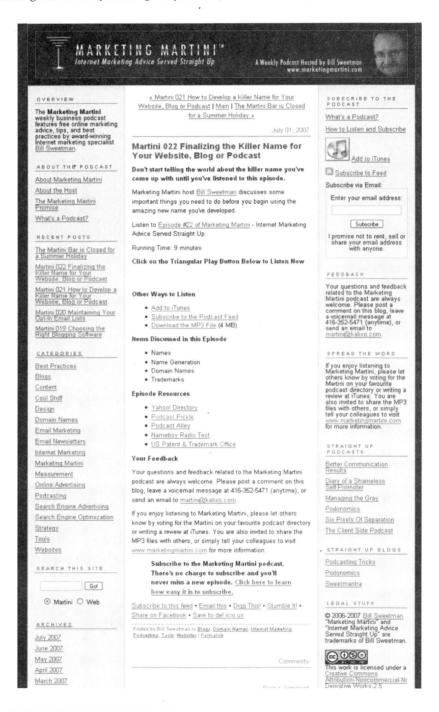

Figure 3.2. Elements of a podpage.

to 100 MB) it may be frustrating to wait and download the entire file, especially if your visitor has a slow connection. Instead, offer a player. This gives people the option to play the audio or video right off your podpage.

2. **Add a page to your blog with step-by-step instructions on how to subscribe.** I typically use iTunes as the player that listeners should download and use to subscribe to my feed. I wrote some instructions, created a separate page, and then linked to that page from the show notes I write for every episode.

3. **Provide only one or two buttons in your sidebar on how to subscribe.** Only provide the ones where it's a simple one click process to subscribe. For me, iTunes and the orange RSS feed button linking to your podcasting feed are the only chicklets I can recommend you list at the top of your sidebar. If you still want to give some love to the other directories you're listed in, list them toward the bottom of your sidebar or put them on a separate page.

4. **Make your podcast visible.** Do not bury your podcast deep on your Web site. Instead, add a button to the front page or a link in the navigation bar that says *podcast.*

5. **Make it easy to access.** In other words, do not require people to register or fill out a lengthy form just to consume your podcast. Make it easy for people to access your podcast, and then use your outro to encourage people to sign up for your ezine, contest, or survey. Build your list after people have had a chance to consume your podcast, not before.

Podcast Cover Art

When you walk into a bookstore, you're greeted with an array of books. You head over to your favorite section, arts and crafts, to find all the books you can on your newest hobby, rock collecting. As you scan the titles on the shelf, you pick up two or three books out of the plethora of titles to skim through on the couch. What attracted you to pick up those titles over the rest that were sitting on the shelf? Most likely the title or the color of the book. Maybe it was the thickness of the book itself or the pictures you saw on the cover. All these elements were carefully planned to make the cover sell itself.

If people judge a book by its cover, people are also judging podcasts by the very same criteria. They will subscribe and choose to consume your podcast if the cover is attractive. Not only does your cover have to be attractive, it also has to speak volumes to the audience you're trying to target. Your podcast cover, or **podcover** for short, needs to have these elements:

1. **Include the name of your podcast.** You'd be surprised how often people forget to do this.

2. **Add graphics.** Use pictures, illustrations, or your logo that convey the theme of your podcast.

3. **Use colors wisely.** Different colors convey different things. For example, if your podcast is related to money, you may want to use the color green. Red, yellow, and orange are associated with food and healthy living, while blue is a more confident color that is useful if you're providing career or sales tips in your podcast.

4. **Save it as a jpg.** iTunes requires that you use this file format for your podcast and many other podcast directories have followed suit. The size of your podcover is important as well. The image should be 300 pixels high by 300 pixels wide.

To get your podcast cover art designed, ask your graphic artist. If you don't have a graphic artist that you usually rely on, use a Web site where you can post details about your project. Web sites such as Elance.com and Guru.com help you to find freelance talent on a shoestring budget. You simply post details about your project, list the maximum amount you're willing to pay, then freelancers bid on your project. You then select a freelancer based on the bid that matches your budget. Figure 3.3 shows you a podcast cover designed for Cubicle Divas.

Unique Podcast Message

When I was a career coach, I encouraged my clients to develop their own memorable pitch. This pitch, otherwise known as the 30-second elevator pitch, helps you to tell others what you do in a pithy, punchy way. The danger with the elevator pitch is that it teaches you to sing your own praises. You drone on and on about how great you are, thereby alienating people with your grandiose self-promotion. For example, when someone asked me what I do, I would launch into my two-minute treatise that went like this:

> *"Hi, my name is Leesa Barnes and I'm a career coach. I inspire women to create the career they deserve. Recently, I helped a*

Figure 3.3. A sample podcast cover.

woman who wanted to apply for a more senior position in her company. After coaching with me, she felt more confident about tackling the interview. I'm happy to say that she landed the job and she's pleased with the additional responsibilities and pay. I'm looking for women who feel stuck in their careers and need someone to help them establish goals for their professional development."

Wow, it's any surprise I didn't clear the room. My elevator pitch sounds like I'm running for office instead of looking for clients. It's all about me, me, and more me. I'm this, I'm successful at that, and I'm looking for this. Who really cares? Too often, I meet podcasters who can't explain what their podcast is all about either. Here's how the conversation typically goes:

Me: "Hi."

Podcaster: "Hi."

Me: "So, what's your podcast?"

Podcaster: "Digital Noise."

Me: "Cool. So, what's it all about?"

Podcaster: "Well, I talk about all the interesting things going on online. You know, like YouTube, SecondLife, MySpace. Then I interview people, like Robert Scoble. You know, that interview with Robert Scoble was so interesting. He talked about *Star Trek* and the impending doom..."

Me: [Yawn and desperately look for someone to save me from the conversation.]

I then walk away still not knowing what that person's podcast is all about. Instead of running around telling all my friends to listen to that person's podcast, I go in search of the buffet table. That's definitely not the reaction you want. Instead, you want people to hear your message in a succinct way and clamor to get your postcard or business card so they can consume your podcast right away.

You need to develop your **unique podcast message (UPM)** that explains what your podcast is all about in 30 seconds or less. Here are a few I really like:

- **Marketing Martini**—Internet Marketing Advice Served Straight Up

- **Cubicle Divas**—Helping Women Manage a Business on a Shoestring Budget

When crafting your UPM, use an approach that I call F.A.M.E. No, this doesn't mean going out and making a song and dance about your podcast. Instead, F.A.M.E. is an acronym that will help you to easily craft and remember what your UPM is. Your UPM should clearly describe who your target market is, what problem your target audience is facing, and what solution you provide through your podcast. Let's work through each one below:

F—Figure Out Your Target Market

It's important that you focus on who needs your podcast. You'll find that if you identify your target market in two or three words, you'll get more interest. I cringe when I hear someone say, "I target everyone." This means the person lacks focus.

For me, I target individuals and businesses, specifically, those who sell a service. Now it's your turn. Take some time to figure out who you're targeting with your podcast. Then write it down below.

My target is _____

A—Acknowledge One Problem They Face

You already went through this exercise in Chapter 2 when you had to target the problem. For me, I target podcasters who have no clue how to make money with their podcast beyond advertising and sponsorship. For you, review the problem you identified in Chapter 2 and write down just one of the pain points below.

Their main problem is _____

M—Make Out Your Role in this Process

What role do you take in this process? What verb clearly describes how you resolve your target market's issues? As a podcaster, I help businesses make money. That's my role, I help. Take a look at the list of verbs below. You'll notice that these verbs I listed below describe you as a guide, a sensei, or a teacher. Remember, your podcast isn't about you; it's about your audience. Since you're using it to educate people about something, the verb you choose needs to reflect your role. Examples are inspire, help, guide, direct, motivate, encourage, assist, support, show, persuade, and promote.

My role is to _____

E—Explain the Solution You Provide

At the end of the day, what solution do you provide through your podcast? Why do you podcast each week or each day? This may be the most difficult part of your UPM. You may have never thought of your podcast as providing a solution to anyone. But you are helping someone, otherwise, why podcast? In my podcast, I provide interviews with people who are making money in clever and unique ways. If you're stuck, review the episode ideas you created in Chapter 2 as a guide, then complete the sentence below:

The solution I provide in my podcast is to _____

Now that you've thought through the pieces, it's time to put your UPM together. The F and A in F.A.M.E. make up the first part of your UPM. This is where you state the problem that your target market is experiencing. You can state this as a question or as a statement. Better yet, if you can find a statistic that shows how many people in your target market are experiencing the same problem, this will go a long way. Numbers make it sound like you're an expert in your field. For example, a professional coach who focuses on bringing balance to the lives of working moms can start her tagline by saying: "Did you know that 45 percent of working women say they're too busy to manage their household?" Or, a social worker can say "Thirty-two percent of teen runaways end up in prostitution."

The M and E in F.A.M.E. make up the second part of your UPM. This is where you state the solution to the problem your target market is facing. You always begin this statement with an "I." The professional coach would end her tagline by saying "In my podcast, I help working moms bring more balance to their lives." The social worker may say "My podcast helps teen runaways develop strategies to return home."

Let's use my information as an example.

[F]igure out your target market. Businesses.
[A]cknowledge one problem that they have. They want to make money
podcasting.
[M]ake out your role in this process (use a verb). Help
[E]xplain the solution you provide to your target market. Make money
beyond ads and sponsorships.

My tagline is: "Think advertising is the only way to make money with your podcast? In my podcast called *Podonomics*, I help businesses find multiple ways to make money with their podcasts beyond the ad."

Now, it's your turn. Put together your UPM based on what you filled out above. Have some fun with it until you get it just right. Then, say it a few times to your colleagues or friends and get their opinions.

"

_____

_____

_____

_____

_____

_____ . "

Podcast Bumper

When you listen to the radio or watch a television show, there's an identifier at the beginning of the program that lets you know what you're about to see or hear. After the show ends, you'll typically see or hear a list of people who worked on the programming, plus information on where to go for further information about the show. In radio, this is called a **bumper.** In podcasting, there are two bumpers—the introduction, otherwise known as the **intro,** and the exit, otherwise known as the **outro** or **extro.** Both are consistent and don't change from episode to episode. You would use the same bumper every week since the name of your podcast and the profitable strategy won't change every time you publish a new episode. Let's take a look at each one in detail.

The Intro

Your sound bite at the beginning of your podcast is used to introduce your podcast to your listeners. For audio podcasts, a voice introduces the podcast and music plays behind it. For video podcasts, most will just show the name of the podcast with music playing in the background, no voice.

Some podcasters make the mistake of making their intros long. It's not unusual to hear intros that are 30 seconds or more that include a mash-up of sounds, voices, and music. Using this approach means that you'll start to annoy your audience. If, at the front of every new episode, I have to be taken through a litany of sounds, after a while I will unsubscribe without even telling the podcast producer why.

Keep it short, silly. Don't drag out the introduction more than you have to. For audio podcasts, keep your intro under 10 seconds. For video podcasts, you have less time to work with, typically five seconds or less.

The Outro

A friend of mine in the radio industry told me that people will remember the last thing they hear or see. After hearing his advice, I started to listen and watch commercials much more critically. I applauded commercials that gave their Web site address when the commercial ended and shook my head at the ones that confused me with their deals and special offerings.

Your outro is your call to action. It's precious real estate at the very end of your podcast where you place that action you want your audience to take after consuming your podcast. Most audio and video podcasts want their audience to visit their Web site and will say or display their URL. For those who are selling ads or sponsorship, they will place the sponsoring company's message at the very end. Whatever you choose, only lead your audience to take one action.

A mistake I see podcasters make is to tell their audience to do two or three different things in their outro. It's not unusual for me to hear the host in an audio podcast encourage me to sign up for their ezine, download their special report, and visit their Web site all in the call to action at the end. Frankly, there's no focus and this works against a profitable podcasting strategy. If you're still struggling with your outro, or if you tell me that you want a portion of your audience to do one thing and the other portion to do another, you have an unfocused podcast. Go back to Chapter 2 and go through each step in planning your podcast.

Your outro not only signals the end of your podcast, but it tells your audience what to do next. They may not take action right away, but after hearing your outro week after week, eventually, they will do what you call them to do. In the sales process, a person needs to hear your message 7 to 10 times before taking action to buy. If you have a consistent message in your outro with one action, your audience won't be confused.

Tone

Being a member of Toastmasters has not only helped me to refine my speaking skills but has taught me the "secrets" that skilled speakers use to craft a memorable speech. What makes a speech memorable are the tools that a speaker uses to convey a message and set the tone. The tone in a speech is critical because the audience experiences the right emotions at the right time. When speaking about the loss of a parent, the speaker wants the audience to feel sadness and will use the right tools to foster this emotion. When speaking about the joy of overcoming a problem, the speaker wants the audience to feel happy.

Less-experienced speakers will only use physical objects and props as their main tools to set the tone. I remember a really bad speech where the speaker spoke about the four keys to being happy. She spoke in a monotone voice, had the most boring expression on her face, and every time she mentioned one of the keys to being happy, she took out her car keys and shook them for emphasis. Experienced speakers on the other hand rely less on physical objects and more on using facial expressions, gestures, and voice inflection to set the tone in their speech. They get louder when they want to emphasize a point, they change their expression to match the mood in their story, and they talk slower if they want to make a point. Martin Luther King Jr.'s *I Have a Dream* speech is hailed as one of the greatest of our time and when you review the video footage, King didn't use any props to inspire an entire generation to seek change. He instead used gestures, facial expressions, and voice inflection to set the tone in his speech.

The tone in your podcast can be conveyed through many things, so you have to choose these wisely. The tone of your podcast needs to match your brand, for example, the music you choose to target teens with your investment podcast will be vastly different from the one you choose if you're targeting baby boomers. Your host or hosts, the music that plays in your podcast bumper, and the way you convey your information all set the tone. Let's take a look at these in more detail.

Selecting a Host or Hosts

Television and radio programs have a main cast of personalities that are consistent from week to week. Typically, these personalities are the hosts and will be responsible for reading a particular segment from week to week. For example, a 6:00 P.M. television news program will always have two anchors who are the hosts each day. Each anchor will reflect the type of demographic that the news program is trying to reach. A male and female anchor in their forties will attract a different type of demographic than an anchor who looks younger.

These techniques also apply to your podcast. The host will be consistent from week to week and will attract a certain demographic. You will need to choose a host who will resonate with the audience you're trying to reach. *Rocketboom* is a great example of this. Although the creator of *Rocketboom* is a man, the host is a woman. The majority of those who view *Rocketboom* on a daily basis are young men who are technically savvy. The host is a young-looking woman who's energetic and pretty. When the first host went off to focus on other projects, it was no accident that her replacement is also a young-looking, energetic, and pretty woman.

The mistake that many new podcasters make is to copy what another podcast is doing. There are many *Rocketboom* knockoffs that hire a pretty woman as their host in hopes of building an audience based on sex appeal. Sure, sex sells, but only to the right audience. A blond bombshell may not work if the majority of your audience will be women between 25 and 50 years old. Just the same, an Oprah-type host may not work for your audience if the majority fall under 25. They don't want to look at or listen to mom; instead they want to look at the girl next door whom they have a chance of dating. With that said, how can you choose the right host? There are several things you can do, such as:

- Watch television shows or listen to radio programs that target your market. They will give you clues as to what appeals to your particular demographic.

- Run a contest and have your list vote on their favorite. In 2004 when Craig Kilborn left *The Late Late Show* on CBS, a handful of replacements hosted the show live for a week and the audience had a chance to give feedback on their favorite host. You can do the same with your list. Launch a podcast, audition potential hosts each episode, then let your audience vote for their favorite.

Another mistake that people make when choosing a host is to hire an actor to play the part. Now, there's nothing wrong with actors. Nothing at all. Yet a podcast should be hosted by someone who's passionate about your topic. While passion can be faked by an actor, he or she will become bored with the topic in the long run. No amount of money can build enthusiasm for a topic that a person has lost interest in. Also, just because someone is the most senior in your company or the most junior on your team or has the most expertise in your industry isn't necessarily a good candidate for being a host. You should choose someone who is charismatic, friendly, and, again, passionate about your topic. The worst thing to do is to drop the hosting duties on someone's lap. Very soon, that person will come to resent the podcast.

Butterball Turkey Talk, a podcast developed by Butterball to give tips on how to prepare and cook a turkey for the holidays, chose its 1-800 operators to host the podcasts.[3] Some of them had worked the phone lines answering customer questions for over 10 years and were a natural choice to host the podcasts. In listening to the podcasts, not only can you hear the passion that the hosts have when it comes to the topic, but they sound natural since they have been talking turkey for a very long time. By not hiring an actor to host its podcast, Butterball avoided the mistake that many corporate podcasts make.

Choosing the Right Music

Everyone has a song that reminds them of their first love, their first dance, or their first layoff. When I was laid off from my job in 2004, I went home and listened to Bon Jovi's "It's My Life." Now, whenever I hear that Bon Jovi song, it reminds me of where I was and what I was doing in the summer of 2004. Music has a profound effect and is a critical ingredient when setting the tone in your podcast. You would typically hear music playing in a podcast in the podcast bumper and when switching between segments. Some podcasters, like Dave Slusher of *Evil Genius Chronicles*, play music in the background throughout the entire podcast.

Although you may love a particular song, your target audience may not. You'll have to pay attention to choose a song that will appeal to your target listeners. Rock music may be fine for one demographic and not the other. Hip-hop music will be loved by some, hated by others. Not only do demographics influence what type of music you'll select to set the tone in your podcast, but so does your topic. If you launch a career podcast giving tips on how to ask for a promotion at work, playing an upbeat song in your podcast bumper will elicit feelings of encouragement while choosing a more somber song will have the opposite effect.

You also have to be aware of copyright laws when it comes to using music. While I love Bon Jovi, I can't use their song in my podcast as I will be violating the record company's copyright. Until the recording industry understands how to treat the playing of songs in podcasts, I would suggest that you don't use your favorite Beatles, Britney Spears or Green Day tune in your podcast. Instead, look for songs produced by independent artists who grant rights for you to use their songs in your podcast for noncommercial purposes. Otherwise known as **podsafe music**, you can play the music in your podcast at no cost as long as you offer your podcast for free. The most popular podsafe music directory is the one managed by *Podshow*.[4] You can listen to music produced by independent artists and use them in your podcast, as long as it's for noncommercial use.

If you decide to sell your podcast content, you can make a deal with the artist or you can use the strategy described in Chapter 8 where you can offer a premium version of your podcast for a fee without the music or ads included. See Chapter 8 for more information on using premium podcasts and paid subscriptions in your monetization strategy.

Recording Audio and Video Content

As mentioned in Chapter 2, content can come from a variety of sources. Workshops, presentations, classes over the phone, webinars, and meetings—all can become great sources of content. You can create audio and video content by repurposing content that you already have sitting in your library (a great value) or create brand-new content from scratch. Either way, you would be wise to ensure the audio and video quality of your podcast is top notch. As more and more content is made available through podcasting, more and more low-quality podcasts will be abandoned for higher-quality competitors. If you want to build an ongoing and profitable podcast, use the highest audio and video production tools within your reach.

That said, there are several options you can use to record your content, everything from the "do everything yourself" approach to hiring a commercial studio. Here are some recording options:

- **Over the phone**—Pick up your phone, dial a number, enter an access code, and talk away. You'll need to use a service that offers recording over the phone. You can record up to two hours and you can use the audio for an audio podcast or to combine with screen captures for a video podcast. One service that offers recording over the telephone is Audio Acrobat. The quality with this approach is low, comparable to the sound of AM radio.

- **Over the Internet**—Plug in a webcam or microphone and you can record your voice or image using a voice over IP service such as Skype and combine it with a recording service such as Pamela or Hot Recorder. The quality with this approach is better than recording over the telephone as it sounds closer to FM radio.

- **In your own studio**—Many podcasters will spend hundreds to thousands of dollars building their own studio at home. To do this, you'll need to purchase microphones, a mixer, a condenser, an amplifier, and a new sound or video card for your computer. For video podcasting, you'll need a lot of what an audio podcaster will buy, but you'll need to include a video camera and lighting, among other things. By selecting the proper equipment, the quality of this approach can be very high, comparable to stepping into a studio. Although your upfront investment is high, you won't have to pay hourly studio fees because you own all your equipment.

- **In a professional studio**—This can be the most expensive option over the long haul and is simply way overpriced for what most podcasters need. Most studios charge hundreds of dollars per hour and you have to book a minimum of two hours. Audio podcasters find that they only need to record 30 minutes of audio at any one time and video podcasters find that they record sporadically, a model that's not suited to the way studios charge. I would recommend that if you choose to use a professional studio, work with one that understands the needs of podcasters. The quality of your recordings will be high, equivalent to what you hear or see on a studio-produced CD or DVD.

Post-Producing Audio and Video Content

The recordings you did are the raw audio or video files. These recordings will include the outtakes, verbal clutter, such as "ums" and "ahs," plus the content you want to keep and turn into a podcast. You will most likely want to mix in music or sound effects to give your podcast more of a professional sound and look. As with a television show, just because the scenes were recorded, doesn't mean you produce it as is. Even reality shows go through a final edit before making it to air and your podcast is no different. Cleaning up your raw files is called **post production** and it will either have to be done by you or you'll need to hire someone to do this for you. Unfortunately, there's no automated process that can do the post production work because it still requires a human being's keen eyes and ears. Detailed post production techniques is a topic worthy of several books and is beyond our scope here, but visit the companion Web site for the book to get help with post production. In the meantime, here are a few things to consider.

Editing

If you plan on editing the work on your own, be prepared to spend some time doing this. If you don't already have a background in audio and video production, your first efforts to edit your raw audio or video files will take a significant investment in time. I promise you that without experience in audio or video production, you will become frustrated with the learning curve. For people with a background in radio or film, this process is easier, but it is still time consuming.

The first time I edited an audio file, I was utterly confused. I didn't know how to increase the sound on my audio file or remove noise. Most times, I would just delete the 15-minute audio recording and start again. Needless to say, my first few episodes weren't my best work. However, as time went on, I became much more proficient in understanding how to edit an audio file. So, if an audio/visual newbie like me can learn how to post-produce an audio file, so can you.

A caution about editing: Bruce Murray, host of Zedcast.com, once said that "A good edit is one that you can't hear."[5] Just because there's a long silence or mumbling from your guest doesn't mean it should be edited out. For example, you may interview a politician for your political podcast. It is election time and you ask the politician a question about taxes. The politician breathes in and out then ponders that question for about five seconds, not saying a word. In post production, you may be tempted to edit those five seconds of silence out. However, the silence sets the mood and gives the impression that maybe the politician is hiding something. Be careful of being too "edit happy," as sometimes the mumbling, stumbling, silence, or other verbal clutter may actually set the tone of the story you're trying to capture.

Also, ambient sounds are often great for a podcast. This includes any background noises such as traffic, chatter from a crowd, or even the wind blowing. Mark Blevis and Andrea Ross host a podcast called *Just One More Book* where they review children's book that you won't typically find in large bookstores. They meet at a local coffee shop and record 45 minutes of their conversations about a book they grabbed from their children's stash of books. If you listen to their podcast, it's not unusual to hear a latte being brewed, the cash register clanging open, or the occasional laughter from other patrons who are sitting close by.[6]

Although many consider podcasts to be the cousin to radio and television, I see podcasts having much more in common with documentary films. According to Wikipedia.org, documentary films are an attempt to document reality in some fashion or another.[7] In particular, documentary films:

- Are narratives from a first- or second-person viewpoint that tell a personal story

- Tend to tell a side of the story that would not otherwise be heard

- Include ambient sounds, or background noises, as part of the story

- Have lower production budgets.

The comparison between documentary films and podcasts is quite striking as most podcasts are narratives that include ambient sound and have low production budgets. That's why podcasts should be loosely edited because ones that sound or look too slick tend to be unbelievable. In 2006, a video podcast named *lonelygirl15* chronicled the life of a 16-year-old American girl. In this video podcast, lonelygirl15 would talk about her life, going to school, and chat about her family and boyfriend. While some questioned how a webcam like the one used by lonelygirl15 could produce such excellent video quality, it was the inconsistencies in her daily life that started to raise questions.[8] By August 2006, lonelygirl15 was outed when an article in the *New York Times* revealed that there was a creative agency behind the development of the series. Although her audience has dropped since it was revealed that lonelygirl15 isn't real, this goes to show you that if you spend too much time editing your podcast, you will produce something that is similar to a Hollywood blockbuster, which in turn will prompt people to avoid your podcast.

Mixing

Being able to insert your intro, outro, music and sound, or visual effects is the process of **mixing**. If you played your audio or video file after the editing process, you'll notice that it starts right where your welcome message starts. That's fine if you're showing it internally to your staff or wanting to show off your masterpiece to a family member. However, if you want to podcast for profit, you'll need to mix in the intro. That way, your audience can be reminded what they're consuming and what is the title of the episode.

You may also want to insert an interview you conducted with someone. Or, you may want to add transitions in-between segments. Or, you may want to play a song from your favorite band. Whatever your needs, knowing how to mix different tracks together will help to enhance the listening or viewing experience.

Be careful as to what type of music content you want to include in your podcast. You may want to include the first few bars from your favorite Brittany Spears song in your podcast, but unfortunately you're infringing on a copyright. Even if you legally purchased the song, you can't use it in your podcast. It's best to find podsafe music, in other words, songs that musicians produce where they give explicit permission for podcasters to use their music for noncommercial purposes. The same is true of sound effects. Using the sound effects that come on your computer may not be legal, so you'll need to do a search in Google for the sound effects that are royalty-free. If you have any questions, consult with your lawyer or download the *Podcasting Legal Guide*.[9]

Publishing Your Content

Pat yourself on the back as you now have an audio or video file that's ready to share with the world. You still have one more step to go through before your file becomes a podcast. You'll have to publish your audio or video file on a podpage that has RSS. In other words, it's not until you syndicate your audio or video file that it becomes a podcast.

I know, this probably sounds like Greek to you, but if you think of this like the newspaper article writing process, it will all become clear (see Table 3.1). For example, just because you wrote an article in a Word document that's sit-

Steps	Article Publishing Process	Podcast Publishing Process
1	Put thoughts and ideas together.	Put thoughts and ideas together.
2	Write an outline in a Word document.	Record content.
3	Conduct interviews.	Record interviews.
4	Edit article and mix in quotes.	Edit file and mix in music, quotes and sound effects.
5	Save completed article.	Save completed audio or video file.
6	Send article to editor.	Send file to FTP server.
7	Update layout with article.	Update podpage with file.
8	Publish newspaper with new information.	Publish podpage with new information.
9	Syndicate article that will appear in many many other newspapers and Web sites.	Syndicate podcast that will appear in podcast directories and subscribers' podcatchers.

Table 3.1. Article and podcast publishing process compared.

ting on your hard drive doesn't mean it'll appear in the *Guardian, New York Times*, or *Globe and Mail* tomorrow. First, you'll need to edit the raw file, in other words, all the notes you put together. Then, you'll need to mix in some quotes and interviews. Once that's done, it's still not published as you need to send it to someone who will do what it takes to get your article in print and will add it to the right resources so it's published in an upcoming edition. On top of that, if your article is really good, it will be syndicated, meaning it will appear not just in one newspaper but dozens across the country.

At step 9, your article has been syndicated, thus appearing in dozens of newspapers across the country. As for your audio or video file at step 9, it too is now a podcast because it has been syndicated, appearing in thousands of podcast directories and other feed readers on the Internet. Now, the big question is how do you publish your file and make it into a podcast? Do you publish your podcast on your Web site? On a blog? Or using one of those all-in-one podcast services? A tough decision if you're not sure how one compares to the other.

While it's confusing, realize that all options fall into one of two categories: hosted or independent. I first came across this concept in Susannah Gardner's book *Buzz Marketing with Blogs for Dummies* when she wrote about blogs that are hosted and blogs that can be managed in-house by a company.[10] For your podcast, you can choose a hosted solution or an independent solution. There are advantages and disadvantages to both and the differences are explained in detail in the next few sections.

Hosted Solution—Benefits vs. Drawbacks

With a hosted solution, otherwise known as an all-in-one podcasting service, you rely on another company to publish the parts of your podcast that can be accessed by the outside world. Most hosted solutions allow you to publish your podcast quickly using a few clicks. You enter information about you and your podcast, select a template, upload your podcast, and you're now podcasting. Hosted solutions will offer some or all of the following:

- **A templated podpage.** Instead of designing a page on your own or hiring a graphic designer, you can choose from a variety of templates.

- **RSS feed.** This is created for your podcast as soon as you create your podpage. This beats you having to code the XML file from scratch.

- **Recording options.** Although most podcasters buy their own headset and video camera, some hosted companies offer an online recording tool that you can use to record your content. Whether you plug a webcam or microphone into your computer and just push the *play* button on the hosted company's Web site, this option is excellent for those who don't want to download any extra software. Another option offered for those thinking about recording audio is to just pick up your phone. Most of these companies have a 10-digit phone number you can call to record your audio. Simply dial the number, enter in your client number, and start talking. When you're finished, hang up and the file will be up-loaded right away to your podpage.

- **Statistics reporting**. You can log in and view how many people down-loaded your podcast, how many subscribers you have, and how many requested your feed. Some even go a step further by offering informa-tion on how long your audience actually consumed your podcast and what the average consumption rate is. In other words, you'll learn if the majority of your audience viewed all 13 minutes of your video podcast, or if 60 percent of your audience listened to only the first six minutes of your audio podcast.

- **Hosting**. Most will store your podcast on their servers. If you know how to attach a document to an e-mail, that's how simple it is to upload your podcast.

- **Flash media player.** If you want to embed your podcast on a Web site or share through a social networking Web site, such as MySpace or Facebook, use a media player.

The drawbacks with using a hosted solution for your podcast are just as numerous as the benefits. Some of these drawbacks are:

- You're stuck with the templates offered by the company, therefore you won't be able to modify it to match your brand, company colors, or Web site.

- Most have bandwidth limits. In other words, if your podcast is really popular, as soon as you reach the ceiling of downloads, it will stop work-ing until you roll over into the new month or new cycle.

- Some will add their identifier to the end of your podcast. This identifier is a three-second score with a voice that says who the company is. This is lousy since people will typically remember the last thing they heard or saw in your podcast. If the hosted company splashes its URL at the end of your podcast, your audience will go to that hosted company's Web site, not yours.

- Some will encode your file at a lower bitrate. This is done to ensure that your podcast is not too large; however, the lower bitrate affects your sound quality. What may sound like CD quality audio on your computer may sound like AM quality audio after you upload your podcast.

- The URL generated to your podpage is a sub-domain. This becomes a problem if you want to tell someone where to find your podcast. Saying *leesabarnes.hostedcompany.com* can be awkward. Plus, from a branding standpoint, this looks lousy. You can alleviate this by purchasing a domain name and pointing it to the URL of your podpage. In other words, you can tell people to find your podcast by going to *leesabarnespodcast.com* and after they plug in that URL into their browser, it takes them to *leesabarnes.hostedcompany.com*, but if you're going to go this route, you may just want to consider an independent solution.

- Read the terms and conditions closely. Some will say that once you upload your podcast to their server, they can do with it whatever they please. Pay close attention to the terms you're agreeing to before creating an account.

- The online recorder may limit how much time you can record. After you plug in your webcam or headset and hit the record button on the hosted company's Web site, you may be limited to just five minutes. If you plan to use a podcast to earn income, being limited to such a short recording time is not good for your strategy.

Table 3.2 provides a summary of the advantages and disadvantages of using a hosted solution for your podcast.

Independent Solution—Benefits vs. Drawbacks

If you're a new podcaster and you're looking for flexibility or if you're an experienced podcaster and you need to upgrade, an independent solution is your best bet. With an independent solution, you can put all the pieces together using

Benefits	Drawbacks
Podcast and video files are hosted.	Template won't match your branding.
Offers online or telephone recording if you don't want to purchase a microphone, webcam, or headset.	There are bandwidth limits that will affect whether people can play your podcast depending on how popular it becomes.
Podpage and RSS feed is created quickly.	The podcast company may add an identifier to the end of your podcast.
Podcast information is submitted to iTunes immediately.	Encoding means loss of sound or visual quality.
Offered free of charge or for a small monthly fee.	A sub-domain is created that could be confusing, long, and won't match your brand.
Technical support offered by the company hosting your podcast solution.	There's a limit on how long you can record using the hosted company's online recording tool.
Online training is available.	Promotional tools are offered to help you market your podcast.

Table 3.2. Hosted solution—benefits vs. drawbacks.

a variety of tools and be able to manage your solution on your own. Some of the benefits to choosing an independent solution are:

- You get to choose which blog platform to use for your podpage (I highly recommend Wordpress).

- You can tweak the design of your podpage according to your company colors and branding. Compare the *Weight Releasing* podcast (*http://weightreleasing.podoptimize.com*) to the *Small Cap Podcast* (*http://smallcappodcast.com*). Both use Wordpress, but the *Small Cap Podcast* has been designed to reflect the company's brand, while the *Weight Releasing* podcast is using a template. Being able to modify your podpage to mirror your Web site, logo, and company colors means that you can keep your brand consistent.

- You can choose where to host your podcast. You can purchase a lot of space with a lot of bandwidth for a low fee. Being able to choose where you host your podpage and podcasts gives you the flexibility to choose according to cost, proximity, or reputation. Some of the hosted solutions have packages where you can use them simply to upload and store your podcasts, while you create your podpage and RSS feed elsewhere. It's also good practice to host your podcasts on a separate server than your podpage. If one goes down for whatever reason, it means that people can still find you. Hence, being able to choose your hosting package makes good business sense.

- You can register a domain name that reflects your brand. Doing this allows you to register a memorable name and one that matches the name of your podcast. One of my podcasts is called *Cubicle Divas*, so it helps that I can direct people to *cubicledivas.com*—an easy-to-remember URL —to listen to my podcast.

- You can edit your RSS feed. This becomes beneficial if you notice any errors in your feed. You can use the one that comes with your blog platform, or if you have XML knowledge you can create it from scratch and use a service such as Feedburner or Feedvalidator to optimize and measure the results of your feed. A hosted solution doesn't offer this flexibility.

Just like the hosted solution, there are a few drawbacks with the independent solution, although the disadvantages focus more on time and technical expertise, for example:

- Technical support. If something stops working, you or someone on your team will have to spend the time troubleshooting the problem. Not a great way to spend your time, especially if you have a business to run or a life to live.

- Statistics will be in many tools. You'll have to log in to your blog, your feed account, and your Web site statistics in order to collect data on the number of downloads and subscribers.

- It will take days, even weeks, to pull your solution together. You will involve many consultants and teams to put all the pieces together. This can drive up the costs, as well as your patience if you want to get your podcast solution up and running quickly.

Table 3.3 provides a summary of the advantages and disadvantages of using a hosted solution for your podcast.

One thing to note is that if you already have a blog and you already have hosting, you are one step closer to using an independent solution to launch your

Benefits	Drawbacks
Podpage can be modified to match your brand.	You will have to troubleshoot any problems.
Bandwidth is only limited based on the package you buy.	Statistics are pulled from a variety of tools.
Domain name will match the name of your podcast.	Timeline to launch is days, even weeks.
While you'll pay upfront in implementation costs, you'll save money in the long run.	You will have to submit your podcast details to iTunes and other podcast directories on your own.
	If you're not technical, implementing this solution will be difficult.

Table 3.3. Independent solution—benefits vs. drawbacks.

podcast. Some podcasters choose to use their current blog to publish their own podcast; however, don't make the mistake I made early in my podcasting adventures. I used a free hosting service (it has since gone under) and I didn't separate my blog posts from my podcast on my blog. If you are considering using the independent solution to launch your podcast, keep these tips in mind:

- Double-check that your current hosting company will allow you to store and share audio or video files off their servers. Although the package you bought to host your Web site or blog is sufficient, hosting audio or video files is a whole different story. A five-page Web site with minimal images will take up no more than 500 KB on your server. Compare that to podcasts: a 15-minute audio file is typically 10 to 15 MB in size (about 10,000 to 15,000 KB), while a five-minute video file is typically 50 to 100 MB in size (about 51,000 to 100,000 KB). If you go over your allotted server space, you will be charged extra money for the increased traffic. Call or e-mail your hosting company or check with your technical staff to make sure that you have enough space and bandwidth to upload and share audio or video files.

- If using Typepad or Wordpress as your blog, create a separate category called Podcast and associate all your podcast-specific posts in there. Both Typepad and Wordpress will generate a feed for that category, separate from the main feed for your blog. This is essential so you can continue to post funny and interesting audio or video content on your main blog that are not part of podcast episodes. You run the risk of confusing your audience if they receive your feed that contains a video you found on YouTube featuring cats yawning when your podcast is all about sales and marketing tips for massage therapists.

Choosing the Right One

In her book *Buzz Marketing with Blogs for Dummies*, Susannah Gardner used a grid to show the difference between using a hosted or independent solution for your blog.[11] I reviewed her list and have tweaked it slightly to make it applicable to a podcasting solution. Here's a checklist you can use to figure out which solution is better suited for your situation (see Table 3.4).

If you answered yes to six or more of the tasks under one of the solutions, you are better to go with that solution to start. Remember, you can always change your mind later. At the end of the day, if you go with the hosted solution, there will be some profiting methods you won't be able to do. For example, because you have limits on what you can modify on the podpage, you

Check If Yes	Hosted Solution	Check If Yes	Independent Solution
	I need it up now.		I can wait a few days.
	I am a low-tech person.		I have some technical knowledge.
	I don't have the time to learn new technical skills.		I want to learn new technical skills.
	I don't have the time to invest in recording tools.		I want my own recording tools for flexibility.
	I have a small budget.		I have some money in the budget to spend.
	My podpage does not need to match my brand.		I want my podpage to match my brand.
	I don't care about bandwidth.		I don't want to be limited by bandwidth.
	I don't have anyone to help me put this thing together.		I have a team of staff members or consultants who can help me put this together.
	Sound and visual quality isn't that important to me.		Sound and visual quality can't be compromised.

Table 3.4. Podcast solution checklist.

won't be able to throw text ads on your page. Most hosted solutions will add their own text ads to your podpage and won't share the money with you.

When choosing your solution, another factor to consider is the technical knowledge of your target market. If your audience is highly technical, they will need far fewer shiny buttons on your podpage compared to a technically ignorant group. Remember that if you're technical, but the audience you're targeting is not, you have to choose a solution that allows you to add as many explanations to the podpage as possible so your target audience knows what to do. Although cost should be considered when choosing which solution to publish your podcast on, the relationship you plan to build with your audience should be much more important. Let's say you choose a hosted solution to publish your podcast. There are many limitations with a hosted solution, one of them being the inability to edit the template of the podpage. You launch your podcast, announce it to your list, and then you spend every minute of every day answering e-mails from your target audience on how to listen to or view the podcast or how to download it. If there's any barrier to consuming your podcast, you will lose your audience.

According to a study released by Forrester Research called *Social Technographics: Mapping Participation In Activities Forms the Foundation of a Social Strategy*, too many companies deploy a blog here or a podcast there without taking the time to find out if their target market is even using them.[12] Too often, marketing departments launch tools that sound cool, but don't take into account how their target market participates online. Forrester grouped the behaviors of consumers online into six levels of participation, otherwise known as **social technographics**. The social technographics transcend age and gender and groups consumers according to how they approach these technologies, not just which ones they use. The six rungs on the social technographics ladder are:

1. **Creators**. At the top of the ladder are creators—online consumers who publish blogs, maintain Web pages, or upload videos to sites like YouTube at least once per month. Creators, an elite group, include just 13 percent of the adult online population. Creators are generally young—the average age of adult users is 39—but are evenly split between men and women.

2. **Critics**. These online consumers participate in either of two ways—commenting on blogs or posting ratings and reviews on sites like Amazon.com. This level of participation isn't nearly as intense as being a creator—critics pick and choose where they want to offer their expertise and often use another blog post or product as the foundation for

their contribution. Critics represent 19 percent of all adult online consumers and on average are several years older than creators.

3. **Collectors.** When users save URLs on a social bookmarking service like del.icio.us or use RSS feeds on Bloglines, they create metadata that's shared with the entire community. Collectors represent 15 percent of the adult online population and are the most male-dominated of all the social technographics groups.

4. **Joiners.** This unique group has just one defining behavior—using a social networking site like MySpace.com or Facebook. Despite the current hysteria about social networks, joiners represent only 19 percent of the adult online population and are the youngest of the social technographics groups.

5. **Spectators.** This group of blog readers, video viewers, and podcast listeners, which represents 33 percent of the adult online population, is important as the audience for the social content made by everyone else. As a group, spectators are slightly more likely to be women and have the lowest household income of all the social technographics groups.

6. **Inactives.** Today, 52 percent of online adults do not participate at all in social computing activities. These inactives have an average age of 50, are more likely to be women, and are much less likely to consider themselves leaders or tell their friends about products that interest them.

I consider myself a creator, yet the audience who listens to *Cubicle Divas* falls into the spectator group. My audience reads my blog and reads the ezine I send to them each month. Yet, it may not be easy for them to understand how to listen to my podcast. For that reason, I need to use an independent podcasting solution so I can add extra instructions to my podpage that give my audience tips on how to listen. On the other hand, my company Caprica Interactive Marketing falls into the creator group and we create a podcast called *Podonomics* where we give tips on how to make money podcasting. Those who listen to my podcast are also creators, some critics, and some collectors. For this reason, I could go with a hosted solution since the Podonomics audience needs a little less handholding. For your podcast, don't choose a solution based solely on your budget. Choose the solution that will help your audience listen or view your podcast without any barriers.

When to Hire a Podcasting Consultant

If you're an experienced podcaster who's spending too much time on the production tasks of your podcast or if you're a new podcaster who doesn't know where to begin, you may choose to hire a consultant to take on the parts of the podcasting puzzle that you're not interested in doing. This becomes evident when you find that you're no longer interested in producing your podcast because you hate doing the production work, or your team is overwhelmed about adding podcasting tasks to their plate of responsibilities. If you find that your podcasting strategy has come to a standstill, it's time to consider hiring a podcasting consultant to help.

You can hire a podcasting consultant to work on only the post production work, such as the editing and mixing, or you can hire him or her to do everything for you. I've worked with agencies that can do everything except the audio production pieces, so they will hire my company to do it for them. Alternatively, I may work with a client who wants to focus on the running of their business and hires my company to do everything. The confusion that arises between the podcasting consultant and you is how to divide the podcasting duties so you're not overlapping each other or stepping on each other's toes. Table 3.5 shows a grid that I often share with the agencies and branding companies I work with that you may find useful. It separates the various podcasting tasks and groups them into a general category. All you'll need to do at this point is agree with your podcasting consultant who will own and deliver that task. The column called *Owner* contains the name of the company that can do the duties for that role. In Table 3.5, this column is left blank so you can fill it in yourself depending on who you are working with.

When you look at this list of duties, determine which ones you can do in house. This will help you save money. Just remember that if you take on these duties or assign them to someone in house, you'll need to determine if you have the time to manage these along with your current full-time duties. For example, let's just say that you want to do the creative pieces simply because you're a creative person or you've always dreamed of creating interesting content. You know that you have a huge marketing campaign launching for your company in just a few weeks. Or, your wife is expecting a baby in just under a month. Will you have time to do that campaign and fuss around with creating a podcover? Can your podcast afford not to be published for two weeks while you stay at home with your newborn? While saving money is a great idea, being stressed or overwhelmed in an effort to save a few hundred bucks makes no sense. Instead, you might save yourself a heap of aggravation by just assigning those duties to your podcasting consultant.

Role	Duties	Owner
Project Manager	Manages timelines, assigns resources, and provides a status on tasks.	
Creative	Designs the podcover and podpage.	
Editorial	Creates content for the podcast, identifies and schedules guests to interview, creates the script, and hires voice talent and chooses a podsafe song for the podcast bumper.	
Audio/Visual Engineering	Provides means to record the content, then edits and mixes the raw file to produce the podcast episode.	
Technical	Integrates podpage design on Web site, creates RSS feed, hosts podcasts, and updates podpage with a link to the new episode.	
Marketing	Promotes the podcast using traditional means and new media channels, including the use of podcatchers. Also, updates the podpage with show notes, show resources, and a descriptive title about each new episode.	
Monitoring	Prepares reports to show how podcasts are positioned online.	

Table 3.5. Podcast solution roles and duties.

Taking Action

In this chapter, you learned how to implement the components of your plan and launch your podcast. Your goal is to leverage your content and share a podcast that reflects your brand, but also meets the needs of your audience. Remember to:

- Choose your host, logo, colors, and design of your podpage.

- Decide on what tool you'll use to record your content.

- Edit and mix your podcast in postproduction.

- Choose a hosted or independent solution for your podcast.

- Hire a podcasting consultant to help you on the tasks you can't do or don't want to do.

4

Grow Your Audience

Building an audience and keeping them as your fans is one of the most important activities you need to master after you launch your podcast. Having a loyal and growing audience for your audio and video podcast will make the profiting stage much easier. In this chapter, you'll learn the techniques that podcasters are using to grow their audience (see Figure 4.1).

The 7 Steps to Podcasting for Profit

Figure 4.1. Podcasting for profit steps—grow.

Introduction

In January 2007, a six-minute video was uploaded to YouTube that showed a woman getting ready for her wedding day with her bridesmaids. The video started off innocently enough. It captured the laughter and the conversations as each of the bridesmaids drank wine while waiting for the arrival of the bride. At about the 1:45-minute mark in the video, the bride walks into the hotel room in a panic. She collapses to the floor, expressing her disgust at how gross her hair looks, complaining that her hair makes her look "like a boy."[1] As her bridesmaids do everything to console her, the bride continues to lament about her hair. In the ultimate act of frustration, the bridesmaids watch in horror as the bride starts to hack off her hair using a pair of scissors.

The video, called *Bride Has a Massive Wig Out,* became one of the most shared videos on YouTube. In just two weeks, between the time the video was uploaded on January 18, 2007, to the time it was pulled on February 2, 2007, the video had been viewed 2.1 million times.[2] Even after it was revealed that the "wig out" was a fake (it was sponsored by SunSilk Canada, which hired actresses to play the parts of the bride and bridesmaids), the interest was still quite high. The four women who starred in the video were profiled in a variety of newspapers and talk shows, including *Good Morning America*.[3] A Canadian newspaper even got renowned director Norman Jewison, who is best known for directing and producing the 1987 Oscar nominated film *Moonstruck*, to offer his analysis of the video.[4]

This YouTube video demonstrates that building an audience and building a buzz go hand in hand. SunSilk Canada wanted to find a clever way to raise awareness about a new line of shampoos and conditioners. However, before they could make any sales, they had to build awareness and they did this by using a video online. This formula is the hallmark of any business. Before you can make money, you have to build a buzz so that people get excited. Part of the excitement is the willingness to build rapport with your audience. It's through this element of trust that your audience will feel more comfortable spending money with you.

In business, people buy from those that they like and trust. I've seen this happen over and over in my own business. My podcast helps people learn more about me and my style. Then, they purchase a product that I recommend in my podcast. Once the person has bought something from me, they're apt to buy something else. Sixty percent of your podcast audience are very or somewhat likely to buy a product or service if the podcast host suggested it.[5] Once your audience trusts you, you won't have to act like a used car salesperson to convince them to buy. Your audience will trust you enough to do so.

Without an audience, you will spend your time acting like a used car sales-person, instead of a genial and likable host. In his book *The Likeability Factor*, Tim Sanders talks about the four critical elements of likeability: friendliness, relevance, empathy, and realness.[6] Because technology has erased boundaries, being unlikeable can prove to be very damaging to your career or business.[7] In particular, Sanders says:

> *"Walk into a local coffee shop that's within a stone's throw of a Starbuck's and I bet you'll find some very agreeable counter people—because they're all too aware that you could walk next door. People with options are empowered people, and empowered people demand a positive environment. They surround themselves with what they choose to buy and whom they choose to spend time with."*[8]

Podosphere, the name used to describe the collection of podcasts online, has grown by leaps and bounds over the past few years. On November 24, 2004, *PodcastAlley.com*, one of the leading podcast directories online, had 484 podcasts listed in its directory; by June 2007, the number had jumped to 32,491.[9] Every-one has a choice when it comes to what podcast they will listen to or view. Some will listen because they like your voice. Others will listen because you're funny. At the end of the day, being likeable helps you to attract the right audience to your brand. As you continue to attract people to your brand, you grow your audience effortlessly. Before you even make your first dollar podcasting for profit, you need to grow your audience. Focusing on growing your audience before making money does three things:

1. It builds trust between you and your audience.

2. It builds likeability.

3. It helps you create a sense of belonging for your audience.

One of my favorite actors when I was a teenager was River Phoenix. I re-member watching him in a variety of movies and especially enjoyed his acting in the 1987 Oscar-nominated film called *Stand By Me*. I remember buying ev-ery teen magazine I could get my hands on that featured Phoenix on the cover. Phoenix, who died of an overdose at the age of 23 in 1993, was a complicated, secretive, and dynamic teenager who acted much older than he was. He was extremely passionate about each role he took on in every film he starred in. It wasn't enough for him just to read the script, he experienced the life of his character by living in a similar environment. In the film *My Own Private Idaho*, which co-starred Keanu Reeves, Phoenix played a gay drug addict. To prepare for the part, Phoenix lived in a home with the other actors and the director in a rundown part of town.[10] Phoenix would talk to street people and even shot up to experience the life of a drug addict. Because of this passion, Phoenix said many things that have become infamous quotes. I found a quote attributed to Phoenix that reminded me so much of podcasting. He said:

> *"It's a great feeling to think that I can be a friend to so many people through my movies."*[11]

I would replace the word *movie* with "podcast." Each of you, whether you're an individual or a business, should strive to be a friend to as many people as you can through your podcast. By developing friendships with your audience, this is yet another way to expand your audience and grow your numbers effortlessly.

While being likeable and becoming a friend to your audience will help you build your audience with little effort, this alone won't bring you the numbers that you can profit from. In order to podcast for profit, you will need more than just your friends, a select number of colleagues, and your mom consuming your podcast. Using both offline and online tools in a strategic way will help you increase your audience faster than just hoping for the best. Without a strong promotional campaign, no one will know about your product podcast. In his book *Promoting Your Podcast*, Jason Van Orden lists a variety of ways to gain a loyal following of podcast listeners or viewers and says:

> *"There are numerous no-cost strategies for marketing your podcast, especially if you know who your ideal audience members are, and create content that they want."*[12]

There are three ways to grow your audience on a shoestring budget:

1. **Tangible promotional tactics that don't require you to use the Internet.** This includes press releases, brochures, business cards, merchandise, and multimedia products—anything that can be sent via snail mail or given to someone at a networking event.

2. **Online promotional ideas that can only be used on the Internet.** This includes tags, podcast directories, and e-mail lists.

3. **Community-building techniques that create a sense of belonging.** When your audience can interact with you and other audience members, this creates rapport and loyalty.

Let's take a look at the three ways to grow your audience so that you constantly increase your numbers, build a relationship, and create a community.

Offline Promotional Tactics

Offline promotions are marketing tools you can use that are not Internet-based. Too often, podcasters forget about the myriad of traditional means to promote their podcast. What works for large corporations, such as Coca Cola and Sony, can work for podcasters as well, no matter your budget. Let's take a look at some proven offline promotional tactics.

Press Releases

Press releases are one of the most effective, yet most tricky promotional tools that exist. They're effective because if your story is picked up, it means free publicity in a newspaper, on a radio program, or on a television show. They're tricky because there's no guarantee that anyone will take interest in your story. I remember sending press release after press release to one media outlet in Toronto that has the largest morning viewership and I still haven't had any luck appearing on television.

I have been on both sides of the press release process. As a business owner, I write press releases to get free publicity for my product or service. As a freelance journalist, I've been in newsrooms where the fax machine never stops churning out press release after press release. Being on both sides, I've learned that there are costly mistakes that I and a lot of people make in a press release that makes it a candidate for the garbage pail.

I know quite a number of journalists because of my past life as a freelance writer and because I do a lot of networking. I did an informal, unscientific survey asking them what bugs them the most about press releases. Here's what they said:

*   **Not relevant to what they write about.** One technology journalist, who focuses on software programs and technology gadgets, told me that he

often gets press releases about new Web site launches. While he notes that this is interesting, he can only discard those press releases because they're not relevant to him.

- **Some lack focus.** Many press releases are written with no focus. They appear to be just a bunch of sentences and paragraphs strung together in an awkward way.

- **One big infomercial.** Although having a positive tone in your press release is important, making it into one big advertisement for your podcast is a great way to have it ignored. I learned this the hard way when I was promoting a contest. I hired a publicist who wrote a press release and used her contacts to try and get me coverage. After six weeks, the story wasn't picked up. I couldn't figure out why until I read the press release objectively. It was one big infomercial.

- **They're overwhelmed.** With fax machines and e-mails, there are now a variety of ways to send your press release to a journalist. But on the receiving end, it can be quite exhausting to go through the volume of press releases that arrive daily. I remember sitting with a journalist in his office one day and out the corner of my eye, I could see the number of new e-mails he received in his inbox. For the 20 minutes I was in his office, he probably got around 100 e-mails. It was alarming.

Now that you know some of the things that annoy journalists about press releases, it's important that you target the right journalist with the news about your podcast. However, just announcing that you launched a podcast in your press release isn't enough. No one really cares, to be honest. There are more important things to write about in a newspaper or talk about on a radio station than your little ol' podcast. Because of this, you need to focus more on the content of your podcast when writing the press release and less on the launch. What will really grab the media's attention is tying in the launch of your podcast into a current event, contest, holiday, or hot news story. For example:

- If you have a gardening podcast and it's spring time, give tips in your podcast on how to get rid of weeds without pesticides.

- If you have a career podcast and there's a transit strike, interview a company that provides work-at-home options for their employees.

- If you're a chiropractor and you want to announce the launch of your podcast, wait for back-to-school season. That way, you can give tips in your podcast on how parents can choose a backpack that won't cause their children injury.

Again, in the three previous examples, the press release will focus on the content of the podcast and tie its launch into a current event (transit strike), a time of year (spring time), or a hot news story (back to school). Using this approach will heighten your chances of your podcast being mentioned or covered by the media. You can also use the press release you're sending to journalists and post it online. There are a number of press release distribution services that help to increase your ranking in search engines. This means that you heighten your chances of a journalist finding your podcast, not because they're using these online press release services, but because they found your press release through a search engine after typing in a keyword. I'll explain more about this in the section regarding online promotional tactics.

Printed Material

It's not unusual to go to many podcasting conferences and get mountains and mountains of printed material. Everything from business cards to postcards to bookmarks will litter the bottom of your conference bags. Podcasters tend to be a very creative bunch and it's not unusual to see strange characters and logos on very colorful material. Business cards tend to have contact details, a logo as well as the address of your podpage. Postcards are typically glossy, 4" × 6", and also have the URL of your podpage. Before designing your promotional material, keep the following in mind:

- **Choose a design that will attract your target audience.** Although you may want to impress other podcasters with a caricature of yourself on your promotional material, it may just turn off your target market. Choose colors, fonts, and images that your target listener or target viewer will find attractive.

- **Be different.** Just because most of the people in your industry design their business cards a certain way doesn't mean you have to as well. For example, lawyers typically put black text on a white or beige background. For your law podcast, you can move away from the plain write background and, instead, try something that's different.

- **Put only your podpage URL and tagline on your promotional material.** Don't be tempted to put all your contact information on your business card or postcard. Your goal is to get people to your podcast page. Too many options may prevent people from taking any action and encourage them to throw away your printed material. Keep it simple and display a clever graphic, your podcover, your URL, and your tagline.

One note of caution is try not to use a template. Some podcasters will get their business cards printed for free and use a template provided by the business card company. However, this is a mistake as it will confuse people. I remember when I attended a podcasting conference in New York, I received a business card from someone. It had a red background with an image of a microphone on one side and the podcaster's contact details on the other. Moments later, I met someone else who gave me what looked to be the same business card with the red background and microphone on the side. Would you believe that I met yet another podcaster about two hours later who handed me what looked like the same business card? Each time I got it, I asked, "Didn't we already meet? Your business card looks familiar."

It wasn't until I got home and while flipping through the mountain of business cards I received, I realized why I was so confused. Five different podcasters were using the same business card template. While I can understand cutting costs, using a business card template will confuse people, especially if there are others using the very same template. Don't make this mistake. If you want people to listen to or view your podcast, make the design of your business cards and postcards unique. The companion Web site list a few companies you can use to get your business cards printed.

Merchandise

Some podcasters use merchandise to give away to people. Everything from T-shirts, stickers, mugs, pens, and buttons. Jim Milles, host of the *CIO* podcast, always hands out buttons. People pin them on their shirts and jackets and become walking promotional tools for Milles' podcast. *Podchick*, a video podcaster based in Los Angeles, always hands me stickers whenever we meet. The colorful stickers can be affixed to any surface whether it be a laptop, a notebook, or some other device. The hosts of *Just One More Book*, an audio podcast hosted by Mark Blevis and Andrea Ross who review their favorite children's books, give away, you guessed it, bookmarks.

There are two ways to create merchandise:

1. Buy in bulk from a promotions company and store the merchandise in your garage or basement. Although the upfront costs will be expensive, you save money in the long run as you can mark up the price. For example, if you had five hundred T-shirts printed at $3 each, you paid $1,500. However, you can sell the T-shirts through your Web site or at conferences for $15, a markup of 400 percent. The drawback is that your investment is tied up in unsold inventory. You could probably use that money for something else.

2. Use an online promotions store and have them ship the merchandise as each individual order comes through. Instead of investing a lot of money up front to store inventory in your garage, you use a Web site such as *Cafépress.com*. Here, you create a free profile, upload your podcast cover or logo, then place the logo on the images of the products you'd like to sell. You can mark up the cost of your merchandise beyond the base price. People can browse your storefront, select a T-shirt or mug, and wait for the order to be shipped. *Cafepress.com* only prints the merchandise with your logo on it once the order is received. *Cafepress.com* takes care of the shipping, the credit card transaction, even the customer service. The drawback is that you get a very small commission.

Multimedia

Although not as popular as printed material or merchandise, copying your podcasts to a CD or DVD and giving them out at events can be an effective promotional tool. People can listen to or view the content on a portable device while travelling back home in an airplane or in their cars. Peter Wood, who hosts a weekly podcast called *Ripple Outdoors*, burns a few episodes of his audio podcast to CD. When he attends conferences and trade shows, he gives people a CD with his contact details on the label. Wood was surprised one day when he received a phone call from a guy who raved about one of Wood's episodes that he listened to on CD. Wood says that it's important to offer a variety of ways for people to consume his podcast so he doesn't alienate anyone.

> *"The older generation is not that savvy technically. I talk to some guys who ask me, 'Well, how do I listen to your podcast?' I say, 'Go to your computer. . .' and they squirm. So I say, 'Well, download it to your iPod,' to which they say, 'What the heck is an iPod?' So, I'll burn it on a CD and say, 'Can you play CDs?'"*[13]

You can create your own CDs and DVDs using your burner on your computer. This will work if you're getting one or two orders a week, but it won't sustain you over the long haul. There are companies that will copy your audio or video data to a disk, print off a cover design that you preselected, then send the disk to the person who ordered it. Otherwise known as fulfillment companies, they can handle orders as little as one a day to as many as one an hour. On the companion Web site, I provide a list of companies that will fulfill your orders and ship them directly to your customers without you having to do anything manual.

Online Promotional Tactics

The opportunities to promote your podcast online are enormous. While you're limited in the offline world by budgets and editorial slants, the only limit you have in the online world is your time. Here's just a small sample of ways to drive people to your podcast and grow your numbers.

Tags

Also known as tagging, **tags** are "one or more descriptive words assigned to an asset, whether it's a photo, Web page, article, person, book, or piece of data."[14] Tagging is similar to the system that librarians use to organize books. The Dewy decimal system allows librarians to use keywords and numbers to catalogue each book before adding it to their shelves. With your podcast, you can assign keywords that describe the content discussed or explored before adding it to the shelf (in other words, before publishing it live).

There are no limits to the numbers of tags you may want to use to categorize your podcast. Tags can be just one word, two words, or more. In Episode 10 of my podcast *Podonomics*, I used almost 30 tags to describe the content. I created tags for the people I interviewed or mentioned in my podcast, as well as the general themes I covered. Web sites such as Technorati and Digg pick up these tags and display your podcast in their directories. This makes it easier for people to find your podcast based on the keywords they're using to search for information. It's not unusual for me to tag a person in my blog post, only to return a few minutes later to see that that very person has left a comment. That's the power of tagging.

Using tags is simple. In Technorati, enter the keyword or the tag in the search field. When the page refreshes, look for a section that says *See Your Post Here*. In the box right underneath it, you'll find a bit of code that you can

See your posts here

To contribute to this page, include this code in your blog post:

```
<a href="http://technorati.com/tag/podcasting" rel="ta
```

Figure 4.2. Technorati tagging code.

copy and paste into your blog (see Figure 4.2). As soon as you publish your podcast with the code in it, Technorati will get the update and list your blog in its directory. If you're using Wordpress, there's a plug-in called Bunny that you can install where you enter in keywords underneath your blog post. This will save you time since you won't have to leave the posting area of your blog (see Figure 4.3).

Podcast Directories

There are a few dozen directories online that only list podcasts. They act a lot like search engines, the only difference is that when you use a podcast directory, the only results you'll get from your search are podcasts. People plug in a keyword into the search field and these directories list podcasts that match the keyword entered. iTunes is considered the Google of podcast directories. According to Podtrac, a podvertising network, 75 percent of podcast listeners use iTunes to find podcasts.[15] Other popular podcast directories are:

- Podcast Alley

- Podcast Pickle

- Podcasts.net

- Pluggd

- Odeo

- Podcasting News.

Figure 4.3. Wordpress plug-in called Bunny.

Promoted in Other Podcasts

Very early in podcasting, many created a 30-second promo and encouraged other podcasters to play it in their podcasts. In the 30-second clip, the host would talk about his or her podcast, what it's about, and who their target audience would be. Often, music played in the background sets the tone. Adam Curry, host of *The Daily Source Code*, would play 30-second promos in his podcast and many podcasters reported an increase in their audience numbers after being featured in Curry's podcast. However, this practice has lost favor and is not as frequently used now as it was back in 2005.

Another way to be profiled in another podcast is to be interviewed as a guest. Many podcasters are looking for interesting people to profile in their podcasts. Some are even looking for that coveted scoop. Use iTunes or another podcast directory and put together a list of podcasts that target the audience you want to attract. Listen or view the podcast for a few episodes to see what their style is and if they even interview guests. Then, contact each host one by one by e-mail to let him or her know that you're available for an interview. Provide a very short bio, no more than 150 words, and let the host know how you can help his or her audience.

Be warned that this is not an opportunity to sell your wares or spam people with information about your new product. I've been on the receiving end where someone e-mails me saying "hi to Lisa" (it's Leesa), that they listen to *Cubicle*

Divas weekly (it's published bi-weekly), that they enjoy the information I provide to business owners (I target women specifically), and that they would love to tell my listeners about their book on gardening tips (I provide tips to women on how to run their businesses better). Obviously, this person is just copying and pasting an e-mail to send to as many people as they can, rather than understanding what my podcast is really about. Often, my suspicions are confirmed when I see someone complaining on one of the podcasting discussion lists I belong to asking if anyone else received a canned e-mail from some dude. If I sense that the e-mail is not well thought-out, I just delete it.

Bryan Person, host of *New Comm Road* podcast, received a canned, impersonal e-mail from someone named Chad who started a new Web site to help podcasters promote their podcasts.[16] Here's a copy of the e-mail (I got a similar one which I promptly deleted):

> *Hi, my name is [name withheld] and I wanted to drop you a line and let you know I really enjoy your podcast.*
>
> *I am starting a new Web site to try to help people find new podcasts and help podcasters get bigger audiences.*
>
> *The site is called [removed].*
>
> *I thought I'd start getting the word out about it by e-mailing the podcasts I listen to regularly. Check it out and feel free to add your show if it's not already on there. If you want to tell your listeners about the site so they can review your site and others it will help us market podcasts and get the word out even more!*
>
> *Take care,*
>
> *[name withheld]*

The author of the message above (a man) probably had good intentions, but because he sent out the same e-mail to me, Person and many others, it was all too easy to classify his e-mail as spam. Like Person, I was not pleased about this guy's approach and Person summed up why this guy's approach was the wrong way to pitch a podcaster. In particular, Person says:

- The author never addressed Person or his co-host by name in the message.

- The author never mentions Person's specific podcast.

- The author says he "really enjoys [Person's] podcast," yet doesn't say why.

- The author asks Person to add his show to the author's site "if it's not already on there." If this were a personal message, he would have taken the time to check his own site to verify that my show isn't already listed, and then would have made a note of that to me.

Person continued to say:

"There was no personal touch from the author in his initial message (nor in his subsequent reply to my reply) that showed any indication that he has ever listened to New Comm Road, *let alone that he truly enjoys it.*

Most podcasters tend to be open to learning about new ways to promote their shows. Heck, there isn't a podcaster around who doesn't want more listeners (I know I do!). But if you want to engage us, you have to take some time to find out what our podcasts are about."[17]

Sallie Goetsch, cofounder of *Podcast Asylum*, writes and speaks about podcasting from the listener's perspective. In an article she wrote called "How to Pitch Podcasters," Goetsch said that "pitching yourself as a podcast interview subject is very different from pitching your book to a publisher or getting on television, with one exception: you have to do your homework."[18] She offers these tips on how to pitch a podcaster so they contact you:

1. **Take a personal approach.** Because most podcasts are a personal and informal medium, most podcasters are suspicious of marketing-speak and press releases, especially if the pitch looks like something that's been sent out on a massive scale. Most podcasters have small, vocal audiences; people who think of them as friends and who will let them know in no uncertain terms if they don't like a show. There's a strong sense of community among podcasters and listeners, and when it comes to doing interviews, podcasters prefer people who are part of that community to people who aren't, unless the interviewee is extremely well-known.

2. **Pick podcasts to pitch.** In April 2006, FeedBurner reported that it was publishing 44,000 podcast feeds. That's good news: it's a pretty safe bet that whatever you're writing about, someone is podcasting about it. And no, you won't have to listen to all 44,000 in order to know which

ones to pitch. Remember the audience profile you had to create when you created your book proposal? You want to find podcasters whose audiences are the same as your ideal reader. These are more likely to be podcasters who talk about the same subjects as your book than book review or literary podcasts, though you shouldn't overlook those either. To find podcasts on the right subject, check out podcast directories like iTunes and Podcast Alley, which allow listeners to rate and review podcasts. Read the descriptions and the reviews and make a shortlist of the most likely candidates. And, of course, don't overlook any podcasts you're already listening to.

3. **Joining the "In Group."** So what do you do after you've gone through and found the highest-rated podcasts on subjects related to your book? First, listen to the podcast. Better yet, subscribe to the podcast and listen to several shows. Read the show notes and the comments. Find out whether interviews are a regular part of the show. (Some shows feature interviews every week, others occasionally, and some not at all.) Next, start commenting. When you leave a comment on the show's blog, you can enter the URL for your book instead of your home page for some subtle self-promotion, but the important thing is to respond thoughtfully to something in that episode. Write a paragraph or two that continues the conversation and shows that you know what you're talking about.

4. **Create genuine connections.** Although podcasters don't necessarily expect people they've interviewed to listen to every show from then on, they'll shy off anyone whose interest seems too self-serving. Just because a podcast has a lot of listeners doesn't mean that you'll like the show or the podcaster. If you don't, don't try to fake it in order to reach a potential market for your book. Make sure the podcast and its host(s) are a good fit for your personality before you try to line up an interview.

   You'll probably have to do this more than once before the podcaster asks to interview you, but if what you say is interesting enough to the listeners (who will usually hear it read out in the next episode as well as have the opportunity to read it on the show blog), the podcaster may contact you immediately. If not, keep listening and commenting for a few shows, and strike up an e-mail correspondence with the podcaster.

   Once you're sure that the podcaster and the listeners know who you are and find your comments interesting, volunteer yourself as an interviewee. And as long as there's enough time before the interview date, send the podcaster a copy of your book. Even if the interview isn't about the book itself (and it probably won't be), having the book in hand helps the podcaster to come up with interview questions.

5. **Keep the discussion going.** Naturally, you'll want to listen to the episode with your interview in it, but don't stop there. Check the show notes to see what listeners have to say about the show. Is there anything you can pick up on and respond to?

It's also a good idea to listen to the next episode for more feedback, and to send in any answers you have to questions which might have come up. Some questions might come directly to you, but many listeners feel more comfortable dealing with the podcast host(s). If enough listeners want to know more, you might get invited back for another interview.

Show Notes

Providing a summary of your episodes with time markers helps your audience to tell at a glance what's included in the episode. Although it may appear that providing show notes is a cosmetic item that you can ignore, shows notes provide much needed search engine traffic. The keywords, names of people, and Web site addresses you include in your show notes will be picked up by search engines and will bring new people to your podcast. Here's an example of show notes from Epidose 53 of Donna Papacosta's podcast called *Trafcom News.*[19]

00:01 Intro and welcome

00:55 Today's topic is based on my article about internal podcasts published in the March/April issue of the *Journal of Employee Communications Management*

01:45 Internal podcasting can be a smart way for a corporation to start podcasting, before venturing into an external cast.

02:25 Internal podcasting at Sedgwick Claims Management (first heard about them on For Immediate Release: The Hobson and Holtz Report)

03:45 Internal podcasting at ALTANA Pharma (Nycomed)

05:55 Podcasts are cost-effective

06:33 Replacing some conference calls with podcasts

07:45 How organizations measure success of their podcasts

08:30 Advice before starting your internal podcast

09:45 Not ready to commit to a podcast? Start with a series.

10:30 Short list of internal podcast applications: peers interviewing peers; leadership communications and interviews; education and training; conference podcasts; visit my new microsite *PodcastYourConference.com.*

13:00 Please share your internal podcasting case study with me

13:33 Comment from Corey Taratuta of the *Irish Fireside Podcast*

15:48 Comment from Luke Armour of the Observations of Public Relations blog

17:55 Comment from Ron Hartman

18:50 Where to send comments: e-mail to trafcom AT gmail.com, call the comment line at 206-338-4200 or post a message to the Trafcom News Podcast blog

19:08 Promo of the new Foreword Thinking Podcast from Mitch Joel of Twist Image

Look for the Trafcom News Podcast on Blubrry.com

Theme music is "Beneath Your Surface" by the Elisabeth Lohninger Quartet from the Podsafe Music Network

Papacosta does a lot of things right with her show notes.

- **She includes keywords.** This is critical since search engines can't listen to audio or view video. To be indexed and ranked high in a search engine for certain keywords, writing show notes helps.

- **She includes comments from her audience.** This is a great community-building tool as most people love to have their egos stroked. Hearing their own voices played in a podcast and seeing their names written in a podcaster's show notes does a lot to build loyalty.

- **She includes time markers.** If her audience can't listen to the entire episode, they can fast forward to the information they really want to hear.

- **She includes Web site addresses and phone numbers.** This is extremely helpful for those who listen to her podcast while traveling or working out. They can just visit her podpage to write down the information just in case a pen and paper isn't near.

What are some other tips for writing really good show notes? Jason Van Orden, author of *Promoting Your Podcast*, provides some tips in the following article.[20]

Summarize/Outline Each Episode

Your show notes should provide, at a glance, an outline of the contents of an episode. This is not only a matter of convenience for your audience but it also serves to lure visitors to your site into listening to your podcast. I'll talk more about this in a bit.

If you carefully prepared and wrote an outline for your podcast before recording, then producing show notes should be easy. You want to include enough information to pull people in without giving everything away.

You can write a paragraph or two that summarize the episode or you can do it in outline form like I do. I also like to include relevant images in my posts. Images add interest and attract the eye.

Include a Captivating Title

The title of your blog post for a podcast episode is important. You should think of this as a headline for that episode. By reading it, a site visitor should want to listen. I would suggest putting more than just "Episode #1" in the title.

Use Popular Keywords

Keywords are phrases that people commonly search for on the Internet. Think about what your potential audience might be searching for on the Internet. Use these phrases in your show notes if they pertain to the episode. This will help your site show up in searches for that phrase, bringing traffic to your site. This is one of the most important purposes of your show notes as audio indexing and search is still a new technology and you cannot depend on this to bring in many visitors yet.

For example, I often mention a variety of New York City dining spots and sites in *GothamCast*. I mention the names of these in my show notes. As a result, my site is getting indexed in the search engines for those phrases. I've started to notice traffic from searches for cafes and other spots that I talk about on the show. In fact, sometimes I show up in a Google search above their official site.

Relevant Links and Resources from Your Show

If you mention Web addresses, phone numbers, e-mail addresses and other such information, it is hard for your listeners to remember this information. They may not be where they can write it down or look at it online right away. It's important to include this kind of information in your show notes. This will enhance the listening experience for your audience.

Each time you post a new podcast episode to your blog, you should include show notes in the blog post. Good show notes enhance your show by offering a convenient outline of the contents of each episode. A good title and well-thought-out show notes will bring new visitors to your site and entice people to listen and subscribe to your podcast.

Transcripts

Transcripts are a written account of the conversation that took place in your podcast. You can transcribe the audio or video on your own, hire an agency to do it for you, or use software. In the 1980s, transcripts were really popular with television talk shows. As a young girl, I would watch *Donahue* and I remember that at the end of every broadcast, there would be information posted about buying the transcripts of the show for a few dollars. Since this model worked for television, many podcasters adopted it for their own podcasts. Many podcasters tried to follow this same model of transcribing their podcast episode and offering it for sale. Although this is an admirable approach to making money, the majority of podcasters I've chatted to no longer sell transcripts due to lack of interest from their audience. Instead, many podcasters are using transcripts to gain search engine traffic to their podcast. You post the transcripts of your podcast on your podpage and as the search engines crawl your new content, they will index the contents contained in your transcripts. This helps you to generate additional traffic to your podpage and convert some of those visitors into audience members.

As I stated before, you can transcribe your rich media content on your own. If you decide to go this route, be prepared to spend a lot of time doing this. I tried to transcribe one episode of *Podonomics* thinking it would take me little time to do it. It took me one hour to transcribe five minutes of audio. Since time is money, I decided to outsource the transcription tasks to a company. When choosing a transcription company to work with, you have to be careful. Price alone shouldn't be the sole factor you use in choosing who to transcribe your audio. Some transcribers will only transcribe the words, which mean you'll still have to edit the transcription for clarity. Although we may sound intelligent speaking, when our conversations are transcribed, it doesn't read well. So, either you have to go through and edit for readability after you receive the transcripts, or for a higher fee you can hire a person to not only transcribe verbatim but also transcribe for clarity.

To give you an idea of pricing, a 60-minute audio file typically takes three hours to transcribe verbatim by a talented transcriptionist who has all the right tools. On the cheaper side, some transcription agencies charge per audio minute. These fees range from $0.27 to $1 per audio minute. If it's 15 minutes of audio, you would pay $0.27 × 15 minutes. If it's 60 minutes, well you get the point. The fees are low because these transcription agencies hire people in India or the Philippines who have a good command of English. Typically, offshore companies will transcribe your audio word-for-word and you'll have to give it a once-over to edit for clarity. On the flipside, transcribers located in North America typically charge by the hour, anywhere from $10 to $50 per hour. For this rate, North American transcribers typically transcribe for readability and clarity.

To decide which company to hire, you're simply limited by your time and your budget. So:

- If you have a couple of hours to spare and you have a large number of audio files to transcribe, you may want to select an inexpensive transcription agency to work with. You spend less in terms of money, but because these companies transcribe verbatim, you'll need to spend a couple more hours editing the transcript for readability.

- If you don't have time to spare and/or money isn't an issue, you should consider hiring someone who can transcribe verbatim and for clarity. You won't have to spend any time editing the transcription for readability as the more costly transcription services do it for you.

E-mail Lists

Over the past three years, I've built a database of around 2,500 e-mail addresses. These are people who have opted-in to my e-mail list. Every time I publish a new episode, I send an e-mail to my list. It's important that you don't spam people. You need to get people's permission to add them to your e-mailing list. If you don't have a database of e-mail addresses, just add an e-mail sign-up box to your podcast page. You can use *feedburner.com, feedblitz.com*, or *aweber.com* to manage your e-mail subscriptions, so instead of doing everything manually, the system takes care of everything automatically. The only thing you'll need to be concerned about is how many people are on your list.

Online Press Release Distribution Services

As I mentioned earlier, you can use the press release you faxed, mailed, and e-mailed to journalists to post in a variety of online press release distribution services. You create a free profile, log in, and then submit the contents of your press release. Most will allow you to post for free, but you get additional features if you pay a little bit of money. The extra features will be worth your money because if you pay, you can upload your logo, a multimedia file, a trackback URL so you know who else published your press release, and a wider distribution of your press release.

- *PRWeb.com*

- *PRNewswire.com*

- *PR.com*

- *24-7pressrelease.com*

- *Newswiretoday.com*

- *PR9.net*

- *openPR.com*

- *Theopenpress.com*

- *emediawire.com*

Online press release distribution services won't bring you an interview right away. Journalists aren't crawling these Web sites looking for their next big story. With that said, don't dismiss these online press release distribution services too soon. Although you won't get a phone call or e-mail the very hour you upload your press release online, you will benefit from how well your press release is ranked in search engines. Include keywords in both the title and body of your press release and you'll reap the rewards with a high ranking. For example, if you're publishing a gardening podcast, you would include keywords in the title and body of your press release that relate to gardening.

Another tactic when using online press release distribution services is to release a series of press releases over a few days. Instead of using the same release over and over, you can write five, 10 or more different press releases that mention your podcast, but each has a different angle. That way, you can attract more attention and hit different markets so that you heighten your chances of generating both a buzz online and coverage in traditional media. This tactic was used in 2006 by Jeffrey and Bryan Eisenberg, the brothers who wrote the book called *Waiting for Your Cat to Bark?* Over a three-month period, the brothers published one release almost every day with different concepts and from different angles. The result? Their book was the first self-published book to make it to the *New York Times* bestsellers list. To get an idea of the different angles they took to generate a buzz about their book, take a look at the titles of their press releases from *PRWeb.com*:

- *New Marketing Book Says Consumer Polls May Not Reflect Actual Spending Behavior* (Published July 12, 2006)—This press release explored what makes a customer stay loyal to a company.

- *Persuasion Architecture Meets Sales to Maximize Marketing* (Published July 13, 2006)—This press release looked at how persuasion and the customer buying experience align in the sales process.

- *Best-Selling Authors Show How to Predict Consumer Behavior in New Book* (Published July 18, 2006)—This press release outlined the four primary consumer behavior temperaments that can help businesses predict customer behavior.

- *New Media Boosts Consumer Confidence; Businesses Must Deliver Best Experience* (Published July 19, 2006)—This press release looked at how the Internet helps consumers make better buying decisions.

- *Evolving Consumer Behavior Means Consumers Win in Expanding Media Market* (Published July 20, 2006)—This press release detailed why businesses are having a hard time reaching their target market because consumers are less trusting of marketing and advertising campaigns.

In all the press releases written by the Eisenberg brothers, their book was mentioned just twice—once at the beginning when the first author provided a quote and again toward the bottom where a summary paragraph offered some information about the book. You can use this tactic with your podcast. Again, focus on creating a story around a major news item, holiday, or upcoming event. Then, to keep the interest buzzing around your podcast, create a series of press releases that cover various angles and upload them to an online press release distribution service over a series of days. With your gardening podcast, you can talk about how consumers can create their own backyard compost to take part in a Green Day event. A couple days later, sum up the expert advice from a recent guest on your show who gave tips on how to prepare your garden for the cold winter months.

Creating a Community

In a keynote address at the 2006 Podcast and New Media Expo, Andrew Michael Baron, creator of *Rocketboom*, said that one of the things he's doing for his audience is creating a sense of belonging.[21] This fact is overlooked by many podcasters. Some are looking for that quick hit, a chance to make a huge splash in very little time. Others want to release 3 episodes, then walk away from their podcasting strategy because they achieved their short term goals. However, when you produce a podcast, you have an obligation to your audience. Your audience looks to you for leadership, entertainment and companionship. As a podcast producer, your audience considers you a leader and leaders know that ditching people is not the way to build confidence in their management abilities. In every Star Trek show I've watched, there comes a point when the crew has to abandon ship. Each Star Trek captain, whether it's Kirk, Picard, Sisko, Janeway or Archer, will stay with the ship until every crew member is in an escape pod. A captain never abandons his or her crew and he or she will go down with the ship until the bitter end.

I'm certainly not suggesting that you go down with a burning ship, however, I used the Star Trek example to show you that as a podcaster, you have a responsibility. Your audience is looking to you to provide a safe, fun and private environment where they can interact with you, meet other fans of your podcast and identify your podpage as their new hang out spot on the Internet. This type of community takes on a life of its own and when people start talking about your podcast, the amount of money you spend on promotions starts to decrease. To cultivate a sense of belonging for your audience, here are some techniques you can use to create a community around your podcast.

Audio Comments

Invite audio comments, then use them in each episode. The hosts of *InsidePr.ca* produce two episodes per week—one that is their main segment, the other that includes only audio comments from their listeners. They have a 10-digit phone number that people can call and leave their feedback verbally. These comments are played in the podcast.

Other services that don't require your audience to dial a phone number and incur long-distance charges are ones that allow people to leave a voice-mail online using a microphone plugged into their computer. Services such as Mobatalk capture both audio and video comments that your audience can leave just by clicking a button. To use Mobatalk on your podpage, you create a free profile on the Mobatalk Web site, then copy and paste the code into the pages of your blog or Web site. When your audience leaves you messages through Mobatalk, his or her name appears in the window of the audio comment system as shown in Figure 4.4.

Written Comments

Not everyone will feel comfortable about leaving audio or video comments on your podpage. You can collect written comments by e-mail or in the comment section of your blog. If you're using a blog, make sure the commenting feature is turned on. Then, in your podcast, invite listeners to leave comments related to the episode. When audience members leave their comments, be sure to read them into future episodes. Donna Papacosta, host of *Trafcom Podcast*, spends a

Figure 4.4.   Mobatalk comment system on *The Engaging Brand* blog.

few minutes at the end of each episode to read some of the written comments that are left on her blog.

For both audio and written comments, you should add a note to your podpage expressing that any comments received will be used by you and edited for length or clarity with no compensation. Although most people won't object to this disclaimer, it's good to include this so people have a clear understanding that their comments will be used for other purposes. Check the companion Web site for an example of this disclaimer.

Wikis

Wikis are collaborative Web sites that allow visitors to add, remove, and edit content.[22] The word **wiki** is a Hawaiian word meaning "quick" and the best-known wiki is Wikipedia.org, the online encyclopedia.[23] These quick Web sites are easy to set up and rely on those who visit the pages to update it with new information. Many podcasters are using wikis to share information with their audience. This is an ideal alternative to HTML pages or e-mails because the information is better organized. If you're asked the same questions over and over or if you find that you need space to display additional information about your episodes, wikis prove to be a viable alternative to a Web site where you have to wait for your webmaster to update.

Shel Holtz and Neville Hobson, hosts of *For Immediate Release*, created a wiki for their podcast to display the show notes.[24] Listeners are invited to update the wiki with information that Holtz and Hobson mentioned in the podcast. Contributors can add time markers, topics, Web site addresses, and the names of people that Holtz and Hobson spoke about. Those who added information to the wiki can then add their name to the contributor section. While Holtz and Hobson can create their own show notes, allowing their listeners to take on this responsibility gives them a chance to collaborate with each other as well as the hosts.

Andrew Michael Baron, producer of *Rocketboom*, uses a wiki to post answers to frequently asked questions.[25] One of the questions he's constantly asked is what type of gear he uses to record and create *Rocketboom*. He recently purchased a new video camera and instead of answering questions about the model number, price, and where he purchased it from e-mails, Baron simply posted the information to the *Rocketboom* wiki. Some felt the need to also correct his spelling mistakes and grammar, but this is a benefit (or drawback) to using a wiki to share information.[26]

There are many tools online to help you create a wiki for free. *Wikimatrix.org* is a Web site that compares the plethora of wiki software tools that are available. It compares wikis based on hosting needs, costs, security, and other features. In choosing a wiki for your podcast, here are some questions to consider:

- **Does it allow me to restrict access?** You may want your audience to edit some pages, but not others. Most wikis allow you to restrict access; however, you may have to pay extra to be able to edit permissions for users.

- **Can I choose where to host my wiki?** Most podcasters use the hosting provided by the company that offers the wiki. This shouldn't be a problem unless you get thousands of people editing your wiki pages at any one time. Once your traffic peaks, your hosting may be affected. Hosting your wiki on another server means you can use a top-level domain instead of a sub-domain as your Web site address. People will remember *cubicledivaswiki.com* (top-level domain) instead of *cubicledivas.pbwiki.org* (sub-domain).

- **Are there statistics available?** Having access to raw numbers that tell you where in the world people are editing from, as well as how many times they edit, can be useful when putting together your measurement numbers (see Chapter 10). Most free versions won't give you access to any statistics.

- **Is it insanely easy to create and edit pages?** Most wikis come with a WYSIWYG editor, meaning you just type text in an area and click on buttons to bold, highlight or hyperlink text. The WYSIWYG editor is similar to a Word document. You type up text and click on the *B* button in the toolbar to make words bolded. If you find it easy to edit the pages, your audience will too.

- **Can I edit the page to reflect my podcast colors and logo?** Consistent branding helps to make a better connection with your audience. Most free versions won't allow you to edit the colors of the pages.

- **Does it provide a multilingual interface?** If you're an English-speaking podcaster, most likely your wiki will be in English, even if you have a global audience. However, if you're a Danish-speaking podcaster, you'll want the pages all in Danish. Some wikis allow you to create pages in the language of your choice. Others are limited to just two or three languages, so double-check what language choices are available.

- **Can I e-mail those registered on my wiki?** If you can send messages to all those registered on the wiki, this is another great way to promote your podcast. Just remember that some of the people who are registered on your wiki are most likely consuming your podcast, so don't bombard them with too many messages.

Facebook, Twitter, and other Social Networking Tools

Whether it's LinkedIn, openBC, Ryze, MySpace, Friendster, Ecademy, Meetup or Facebook, networking online has helped many to gain new business contacts and form new friendships. In their book *The Virtual Handshake*, David Teten and David Allen use the term **social software** to refer to these Web sites and define it as:

> *"[The] tools which help you to discover, extend, manage, enable communication, and/or leverage your social network."*[27]

In its simplest form, social networking Web sites allow people to network with one another based on a specific interest. Using social networking Web sites to connect your audience makes sense because you can create groups, networks, and forums around the one thing you care about—your podcast. As explained in the Introduction, no matter how weird, bizarre, or odd your interests are, you are bound to find a group of people online who are just as weird, bizarre, or odd as you are. If you love your podcast, chances are there is a group of people who love it just as much.

Mitch Joel, host of *Six Pixels of Separation*, created a group on Facebook to connect his listeners and "centralize people interested in the podcast."[28] He explains on his blog why he selected Facebook over other social networking Web sites:

> *"After looking at groups on LinkedIn, frappr, and the like, it seems like joining a Facebook group is the lowest barrier to entry. We've got well over 90 people—in less than 12 hours of creating the group—as part of the community and my hopes are that you will join. It's free (always the right price)—all you need is to create a Facebook profile of yourself—but, more importantly, it's a chance for you to dive into online social networks, meet like-minded people and better understand how communities like Facebook and other online social networks operate."*[29]

Not only does Joel want to create a community for his listeners using Facebook, but he hopes that his target audience, marketers, will feel less fearful of Web 2.0 while participating in Joel's Facebook group.

"Facebook is also crazy hot right now, so my hopes are that marketers will dive in, connect, co-create and share. I'm also hoping that you'll check out your brand, products, services and competitors to see who's been talking (and creating) content out of love (or hate) for you. Another immediate opportunity is to see how the user interaction is on Facebook. The days of clicking and reading are long gone. It's a heavily immersive experience."[30]

Twitter is a social networking tool that provides short, text-based updates that are sent to other users who want to receive them. Anyone can be your friend and view what's going on in your world. Some choose to read the updates of what their friends are doing on the Twitter Web site, others choose to receive them via a text message to their mobile phone and another option is to add a plug-in to a blog that will display your status to all who visit.

Although most people will use Twitter to communicate random meanderings, podcasters are using it to generate feedback or update fans on the production status of an upcoming episode. Shel Holtz and Neville Hobson, hosts of *For Immediate Release*, use Twitter to communicate with their audience.[31] You'll see the variety of comments left by the hosts, as well as by their fans.

Taking Action

When using these tools to promote your podcast and grow your audience, remember not to create a barrier to participation. If a tool requires too many forms to fill in or requires too many downloads, abandon it for something much easier. Your goal is to encourage your audience to create a relationship with you and your podcast, not to add yet another piece of digital noise to their already busy lives.

1. Choose an offline promotional tool to market your podcast.

2. Then, choose several online promotional tools to use to market your podcast. Remember, you're only limited by your time.

3. Decide on how you'll use your podcast to create a community for your listeners.

Part II

Generating Profit

Earning an income through your podcast can be a reality if you apply the right tools. There are a variety of ways you can generate money with a podcast and choosing the right one will depend only on your time and creativity. All the scenarios you'll read about in the following chapters are actual strategies used by podcasters. You won't find strategies that are based in theory. Instead, you will read about practical examples that are generating a solid return on investment for both individuals and businesses. The money earned is enough to pay for incidental fees, such as hosting or new podcasting equipment, while other podcasters are earning enough to quit their day jobs. I would suggest that you read through the following chapters so you can understand the possibilities before applying a specific strategy to your own podcast.

5

Selling Products and Services

We have now reached the profit stage in the seven-step process (see Figure 5.1). The most obvious way to make money podcasting is to encourage your audience to buy your products and services. However, if all your episodes sound like infomercials, you'll scare your audience away. Whether you're already sell-

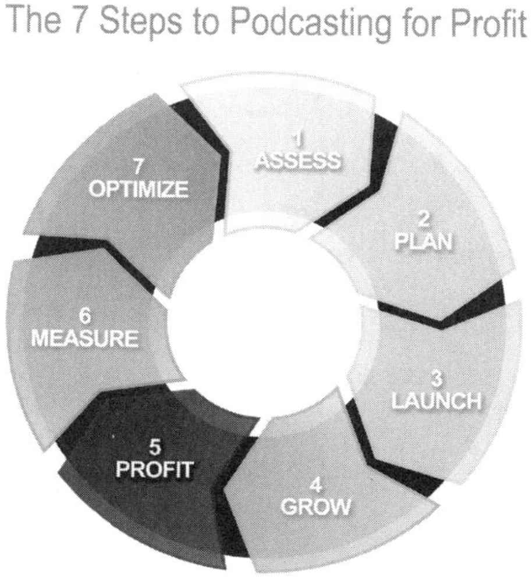

The 7 Steps to Podcasting for Profit

Figure 5.1. Podcasting for profit steps—profit.

ing products or services in your business or if you're interested in selling other people's products or services (a very viable alternative), this chapter will teach you the techniques to use to sell to your audience without coming across like a used car salesman or a pushy telemarketer. Always remember you must create value for your audience first and sell second.

The Breadcrumb Podcasting Approach

Late-night television is filled with infomercials. Products are being sold to satisfy a common problem. Promises are made to help you lose weight, tone up, make money, and free up your time. Typically 30 minutes in length, these infomercials sell everything from juicers to eyebrow tweezers to workout machines. According to the Electronic Retailing Association, direct response television and infomercials form a $150 billion industry.[1]

What makes these infomercials so successful is that they follow a specific formula in order to translate those eyeballs into billions of dollars in product sales. First, you have to find the energetic host, that person who will say, "Amazing," or "Incredible," to everything being said. Then, you have to find the product specialist, that person who has used the product and can attest to the results. After describing a problem, the product is presented as the solution. A bonus is offered, a price is shown, and the guarantee is offered.

Although this formula works for late-night television, it's typically a lousy process for podcasts. If you hype up your products and services in your podcast, this will do more to discourage people from subscribing to your podcast. The infomercial model on how to sell products and services is not likely to work with your podcast.

To be successful selling your products and services through a podcast, you need to think of it as a lead generation tool. That is, to find people who are likely to buy your products or services so you can turn them into customers. You should use your podcast to give a teaser and lay the breadcrumbs that will lead your listeners to want the full course meal. This full course meal will be your products and services that are available on your Web site or blog. A 2006 report released by Marketing Sherpa showed that 22 percent of managers listed podcasting in their top five lead generating tools.[2] A year earlier, podcasting didn't even show up in the top five. This shows that many businesses and individuals recognize that podcasts are an effective tool in turning listeners or viewers into customers.

You use your podcast to generate leads, then you direct listeners or viewers to your Web site for more information. I call this model the breadcrumb podcasting approach, or BPA for short, borrowing from the children's fable *Hansel and Gretel*. In that story, the children were led into the forest and abandoned. To find their way back home, Hansel had laid breadcrumbs along the path so they could simply follow the trail of crumbs to retrace their steps. Unfortunately, the birds and other animals in the forest ate all the breadcrumbs and poor Hansel and Gretel had no other choice but to go to the big candy house to fill their hungry bellies.

Although it was unfortunate that the forest animals ate the breadcrumbs that the young children left behind, you will want people to consume the breadcrumbs you leave behind online so they can follow the trail back to your online shopping cart or Web site. If you want to sell products and services using your podcast, the BPA is the best method to use. You want to use your podcast to lay the breadcrumbs. After they consume the breadcrumbs along your path, in this case, your podcast episodes, you will lead them to the end, in other words, your Web site, e-mail, toll-free order line, or whatever. Because the breadcrumbs are free and are simply the appetizer, people will want more. They will hungrily go to follow the trail and purchase the full course meal, in other words, a product or service that will help them solve their problem.

The BPA was the first model I used to make money podcasting. I didn't like ads, nor was I interested in pitching products. Instead, I would hold a live 60-minute seminar over the phone and charge those who attended a fee of $19. On the date and time of the seminar, attendees would call into a number, enter in an access code, and hear me interview a guest. Because my audience was mainly female entrepreneurs and career women, I would interview people who also targeted women. One of my guests was *The Sales Diva* and she helped women take the fear out of selling.[3] I would record the entire call and then edit the recording to include my intro and outro, plus remove any other verbal clutter, such as "ums," "ahs," or "you knows." I would add the recording as a digital download to my shopping cart and send out an e-mail to my mailing list to let them know that a new product was for sale.

I'd also update my podcast with the recording of the seminar. Now, I wouldn't produce the entire 60-minute recording as a podcast. Because I wanted to encourage people to buy the recording in my shopping cart, I used my podcast to give a taste of what people missed by not attending the live seminar. Instead, for my podcast, I would cut out a 10-minute selection from the seminar recording, typically the most interesting and emotional part of the interview and produce that into a podcast. At the end of the 10-minute podcast, my call to action was to invite listeners to my Web site to purchase the entire 60-minute recording on CD or as a digital download.

Using the BPA did three things:

1. *It increased sales.* While I would typically make just under $200 for the live seminar, once I added podcasting as a tool to market the recordings, I was soon pulling in just under $2,000.

2. *It built my list.* Every time someone bought a product from me or visited *cubicledivas.com*, he or she made a choice to give me their e-mail address. This helped me increase my mailing list by 30 percent in five months.[4]

3. *It increased the trust and interaction between my audience and me.* My podcast allowed me to not only share the recordings from my live seminars but it gave me a chance to update listeners on my goings-on. My listeners started to reach out to me by leaving comments on the audio comment line or e-mailing me about their issues. I no longer seemed untouchable and my listeners started to crave interaction with each other and me. My trust level went up because now my listeners could hear the more human side of Leesa Barnes.

A word of warning: If you give away too much in your podcast, your listeners will be full and won't have a need to spend money with you. I remember going to a mixer and the appetizers were to die for. Slivers of beef wrapped around a thin breadstick. Rice balls stuffed with pink salmon. Gourmet pizza with sprinkles of parmesan cheese and pieces of spicy chicken. Miniature hamburgers dressed with mango relish. There was no need to hit the restaurant afterward as these appetizers filled me to the brim.

Had the event organizers chosen to feed us simple cheese, crackers, and vegetable sticks, I would've excused myself after 90 minutes to dine in the restaurant on a $40 plate of Grade A steak and mashed potatoes. Hungry people will never be satisfied with the free crackers and cheese. If you stuff people with too much information at the breadcrumb stage, they will leave you feeling satisfied without having spent a dime with you. For example, if you went to an ice cream store and they gave you a whole scoop as a free sample instead of on a teeny tiny pink spoon, would you bother to spend any more money with them? Of course not, because your needs have been satisfied with the large scoop.

Another thing to remember when selling products and services through your podcast is that your content needs to be interactive and infotaining. In other words, the way that the BPA can work is to offer your content, which is packed full of information and is also entertaining. Whether you're producing an audio or video podcast, giving your audience tips and tricks in an entertaining way that will prompt them to crave more.

Selling Intangible Items

Selling the intangible can be tough. It takes a lot longer to convince someone to invest their money in something they can't see or touch. There are many honest entrepreneurs selling intangible items through a Web site, but unfortunately, there are equally as many dishonest entrepreneurs. According to a survey conducted in 2006 by CyberSource, online merchants lose $3 billion a year due to scams, an increase of 7 percent from the year before.[5]

Those who use a podcast to communicate to prospects and customers stand way ahead of the pack as it shows that there's a live person on the other end. Your podcast will make prospects comfortable spending money with you. If your prospect can hear you before they buy, this will increase their comfort level. In a survey of 928 Canadians, 54 percent of podcast listeners would be somewhat likely to buy a product or service based on the host's recommendation.[6] Using audio in your marketing and communications strategy also helps to:

- Build trust.

- Build rapport.

- Target the right person.

Because of the low cost involved in packaging and distributing intangible items, the profit margin is quite high. There's nothing to ship, the production costs are minimal, and there's no money to spend on packaging. All you need to do is record an audio or video file, save it in a format that can be consumed, and sell it on a Web page or Web site. A person pays a fee and after their purchase is approved, they're given additional information on where to download the file. As soon as the person downloads the digital product, he or she can consume it right away. Here are a couple of ways podcasters are using their podcast to sell intangible items.

Marina's Fitness

Marina Kamen is a New York-based recording artist who produces unique fitness beats and sells them on CDs. The winner of the 2005 People's Choice Podcast Award, Marina's High-nrg Fitness audio workouts come complete with verbal training instructions as well as original music written, produced, and performed by Kamen at the proper tempo for each workout (see Figure 5.2).[7]

She describes why podcasting became a natural extension of her business:

Figure 5.2. Marina's Fitness podcast.

"When podcasting started, I created 10-minute segments because it took forever to download a half-hour show. So, I created these 10-minute walking programs where I would write the music, sing to you, talk to you, and get you to walk. Podcasting was a natural transition of my audio musical fitness entertainment product. It was a perfect marriage because, let's face it, people with an iPod can't walk or run while looking at a video."[8]

Her podcasts are now offered in six-minute segments where she interviews people asking them about their fitness challenges and successes. Past guests include singer Carnie Wilson, actress Liza Minnelli, as well as doctors and physical trainers. These interviews have a fitness beat that plays behind it so while listening to the interview, you can workout at the gym or take a brisk walk. These short interviews are offered through iTunes and at the end of the interview, Kamen invites listeners to go to her Web site to purchase a full-length workout on CD or download individual tracks at 99 cents each. Kamen credits her success not only to her 20 plus years as a recording artist, but also because of the type of audio she produces:

"I own an 11,000 square foot studio in Times Square. I produce [my audio] in top-of-the-line studios that I own. I make sure it sounds as good as any record you're hearing out there. It has to. The public is very fickle and no matter what anybody says, the

reason most podcasts do not get listened to is because the audio quality is so poor. We're all spoiled, we're all used to hearing incredible audio quality on everything."

Kamen herself lost over 100 lbs. and uses that experience to motivate others to lose weight. Her story has appeared in the *New York Times, Billboard Magazine,* and *Women's Own Magazine.* Kamen can produce up to 27 new tracks in one day and the revenue she generates from single track downloads at *MarinaOnline.com* and shipments of her audio workouts on CD now make up a good portion of her business:

> *"It is increasing daily. I would say now that it's probably up to 40 percent. In 2005, I had over a million downloads internationally."*

Work At Home Moms Radio

A Web-hosting disaster took Kelly McCausey, host of *Work At Home Moms Radio,* to an online forum where all the clients from the now defunct Web-hosting company met to cry, lament, and talk about what happened. McCausey, whose background is in desktop publishing, decided to help work-at-home moms (WAHM for short) move their Web sites to her newly launched Web-hosting company. Eventually, McCausey realized that she could use her Internet savvy to teach other moms how to run a successful business while staying at home with their children. McCausey illustrates what issues WAHMs have that is unique to this market:

> *"We're small business owners... and we're balancing this with a desire to be home with our kids. A huge percentage of WAHMs have small children at home, under their feet, nursing babies or they're expecting another one. That changes the dynamic of running a small business in a major way. The importance of building a business that can run large chunks of itself on its own using automation becomes really important. What unites the community are the values. The main goal is being home with your children. We want Internet success, of course we do. I'm a single parent so if I don't succeed, we're not going to eat this week."*[9]

McCausey started producing a weekly Internet radio program called *Work at Home Moms Radio* in which she doles out advice to WAHMs on how to build a

Figure 5.3. Work at Home Moms Radio.

successful business using the Internet (see Figure 5.3). When she first started her weekly Internet radio program back in 2005, she sold advertising spots to businesses that wanted to promote their products or services to the WAHM community. Through advertising, McCausey was pulling in anywhere from $700 to $800 per month. Once her podcast was launched a year later, which was simply the syndicated version of her Internet radio program, McCausey saw her audience nearly double. Although she has a couple hundred subscribers, McCausey finds her download statistics much more valuable. She tracks her downloads off her Web statistics and she's reaching 1,000 plus listeners per week.

McCausey quickly saw that she could make more money from using her podcast to lead listeners to her other products and services than from selling ad space on her Internet radio program and in her podcast. McCausey abandoned the advertising approach because she found another alternative that proved to be more successful:

> "In 2004, my [business partner] Alice Seba and I launched Mom Masterminds, which is a private mentoring membership site for WAHMs. That boosted my income significantly. In 2005, I launched a print newsletter for WAHMs that had a paid subscription. So, my other income was growing to the point that the advertising income no longer seemed all that significant. In the summer of 2006, my little print newsletter turned into a magazine and my subscribers leveled off at three hundred for months. I was

a little disappointed because I wanted to reach thousands. So, I decided to make the magazine free to "Mom Masterminds" subscribers and make advertising in the magazine so attractive that advertisers would cover my costs. In making that decision, I stopped selling advertising in my radio show and used it to stop promoting other people's messages and to promote my own."

McCausey earns a five-figure income from home selling everything from coaching services to digital products. The audience she attracts to her Internet radio program and podcast are fed directly into her monthly Mom Masterminds program. This service is a hands-on mentoring community for mothers who are ready to work past the fluff and re-focus on making real money from their online businesses.[10] For just $39.97 per month for 12 months, those who join the Mom Masterminds get access to a membership Web site that includes special reports, audio content, and worksheets. In addition, members get to call in to special conference calls where they receive information from McCausey on how to make the most out of their Internet-based business. With 180 members in this program, most find out about Mom Masterminds through McCausey's Internet radio program and podcast.

McCausey herself was able to become debt-free and leave her full-time position as a result of setting up a business online. McCausey was in debt ever since her divorce 15 years ago. She was working full-time at the time and when she finally paid off her last bad debt, her outlook started to change on her Internet-based business:

"When everything you make is going somewhere, you get a defeating attitude. Nothing is ever going to change. It was the next month that I saw my checking account actually getting fat, I thought, 'Oh my goodness! I might be able to make a decision based on what I want to do, not what I have to do.' And that's when I took a really good look at the numbers and I discovered I was making as much at home as I was making at my day job."

Meshcasts

Billed as Canada's Web 2.0 conference, Mesh was founded by five ordinary guys who are passionate about the Internet and how people use it to make money and socialize with one another.[11] The annual conference held every spring attracts close to 400 attendees who are equally as passionate about Web 2.0. Keynote addresses, workshops, and the opportunity to network—or "mesh" as the organizers call it—are what drive people to register for this yearly event. Once the conference is over, the organizers continue to engage attendees and attract new fans by keeping the blog on the Mesh Web site fresh with information.

In the months leading up to the second conference held in May 2007, the Mesh organizers decided to do something a bit different. Instead of just posting text-based posts on their blog, they put in plans to post audio podcasts called Meshcasts (see Figure 5.4), a hybrid between Mesh and podcasts. To gather content, the Mesh organizers held informal networking events and interviewed some of the attendees about their reaction to the most interesting things happening in technology. With the attendees' permission, these interviews were then produced as podcasts and posted to the blog. Attendees who heard their voice in the episode would comment about the Meshcasts on their own blog and send the link to friends and colleagues. This not only created a buzz, but also helped to keep the community involved in an event that was weeks away from going live.

While the outro in the podcast did not explicitly tell listeners to go buy a ticket to the event, it did encourage listeners to go to the conference Web site to find out more. Tickets were virtual, in other words, attendees were not mailed a ticket, nor were any printed out for the event. Instead, the conference organizers used an online ticketing system called *Eventbrite.com* to sell virtual tickets and manage attendee information. The event sold out 10 days before it was slated to start.[12] The conference organizers relied on a number of

Figure 5.4.   Mesh conference podcast.

tools to keep the energy going in the 11 months between each conference and podcasting only helped to enhance their relationship with attendees and create anticipation.

Selling Tangible Items

Tangible products are physical products that someone can touch and feel. Merchandise, such as T-shirts, mugs, caps, and computers, and information products, such as books, CDs, workbooks, DVDs, and videos, are just some of the examples of the physical products that you can sell on your Web site or blog. Consumers tend to put more value on tangible products because they can carry them wherever they go and because they're perceived to have more value. It's harder to curl up by the fireplace with a downloadable book in PDF. Most likely, it's sitting on your computer and to make it transportable, you'll need to print it out. With a hardcopy book, there's no waiting for your printer to print two hundred pages. Instead, you grab the book and head out to the pool for a little rest and relaxation. From the seller's standpoint, tangible products increase your credibility. In his book *Book Yourself Solid*, Micheal Port indicates that creating information products is one of the seven core self-promotion strategies that help small business owners get more clients than they can handle.[13] Review the case studies below to find out how these podcasters sold a tangible product through their podcast.

Justice League Podcast

A new video game called *Justice League Heroes* was being released worldwide. According to Julian Hollingshead, director of marketing at Warner Bros. Interactive Entertainment, podcasting provided the best medium to help set the prequel to the story that will be completed in the video game.

> *"We told an interesting, but brief, background story to the* Justice League Heroes *video game with the podcasts—and the game tells the rest of the story—a much longer one at that."*[14]

Both an enhanced audio and a video podcast were produced so that people could consume the podcast according to what worked best for them. The storyboards, sound effects, and voiceover artists used in the video game were used to craft the storyline for the podcasts. Each video podcast was no more than five minutes and viewers were encouraged to go to the Justice League Heroes Web site to find out more about the video game. While Hollingshead couldn't disclose the number of downloads for each of the three episodes, he did say that his team was happy with the results as word-of-mouth and a top ranking in iTunes helped generate a buzz.

> *"The podcasts were high-ranked among the iTunes Store's Top Podcasts list for over two weeks, which we believe added to the strength of our promotional campaign for the video game."*

Irish Roots Café

Mike O'Laughlin has a passion for Irish history and has written over 39 titles on the topic and has published a few of his own. Before he started his podcast called *Irish Roots Cafe* (see Figure 5.5), Mike would use direct mail to send postcards to people to promote his books. With only a 1 percent response rate, the return on his investment was quite low and the cost to do these mailings was quite high.[15]

O'Laughlin discovered podcasting and immediately saw a way to replace the direct mail pieces. In each episode, O'Laughlin talks about some aspect

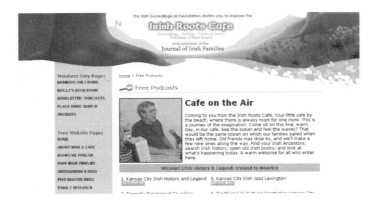

Figure 5.5. *Irish Roots Cafe* podcast.

of Irish history, content that can be found in his books. He even pulled up an interview he did 20 years ago with a few of his colleagues that he was able to transfer from tape to digital and use in one of his podcast episodes. While some were obviously inebriated, O'Laughlin was pleased to have a chance to repurpose an interview from so long ago for his podcast. The results? O'Laughlin has orders coming in from all over the world. Compared to the direct mail pieces, O'Laughlin not only saves money, but he now gets an opportunity to communicate with his audience through e-mail and his audio comment line.

Evil Genius Chronicles

Dave Slusher calls himself a contrarian, someone who doesn't think like everyone else and tells everyone as such. Slusher's podcast, *Evil Genius Chronicles*, is updated on an irregular schedule and contains his thoughts on anything. To him, he makes money podcasting not for profit, but to avoid loss:

> *"If the money didn't come in, I'd just reach into my pocket [to cover the expenses]. But that's not the kind of thing that builds up a lot of karma for you in the house. You have this little thing that you're doing and it ends up being a really expensive hobby. One of my goals fairly early on was to run at no worse than breakeven."*[16]

His very first sponsor was iPodderx and they sponsored Slusher's podcast for six months. With the money he got from this deal, he bought a whole bunch of T-shirts to sell to his audience; however, Slusher didn't feel right about pocketing all the money:

> *"Integral to my show is music that runs underneath the whole show. It's the same song every time. At that point, it seemed kind of wrong for me to make money and not somehow compensate the musicians behind that song. I worked out a deal where I only sold the T-shirts as a package deal with the CD that that song is on. I bought the CDs wholesale from the band. So, the band is seeing a couple dollars of every one of those sales. Since my show is synonymous with that band's song, the band is sort of like a co-creator of my podcast. I make money, he makes money. I'm inviting them to eat at the table."*

Selling Other People's Products or Services

Let's just say that you don't have any products or services. Or maybe you have a product or two, but you want to offer your audience a bigger selection. You can still make money by becoming an affiliate of a company that sells products or services you believe your audience would be interested in knowing about. One popular example is the Amazon.com associate program. You can sign up easily for this affiliate program and using a special code, you can sell any of Amazon's products on your Web site. Let's just say that you interviewed a marketing expert who just wrote a book called *Marketing Gym for Overweight Egos* (not a real title). After the interview is over, you recommend to your audience to go to your podpage to purchase the book. As your visitors click on the link and purchase the book, Amazon.com records it and sends you a check for the referral.

This doesn't stop you from offering related products for sale. If you know of a companion book that would complement *Marketing Gym for Overweight Egos*, then feel free to create the affiliate link and offer that related product for sale as well. Your audience will appreciate your research and will reward you in a slew of affiliate sales that can only help your bottom line.

Of course, Amazon isn't the only company that offers an affiliate program for their products. There are thousands of entrepreneurs, small business owners, hobbyists, and corporations that offer products or services for sale and give a commission for any referrals. Going this route means that you'll discover little gems, in other words, products or services your audience has never heard about.

Also, you'll find great guests for your podcasts as these individuals are always looking for ways to promote themselves. Here are just a couple of podcasters who are using affiliate marketing in their podcasts to sell other people's products and services.

Deserve What You Want

Four years after divorcing, Scot McKay never believed he would be ready to date ever again. After dating online, he not only met the greatest woman of his life, but he married her in December 2006. McKay, who produces four podcasts all related to dating (see Figure 5.6), teaches men the secrets to attracting and keeping women. With a background in life coaching, McKay helps men answer the question: "How can I craft myself into being the greatest man that I can possibly be so that I actually deserve the greatest woman whom I dream about. Not just deserve her, but attract her as well."[17]

Figure 5.6. *Deserve What You Want* forum.

McKay has a ton of products and uses his podcasts to lead people to them. However, what he found more valuable is promoting other people's products and services in his podcasts:

> *"What we found out having read some marketing literature and some Internet marketing stuff is that an advertisement will be marginally successful. However, a testimonial from a third party is up to 10 times more effective than an advertisement. Your advertising efforts may be successful, but if someone who's a third party says to a magazine readership or a television viewership or a podcast listenership, 'Hey, we like this product and we think you ought to go get it,' that manner of marketing is up to 10 times more effective than saying, 'Hey, we're the podcasters, go buy our product.'"*

McKay interviews people who have an expertise in an area that would interest his target market. Whether they're a big name self-help guru or an entrepreneur, McKay's podcasts provide these experts access to a highly niche, highly targeted group. He double-checks that his guest has an affiliate program. If so, McKay signs up for it. Because most affiliate links are difficult to remember due to the variety of words, numbers, and symbols they contain, McKay creates a directory on his server using the first name of his guest, then uses simple HTML redirect to send people to the guest's product or service. That means in every episode, the listener will hear *http://www.deservewhatyouwant.com/ nameofguest*. For every person who clicks on the link or types it in their browser, if they then purchase the item, McKay gets a commission for the sale.

Using this model, not only did McKay leave his full-time job to work on his podcast and Internet-based business full-time, but he was able to get rid of some debt at the same time:

> *"I paid off my pickup truck last month just from the guest from that podcast. It's that effective. You have to have people with good products, because chances are, people in the dating field have probably heard of a few people I've had on before. [The person may say], 'You know, I was wondering about that guy's book and now that I've been kicked over the fence, I might as well go check it out.' Everything's transparent and [my listeners] just go to it."*

Some other tips that McKay gives when using affiliate products:

- Don't mention the product every second of the podcast. Mention it toward the end of your podcast in your call to action.

- Give an easy to remember URL. Most URLs contain words, symbols, and letters. This will make it difficult for your audience to remember. In this case, register an easy-to-remember domain name, then forward it to the affiliate URL. Services like Tinyurl or Snipurl can help you do this. With Snipurl, if you create an account, you can even track the click-throughs.

- Say or display the URL at the absolute end of your podcast. Most times, the last thing your audience will remember is what they heard or saw at the end of your podcast.

- Check out the product before you endorse it. Nothing is worse than suggesting a product to your audience and it turns out to be a waste, or worst yet, a scam. Often, the person who created the product or service won't mind giving you a complimentary copy or free access if they know that in return you're going to bring them a slew of sales. So, ask to review the product first.

- Set the expectations with guests as to what you can deliver. McKay calls potential guests and lets them know that he can connect them with a highly targeted audience who wants to buy his or her product. McKay lets his potential guest know that his requirements are that he or she must have an affiliate program and the marketing should be left to McKay. He rarely has anyone saying no.

- Try to work out cross-promotional opportunities. McKay not only invites people on his show but encourages his guests to promote his products and services on their show or in their ezine. He doesn't force them to do this, but does suggest it.

And one other tip is to tell your guest that your podcast isn't an infomercial. It's not the time to talk about the product or service for 30 minutes or more. Instead, your guest should offer how-to information that your audience will find useful. For example, if you're interviewing a relationship coach, don't talk about her 250-page book. Instead, design your episode to talk about the "Seven Ways to Maintain a Happy Marriage." Let your guest's expertise sell the product, not the other way around.

Financial Aid Podcast

Affiliate programs are not just relegated to products and services sold by individuals. Large institutions and organizations also have affiliate programs that pay a commission for referrals. The *Financial Aid Podcast* hosted by Christopher Penn is published daily and offers information to students on how to get grants and loans to further their education (see Figure 5.7). Initially, Penn started recording information about the financial aid process for reasons that had nothing to do with podcasting:

> *"I started it as an internal training tool. We had one employee, to be charitable, who needed things explained more than once. At the same time, I got a new Mac Powerbook and an iPod. I started to record some of the things, some of the financial aid process."*[18]

After listening to *The Dawn and Drew Show* as well as *The Daily Source Code*, Penn felt that he too could produce a podcast. Using a microphone and software he found on his laptop, Penn started recording content for his podcast. The *Financial Aid Podcast* doesn't offer loans. Instead, Penn refers his listeners to loans that are offered through the company he works for, the Student Loan Network. Penn explains how it works:

Figure 5.7. Financial Aid Podcast.

"The company I work for, the Student Loan Network, has a series of federal and private student loan products in the United States. I'm essentially signed up as an affiliate for my own show. I have affiliate links on the Web site that go to the loans. So, when someone listens to my show and says, 'I should probably take out this loan,' I receive credit for it."

What to Use to Sell Online

There are several ways to sell products and services online. Some solutions are more robust than others and the solution you choose will depend on your budget and whether you'll sell your own items or someone else's.

The Nuts and Bolts of Selling Your Products and Services Online

Whether you sell a service or a tangible or digital product online, you would use the same tools to sell your item. The key here is to automate your sales as much as possible. In my business, any task that is done the same way again and again is made obsolete through a tool that automates what I'm doing. Automation is key as it helps to save time, money, and resources. After a sale is made, the less manual things you have to do to deliver your product, the more enjoyable the buying experience is for your customer. Here are a few tools that help me automate my sales so that I'm free to do other things:

- **Online Shopping Cart System**—This allows you to create links for your sellable items that you can easily add to your Web page, blog, or podpage. You create your profile in one of these systems, pay for a monthly service, then log in. The next step would be to input details about your product or service into a number of fields, including the name of your item, the price, taxes, and shipping options. After clicking *save*, the online shopping cart system displays a URL that you can copy and paste and add to the show notes on your podpage. For digital products, you want to choose a shopping cart that will deliver the item to customers as soon as their credit card has been approved. If the customer has to wait until you wake up the next morning to send an e-mail with the PDF or MP3 attached, he or she won't be happy. Of course, if you get too many of these orders, you could spend the whole day just sending e-mails with the digital product attached. Choose a shopping cart system that will send digital products to your customer immediately without any manual intervention on your part. I provide links to some recommended solutions for this on the companion Web site for this book.

- **Online Payment Gateway**—If your customer can't exchange money with you online, then you'll lose the sale. This is similar to going to a store, stuffing your shopping cart with items, but there are no cashiers anywhere. It would be impossible to pay for what you want if cashiers aren't there to take your money. It's the same online. You need to provide your customers with a way to pay for your items and signing up for a payment gateway will help. These online payment gateways allow you to accept credit card payments over the Internet. If you already accept credit card payment in your business, call your bank to find out if it will allow you to use your same merchant account online. If not, there are many payment gateways to choose from and you will find a list on the companion Web site for this book.

- **E-mail Autoresponders**—Being able to follow up with your customer through a series of e-mails can be automated as well. Instead of sending e-mails manually, you can use a program to create a series of e-mails that can be sent out on a predetermined schedule. If you're selling a service, you can send an e-mail to the customer on day 1 letting him know about an assignment he has to finish before calling into your consulting session, then on day 3, another e-mail is sent reminding him to finish the assignment. For products, you can create a series of 5, 10 or a dozen e-mails that are sent automatically to your customers every two or three days to help them use the product effectively. Some online shopping cart systems offer autoresponders as part of their package, so look for a bundled service. Otherwise, you'll have to login and manage two completely different systems.

Selling a service or digital product won't take up space in your office or your garage. Tangible products on the other hand will need to be stored. Not just that, but you'll have to buy boxes, postage, insurance, and spend the time to assemble the order for shipping. If you're going to sell tangible items, I highly recommend that you work with companies that will fulfill your orders after they're placed. For example, you can use a service such as *Cafépress.com* to sell T-shirts, mugs, hats, and tote bags with your podcast cover on it. You simply create your profile, upload your podcast cover, choose the inventory that you want to sell, then place a link to your virtual store somewhere on your podpage. When one of your audience members buys a T-shirt from your virtual store, *Cafepress.com* will handle the online payment, print, and then ship the item to your customer. You receive a small commission for the referral.

For CDs, books, and DVDs, you can use companies that will ship the item out to your customer once the order is placed. You pay a setup fee, then send the digital information to the fulfillment house. You will also have to send them the creative to print on the cover of your book, CD, or DVD. You process the order and take the payment through your Web site, then send the information to the fulfillment house by e-mail. If you use the right online shopping cart system, some fulfillment houses have integrated their system to take action as soon as the credit card has been approved. This is a better alternative than having to wait for you to return from vacation to manually e-mail the orders to the fulfillment house.

The Nuts and Bolts of Selling Other People's Products or Services

To sell other people's products and services, you won't need to buy products at a wholesale price then store them in your house or office. Instead, you simply sign up as an affiliate and then refer sales to the creator's Web site. To find affiliate programs, you first need to understand who they are. Affiliate programs can be grouped into three major categories:

- **Affiliate Network**—These Web sites act like a marketplace and list hundreds, even thousands, of products and services from sellers around the world. Typically, the creator of the product or service uploads information and sets the commission rates. Some creators will pay out as much as 75 percent of the price of the item to the person who referred sales to him or her. *Clickbank.com*, Commission Junction (*cj.com*), *Shareasale.com*, and *Linkshare.com* are just a few of the online affiliate marketplaces where you can find and sell quality products.

- **Large Online Merchant**—Most of the popular Web sites online, such as Amazon.com, eBay.com, and Expedia.com all have affiliate programs. Large online merchants typically sell a lot of products in one vertical, in other words, they may sell only books or vacation packages and nothing else. The commissions paid out are low, typically under 20 percent; however, the name recognition alone is worth being a part of their affiliate program.

- **Individual Merchant**—Many entrepreneurs and small business owners sell products and services that service a specific niche. For example, if you find a Web site for a negotiation expert, the products and services he sells will all have to do with negotiation. To find the products that individual merchants are selling, plug in a specific keyword into a search engine, then visit the links that are displayed. While this may be time consuming, you will find original and unique products and services that provide value to your audience. Most individual merchants set their commissions anywhere from 15 percent to 55 percent.

No matter which product or service creator you choose, the steps to become an affiliate are the same. First, look for the *Become an Affiliate* link on their Web site. Create a free profile and then log in to their affiliate center. There, you can copy and paste a URL that contains your referral ID. You then put this URL in your show notes so that when your audience clicks on the link, the affiliate network records this. As soon as your audience purchases the product, the sale is recorded and you receive a commission for it. Other items you will find in the merchant's affiliate center are banner ads, text links, and e-mail marketing messages you can use to promote the product or service.

Most affiliates will pay commissions on the first day of every month or once you hit a certain dollar amount. Some will send you a check in the currency where the company is located, by PayPal, or through direct deposit. The most favored payment method is electronically through PayPal or direct deposit as there's no waiting for checks to arrive or for checks to clear in your bank account. When you create your profile, you will have an opportunity to choose how you want to receive your commissions.

The Rules of the Breadcumb Podcasting Approach

Remember the BPA discussed earlier? All the case studies in this chapter follow the BPA where they offer infotaining content and lead their audience to the item that they're selling. If you go for the hard sell and turn your podcast into an infomercial, you might as well take your podcast off-line and focus on another strategy. As a reminder, here are the steps to follow so you can successfully sell products and services through your podcast:

1. **Keep your podcast interactive**. Talking head video podcasts or rambling audio podcasts will bore your audience.

2. **Present infotaining content.** Focus on providing tips, tricks, and techniques to your audience.

3. **Have one call to action.** Don't ask your audience to leave a comment on your comment line, visit your Web site, and sign up for your e-mail list in your call to action. With too many options, your audience will do nothing at all. Remember, a confused mind always says no, so make it simple for your audience to follow up with you.

4. **Automate your sales online.** Use tools that put your computer to work, not you. Use a shopping cart, an autoresponder service, and an online payment gateway to sell products and services online.

5. **Fulfill your orders using someone else.** While you can burn a few CDs on your computer or print a few T-shirts at a photocopying store, this solution will not scale once you start receiving hundreds of orders per week. Look for a service that doesn't require you to store inventory in your home.

Taking Action

When you're trying to sell products and services using your podcast, remember these tips:

- **Use the breadcrumb podcasting approach.** Don't do the hard sell in your podcast or you'll alienate your audience.

- **Develop interactive and infotaining content.** Provide tips and allow your audience to learn something new and to be entertained. Entertainment could mean a sketch comedy skit or two hosts who are disagreeing on a topic.

- **Provide only one call to action at the end of your episode.** Don't confuse your audience by giving them too many things to do. Keep the language consistent and simple. You either want them to go to your Web site or sign up for your e-mail newsletter, but not both.

- **Keep it short, silly.** Ensure that your podcast content isn't too long. You want your audience to get to the end of your podcast to follow up with you. In the *2006 Canadian Podcast Listeners Survey*, the majority of respondents selected under 10 minutes as their preferred length for an audio podcast.[19]

6

Podcast Consulting and Teaching

After you learn how to do a task, there are many who will want to pay you to teach them how to do it. Podcasting is no different as many podcasters are seeing an income stream from helping others launch their own podcasts. In this chapter, you'll learn how to make money through consulting and teaching others how to podcast (see Figure 6.1).

The 7 Steps to Podcasting for Profit

Figure 6.1. Podcasting for profit steps—profit.

Introduction

Jonny Goldstein is a funny guy. Using a video podcast posted to his personal blog, Goldstein chronicled his quest to get paid for a consulting job that he did. He recorded himself making phone calls, pacing across his floor in his home, everything just to show the unglamorous side of being a freelancer. At long last, the check came through the mail. What did Goldstein do with his hard-earned and well-chased cash? He bought boxes of Twinkies, threw them into his bathtub and took a Twinkie "bubble bath." Of course, it was a tasteful video podcast as Goldstein filmed his celebratory Twinkie bubble bath from the neck up.[1]

Although freelancing as a video podcaster has both its ups and downs, nothing prepared Goldstein for the biggest job of his life—teaching low-income high-school students from the Bronx, New York, how to create their own video podcast. It's not because the kids were hard to manage, because they weren't. The biggest challenge for Goldstein was the scope of the project. What started as an after-school program turned into a seven-month curriculum funded by the federal government. As program director and curriculum developer of BX21, the name of the program, Goldstein managed 10 mentors who helped him teach a hundred students how to plan, shoot, and edit video using off the shelf point-and-shoot cameras. Students created dramas, documentaries, and news features and posted them online.

Consulting and teaching are just some of the indirect ways podcasters are making money. Whether it's holding a workshop, organizing a trade show, or walking into someone's office and presenting a solution to a group of executives, getting paid to design and implement a podcast solution for an individual or business is an indirect income stream. And it is often overlooked. The major reason is that many podcasters see themselves as an evangelist, someone who's spreading the good news about podcasting to the masses. For many, they would rather educate through a free session at a local high school than accept money for their time and expertise. As podcasting continues to grow, more and more podcasters will see that their unique skills and expertise are something that can no longer be given away for free. Here's a selection of podcasters who are charging others for what they know.

Trade Shows, Conferences, and Expos

According to the International Congress and Convention Association (ICCA), the United States and Germany ranked number one and number two respectively as the most popular countries for international conventions and meetings.[2] The ICCA also identified 5,838 events that took place in 2006, an increase of 523 events over 2005. The conference and trade show market continues to grow. By running a trade show or conference, you can educate a lot of people at once about podcasting. You can just organize all the details for the event and invite speakers to lead sessions on how to podcast. Exhibitors who are eager to showcase their product or service to those willing to buy will pay for space at your expo. Collecting fees for booths from exhibitors, plus getting advertising from companies to have their logos prominently displayed at the event, are just a couple ways to cover expenses.

The tools you use to hold your trade show or conferences are varied. You can go the traditional route and hold your event in a large auditorium or you may choose to hold an expo online using an online meeting tool or even the telephone. Here are some ways you can use the trade show and conference model to make money indirectly from podcasting.

Offline Paid Events

Early in 2005, Bourquin saw a need to bring together some of the best minds in podcasting to share their knowledge about this new media. The first Podcast and New Media Expo was held in Ontario, California, in the fall of 2005 and a small contingent of attendees, exhibitors, and speakers made it to the Expo (see Figure 6.2). Although it was small, the Podcast and New Media Expo attracted enough attention to receive the 2006 Best New Show Award from *Expo Magazine*.[3]

Figure 6.2. Screenshot of promoting Podcast and New Media Expo.

The Podcast and New Media Expo now attracts close to 3,000 attendees and many exhibitors. Speakers lead sessions on everything from podcast monetization to video podcasting techniques. There are different tracks and different sessions occurring concurrently during the three-day event that typically takes place the last weekend in September. Many podcasters have hailed Podcast and New Media Expo as the only conference to attend in podcasting if you can't go to anything else. And while Bourquin wouldn't reveal how much revenue he earns from Podcast and New Media Expo, he did share that it costs $400,000 USD to stage the event.[4]

Online Paid Events

While the Podcast and New Media Expo is an offline event, some podcasting expos are held online. These virtual events are held via a Web-sharing tool where people can see each other, hear each other, and view slides from presenters. A fee is charged to attendees and once they pay, they get the login details. On the day of the event, attendees launch their browsers, go to the Web site address, enter the login details, and they can network with other attendees, exhibitors, and speakers. Sessions are led by experts and consultants who teach attendees how to publish a podcast, how to promote, and how to make money.

Penny Haynes is a podcaster and founder of the International Podcasting Expo (IPE). Every quarter, she focuses on a different theme and invites speakers to lead sessions on how to create a better podcast. Attendees are charged $50 to attend and on the day and time that the International Podcasting Expo begins, attendees launch their browsers and go to a Web page, then plug in their user name and password. Since launching IPE in the fall of 2005, Haynes has seen a significant growth in attendees, sessions and revenue. Past topics include:

- Promoting Your Podcast

- Podcasting for Profit

- Podcasting for PR

- Podcasting in 2006: What We Learned

- Vocal Techniques for Podcasters

- Conversational Podcasting: Letting People Add Their Own Audio and Video to Your Podcast.

Workshops and Seminars

Trade shows and conferences are designed to bring together sellers, buyers, and educators all under one roof. Workshops and seminars on the other hand, bring together people who want to learn a specific skill in a more intimate environment. Here are some ways that podcasters are using workshops and seminars to teach people hands-on about podcasting and earn some income while doing it.

Over the Telephone

This is perfect if your educational material doesn't involve a visual element. Sessions held over the phone are called many things—teleclass, teleconference, teleworkshop, teleseminar, or telesummit—and are easy to organize given that there's nothing to download. The only thing people need to do is pick up their phone, call a number, enter an access code, and gain access to the "class." A facilitator, typically the person who created the content, will greet people to the class. I train hundreds of people per year using the telephone. One of my more popular podcasting courses held over the telephone is my Six-Figure Podcasting mastermind group (see Figure 6.3). Each month, we dial into a phone number where participants are trained on a specific podcasting skill.

In a Classroom

Podcast Academy, organized by the Gigavox team, is typically held at a university in the United States. Podcast Academy brings together presenters who lead

Figure 6.3. Logo for the Six-Figure Podcasting Gold Success Club.

classroom sessions about podcasting and participants eager to learn about it. Typically held over one or two days, Podcast Academy is a hands-on approach, teaching people step by step how to do something in podcasting for just under $200 for admission. Past sessions include:

- Understanding Authentication and Personalized RSS Feeds

- Recording: Microphones and Telephones

- Music Licensing for Podcasts

- Recording and Editing Interviews.[5]

In a Conference Room

Podcasters Across Borders is an annual conference held in Kingston, Ontario.[6] Organized by Mark Blevis and Bob Goyetche of the Canadian Podcast Buffet, along with Cat Goyetche, host of *The Cat Fish Show*, this three-day conference brings together podcasters from across Canada and the northeastern United States. What makes Podcasters Across Borders unique compared to other conferences is that:

- There are no exhibitors.

- Attendees are mainly hobbyists.

- There is only one track of sessions.

- Sessions focus more on how to create great content and not how to profit from it.[7]

Speakers lead sessions, but are more like facilitators guiding the discussion, rather than presenters. The cost to attend the three-day event is $100 and at its first conference in 2006, Podcasters Across Borders attracted over 80 attendees.

In a Studio

There's no better place to teach people how to podcast than in a place where the tools of the trade are being used. Most podcasters will use amateur tools to podcast, however, nothing will make the eyes widen more than to go into a studio to learn how to get a professional sound from the professionals without spending like one. Gear Media Tech is a two-day workshop taught by the award-winning team that produces one of the top-rated podcasts in iTunes, *This Week In Tech*. For $297 USD, Gear Media Tech teaches podcasters how to produce a video podcast, everything from lighting to audio production.

Over the Internet

Dave Jackson's School of Podcasting and this book's companion Web site include video and audio tutorials teaching you how to podcast. For a nominal monthly fee, you can access a wealth of tutorials that will teach you how to produce, publish, and profit from a podcast. As long as you continue to pay the monthly fee, you get access to the educational materials.

Managing Guest Speakers

Whether you plan on organizing a large-scale event for thousands or a small workshop for hundreds, your speakers can either make or break your event. While exhibitors will pay for booth space and attendees will come and go, if your speakers are not selected carefully, you will get a reputation of putting on really lousy podcasting events. Attendees will stop attending and exhibitors will avoid your event like the plague. Here are two things I must suggest if you plan on organizing a podcasting event:

1. Release forms

2. Paying speakers.

Get Speakers to Sign a Release Form

If you plan on organizing an expo, trade show, or conference, you have to cover your legal bases. As the event organizer, if you want to record any or all the sessions and speeches, get the speakers to sign a release form. This release form should state to the speaker that you plan on recording their presentation and that you plan to use it in your marketing material and possibly for sale later on. Stating up front through a release form what you intend to do with the speeches after the event is over will save you headaches in the long run. A sample release form is available on the companion Web site.

I remember presenting at an annual general meeting and was horrified when my speech was for sale immediately after I finished my talk. No one told me this would happen as I didn't sign a release form before the event. I was even more horrified when I asked for a copy of my own speech and was told I had to pay the $20. After going into a slight hissy fit, the event organizer apologized for the oversight and allowed me to have a copy of my own speech on CD. I then gave her some friendly advice to always get your speakers to sign release forms prior to the event so they're not surprised when their speech goes on sale later on. Let's just say I won't present for that group ever again.

Experienced speakers and presenters won't mind signing the release form. In most cases, they expect it and will put up little—if any—resistance. Plus, many speakers and presenters welcome the added exposure of having their face, Web site, and speech getting into as many hands as possible. So, don't be nervous that someone will say no to your insistence that they sign a release form. At the end of the day, you'll give the impression that you are a professional event organizer for being so thorough.

On the flip side, more and more event organizers need to be mindful of attendees as well. Wherever podcasters are, you're sure to find people with their recording equipment. Although I have yet to see this, conferences, trade shows, and expos will need to develop something that lets podcasters know that they can't record or disseminate the keynote speeches or presentations. Or, if they record them, they can't share them on their blog, podcast, or any other distribution media. This might be tricky if the language isn't crafted carefully; however, if anyone can record and share the very sessions only you as the event organizer have the right to sell later on, your product (the recorded speeches) now has little value.

Paying Speakers

Speakers travel far and wide to attend events. They prepare a presentation, they give up their time to attend your event, then they deliver a memorable speech. While standing in front of a group for 30 minutes and delivering a speech may seem easy to do, it's the preparation that's the most difficult.

Recently, I did a keynote address for the Women in Trade and Technology Association called *What Technology and a Cute Guy Taught Me About Taking Risks and Being Myself.* I received a four-figure sum for that keynote address and I only had to speak for 45 minutes. Although getting paid that amount for only 45 minutes of work may seem silly to some, it took me 20 hours to prepare for that event.[8] Here's what I had to do:

- **I researched my topic.** Because it was a keynote to an audience I wouldn't normally speak to, I had to do some research to make my speech even more interesting. So, I pulled up some statistics, grabbed a few quotes from some books I read, and found some material online to make sure my points were well supported. I even had to ask my younger sister (age 21) about the street lingo used by high-school students just so I could look current. I mean, using the word "cool" would probably date me about 15 years, so I had to know what the kids are using these days.

- **I practiced my speech.** I spent about an hour a day the week prior to the event going through each point, timing myself with a stopwatch, just to make sure I got it right. A few times, I would be in front of my computer while I practiced so I could type out what I said and edit my notes as I was rehearsing.

- **I made my speech edutaining.** I knew that if I were to maintain the attention of a group of young women for at least 30 minutes, I had to make sure my speech included characters, gestures, and vocal variety that would make them laugh, smile, and sit on the edge of their seats.

- **I prepared an activity sheet.** I love interaction from the audience when I present, so I included an activity sheet that the young ladies could work through in between the end of my speech and right before the Q&A.

- **I drove a total of four hours to and from the event.** I went from Toronto to Brantford, a distance of about 120 km one way. I would've gotten there sooner, but the weather was miserable for driving that day.

- **I hired my assistant and cameraperson to accompany me.** I videotape all of my speeches. It gives me an opportunity to review them later on. The more times I review my speeches, the better it gets as I can make improvements. If I rely on my memory to try and recall my entire speech, I will do a poor job, so having the video really helps. Also, my assistant totally understands what I do at events, so I absolutely need her when I do a speaking engagement.

Overall, I believe I spent about 20 hours preparing for and doing this keynote. When you consider what I was paid in relation to all the preparation I did and the people I had to hire, my speaking rate is now spread out over several hours.

If you're planning to organize a podcasting event, take a look at the steps that a speaker needs to do to prepare for your event. There's a lot of work that goes into crafting an entertaining and educational speech, one that will wow your audience and make you (the event organizer) look like a star. Skimp on the cost to put flowers on each table, but don't skimp on compensating a speaker to speak at your next event.

What if you can't pay a speaker? Then here's a list of things I suggest you consider before sending those invitations out:

1. Look for experts close to the event. Travel and accommodations costs will be cheaper if you invite speakers who live close to the city where you plan to hold the event.

2. If you can't pay his or her speaker's fee, offer to pick up the tab on travel and accommodations. There have been a few conferences I have said yes to simply because the only thing out of pocket would be my meals.

3. Offer an honorarium. A small amount of money would show the speaker that you are appreciative of their efforts. Whether it's $25 or $250, choose an amount that will say thanks, but that won't break your event budget.

4. Choose a gift that will improve the speaker's craft. People who present are constantly looking for material to add to their speeches. As an event organizer, the best gift you can give is a gift certificate from a national bookstore. I racked up so many of those gift certificates one year that I had a field day buying every book on my wish list. Statues, pins, and bookmarks are lousy gifts as they do little to improve the speaker's craft, so choose wisely.

Consulting and Coaching

"How do I do this podcast thing?" I remember getting this question from a colleague of mine about two months after I launched *Cubicle Divas*. I coached her through the process and didn't think anything of it until a week later when another colleague asked me the very same question. Soon, the number of people asking me how to podcast was greater than the number of hours I had in the day. I recognized that this was an opportunity for me to offer podcasting services for a fee. After only podcasting for three months, I quickly put together a business plan, I looked at what my competitors were charging and in March 2006, I started my podcast consulting company called Caprica Interactive Marketing. Now, anytime someone asks me, "How do I do this podcast thing?" I direct them to my Web site for more information on my products and services.

Helping a Politician

Other podcasters have also had the very same experience. Steve Garfield, a Boston-based video podcaster, found that he was receiving many requests from companies to help produce a podcast. Not only is Garfield a correspondent with *Rocketboom*, but he also produces a few of his own video podcasts. He recently did a video blog with a Boston, Massachusetts, city councilor named John Tobin. Garfield shared his insights about the project:

> "[John Tobin] is one of the first elected U.S. politicians to have a video blog and he loves it. One exciting thing we did was a seven-day video blog where he addressed an issue that he wanted to talk about. When Tobin looked at his opponent's Web site, it was just about taxes. A lot of people wait until Election Day to decide who they want to vote for. If you went to the opponent's Web site, you would just see text. If you went to John Tobin's site, you would see him and he would be talking to you."

Did Tobin win the election? Garfield says yes and Tobin's now up for re-election.

Helping Disneyland

Seven days before Disneyland celebrated its 50th anniversary in May 2005, Michael Geoghegan's telephone rang. "Hey, do you want to spend next week at Disneyland?" Two days after that phone call, Geoghegan, the co-author of *Podcast Solutions*, was sitting around a conference table at Disneyland with other marketing executives. Geoghegan said that what happened next seemed like a whirlwind:

> "We worked about four or five days at the park from literally seven in the morning until almost midnight each night. [The

*Disneyland folks] took it seriously, which I think was really
important and helped to drive its success. We put out a podcast
that was really from behind the scenes."*[9]

Geoghegan and his team would record some of the events, prepare the
podcast, upload it to the server at three in the morning, then be at the park
bright and early to record more events during the 50th anniversary celebration.
Although Geoghegan no longer produces the Disneyland podcast, it is still being updated with new episodes and is available at iTunes.

What Skills Do I Need?

While Michael Geoghegan, Steve Garfield, and I are just some of the people
who get paid to produce a podcast solution from beginning to end, not everyone is cut out to do this. Some podcasters are realizing that there are certain
aspects of producing a podcast that they enjoy and others that they completely
hate. In fact, many have started to sell their skills not as podcasters but as
experts in skills that are related to podcasting.

Hard Skills vs. Soft Skills

In podcasting, the skills needed to produce a podcast can be divided into soft
skills and hard skills. **Soft skills** refer to the cluster of personality traits, social
graces, and personal habits that mark people to varying degrees.[10] Also known
as people skills, soft skills are the ones you use to communicate, problem solve,
engage in dialogue, and express yourself. **Hard skills** on the other hand are the
technical and administrative skills you use to operate machinery, crunch numbers, and program computer software.[11] These skills are easier to train, but
difficult to master. Table 6.1 details this further.

Where to Find Skill-Specific Podcasting Jobs

Finding opportunities can take a bit of work, however, they do exist. Some, like
me, get podcasting projects through word of mouth and from existing clients. If
you don't currently have clients, here are some ways to tell others that you are
looking for podcasting projects to work on.

Soft Skills	Hard Skills
Interviewing	Audio or video production
Voiceover artist	Installing or configuring a blog
Script writing	Audio or video recording/encoding
Vocal training	Measuring statistics
Creative services	Creating an RSS feed
Content creation	Technical project management
Transcribers	

Table 6.1. Podcasting soft skills vs. hard skills.

- **Podcast Directories**—Some will have a section for people looking for podcasting work and those offering it.

- **Google**—Type in the keyword *podcast jobs* or *podcasting job* and visit the Web sites that pop up in the search results. Chances are, you will find a Web site where you can list yourself as a contractor for hire.

- **Freelance Web Sites**—*Guru.com, eLance.com,* and *Craigslist.org* are great Web sites to use to post information about you and your skills.

- **Skill-Specific Job Boards**—For voiceover artists, you can create a profile at *voices.com* or *voices123.com* and wait for the opportunities to come to you.

- **Launch a Blog or Podcast**—I found the transcription company using this method. It can be quite effective, especially if you use it to dole out advice on how individuals and companies can use your skill in their day-to-day lives.[12]

- **Attend Events and Network**—If you want to work with podcasters, you have to go where podcasters are. Attending podcasting events and handing out business cards is an excellent way to raise your profile.

- **Cold Calling**—I know this is the most dreaded way to find new clients; however, it can be effective if done right. Put together a list of companies that offer podcasting services and call them to see if they could use your services.

- **Informational Meetings**—Send an e-mail to a podcaster who lives close to you or who will be attending the same event you'll be at and request to meet over coffee. Use the meeting to find out more about what podcasters need, rather than use it to talk endlessly about yourself. And don't forget to pay for his or her coffee.

How Much Do I Charge?

When I first started my company, I had no clue what to charge for podcast consulting. So, I started to ask my peers what they were charging. Although I can't share with you specific numbers, I can give you a strategy to help you determine what your rates will be.

1. Look at who else is offering podcast consulting in your area. While the nature of podcasting means that a person can choose anyone in the world to produce it for him or her, most businesses would rather choose someone closer to them to manage their podcast solution. So, take a look around and if you're the only one in your city offering podcast consulting, you can charge a lot higher.

2. Look at whom you're attracting to your business. If you work mainly with corporate clients, charging a paltry $1,500 for an audio podcast solution will raise suspicion. Similarly, if you work mainly with solo entrepreneurs—businesses with just one person—you'll have to adjust your prices so they can afford your services.

3. Determine if it's a one-off opportunity or ongoing. Someone may hire you to help him or her get started. This is a one-off opportunity and, therefore, you'll need to charge higher for this type of work. If it's ongoing, meaning you'll be doing something every month for this client, then you can charge a rate that gives a preferred discount for the consistent work.

4. If you hire others, your prices need to be higher. When I first started my podcasting company, I did everything from business development to editing podcast files. Now that I have more clients, I focus solely on business development and hire contractors to do the editing of podcast files and the implementation of podcast solutions. Because of this, I had to increase my prices to cover what my contractors charged me and to cover my administrative tasks.

At the end of the day, don't sell yourself short, but at the same time, be mindful of who you want to attract to your business as clients. Set your prices accordingly.

Final Words of Caution

Out of all the profiting models, making money from consulting and teaching can be one of the most profitable income streams for podcasters, but it takes a long time to happen. Although you can make money within a few weeks of launching your podcast through advertising and sponsorship, consulting and teaching rely on your experience. From my interviews with podcasters and from my own experience, it will take on average 6 to 12 months from the time you launch your own podcast to the time you secure your first paid consulting or speaking gig.

Being able to teach others how to podcast can only come if you've been doing it yourself. Too many times I've seen people jump on the podcasting bandwagon in an effort to make fast cash, yet they make mistake after mistake because they have never produced their own podcasts. Avoid this mistake yourself by taking the time to learn the ins and the outs of podcasting by producing one for yourself. Your future clients will appreciate your knowledge and will pay you accordingly. As Geoghegan said in my interview with him:

> *"If your goal is to make money right away, then I would say you need to stop and think for a minute because like anything, obtaining some level of success in podcasting is important."*[13]

Look at the following points and assess whether you're ready to make money podcasting through consulting and teaching:

- **Do you have case studies or testimonials from people who hired you to produce their podcast?** Let the solutions you produce speak for themselves. If others are saying great things about you, people will hire you to get those results for their own podcast. If you don't have case studies or testimonials, start by developing someone's podcasting solution at no charge on condition he or she writes a testimonial that praises your work.

- **Do you have your own podcast?** Again, producing your own podcast helps you to make the mistakes on your own dime. You can then advise others with confidence since you've probably been through a lot of equipment—and experiences. If you don't have your own podcast, go back to Chapter 3 to learn how to launch your own.

- **Have you been podcasting for at least six months?** While anyone can talk a good game, it's the results that people want to see. It will take about six months to generate a following, to become a pick of the week in a podcast directory, or to test out some of the strategies in the following chapters on your podcast. Take the time to develop yourself as a case study before selling your podcasting skills to others.

- **Are you involved in the podcasting industry?** Speaking at conferences, doing interviews in the media, writing articles on the subject, and developing ventures all related to podcasting can only help set you up as an expert in the field. A good test is to plug in your name into a search engine and see what pops up. Are the majority of links proving that you are a podcaster that people can hire? If not, start networking with other podcasters and get your name out there.

- **Can you support others' podcasting solutions during normal working hours?** I can appreciate that most people start a business on the side while working full-time for someone else so they can eat and have a roof over their head. Unfortunately, technology runs 24 hours a day and if there's a problem with someone's podcasting solution, they will call you at 9 A.M. or 9 P.M. If you work for someone else full-time, can you reasonably provide the customer service your clients will be looking for if the audio sounds poor or if the flash player doesn't work on their podpage? If not, you will have to rethink how you'll be able to provide podcast consulting without compromising your day job.

If you've answered *yes* to all five questions above, put together a rate sheet and start pounding on the doors. It's time for you to indirectly make money podcasting through consulting and teaching.

Taking Action

Being able to help people podcast and get paid for giving them valuable advice is an indirect way to make money podcasting. It takes anywhere between six to 12 months to realize an income stream from consulting and teaching, so build your experience first by publishing your own podcast before you offer to do the same for others. Here are some tasks to follow:

1. Start podcasting so you understand the ins and the outs of podcasting production.

2. Decide how you'd like to teach people to podcast. If you prefer one-to-one interaction, you'd be better as a consultant. If you like to teach groups, holding a workshop or seminar might be better. If you'd rather bring experts together, organizing a trade or conference might be up your alley.

3. Determine your fees based on location, availability, expertise, and type of clientele.

7

Advertising and Sponsorship

Providing a venue in your podcast for other companies to promote their products and services is one of the earliest ways some podcasters made a four-, five-, and six-figure incomes. While advertising and sponsorship in podcasts are popular, so too are the number of tools available to help sell ads. Figure 7.1 shows

The 7 Steps to Podcasting for Profit

Figure 7.1. Podcasting for profit steps—profit.

that we're still looking at the profit step in the seven-step process, and in this chapter you'll learn the various ways podcasters make money using advertising and sponsorship, whether they seek it on their own or as part of a network.

Introduction

Frasier, a popular U.S. situation comedy television series that starred Kelsey Grammer, centered around the character of psychiatrist Dr. Frasier Crane, whom Grammer played on the show. Frasier, who hosts a daily radio program on the fictional KACL in Seattle, Washington, takes calls from his listeners, helping them solve their mental health issues over the airwaves.

In one episode, Frasier felt uneasy about reading an endorsement for a Chinese restaurant at the end of one of his radio shows. He was so against the idea that he asked his producer, Roz Doyle, to play a previously recorded advertisement instead. He quickly changed his mind after he found out how much extra money he could make just for making a host recommendation.

Frasier's situation gets a little bit more complicated when he acquires a new agent, Bebe Glazer, who gently pushes him into endorsing other products, everything from hot tubs to peanuts. While Glazer continues to obtain more endorsement deals for Frasier, he confides in his brother Niles that he can no longer endorse products because it compromises his integrity as a psychiatrist. Frasier finally decides not to take the five-figure endorsement deal with a peanut company simply because he finds that his ethics are being challenged.

Like Frasier, many podcasters are concerned over accepting advertising or sponsorship deals for their podcasts. Many believe that they will lose the freedom to craft the content they want if they start accepting money to profile another company's message and brand. Mark Blevis and Andrea Ross, the husband-and-wife team who host a hobby podcast called *Just One More Book*, recently recorded a conversation explaining why they will never accept advertising or sponsorship deals for their podcast.[1] Blevis explains why being independent is important for their podcast:

> *"You want to have a certain amount of independence. If, for example, we took sponsorship or advertising dollars from a publisher and we happen to review a few books that month by that publisher and we give raving reviews, people would be suspicious about what we're doing."*

Ross adds:

> *"And it's not because if we took money from people we would be influenced by them because I really don't think we would. I know there are a lot of people who can accept money and still do exactly what they want to do. It just so happens that we don't take in one single cent from this endeavour. If you're powered by passion, you're not accepting money at all. Sometimes I feel like a big sucker because people are buying lots of books because of us and we're not making a single cent. But this is the way I like to do it."*[2]

There are many podcasters who share the views held by the hosts behind *Just One More Book*. Individual podcasters such as Dave Slusher and Robert Walch, who are considered some of the top minds in podcasting, also feel strongly against accepting any advertising. Even prominent podcaster, Leo Laporte, who owns one of the biggest independent podcast networks called This Week in Technology (TWiT), was reluctant to accept advertising on his network. In September 2006, Laporte finally relented and accepted Visa and Dell Computers as his first corporate advertisers. In a blog post dated September 5, 2006, Laporte explained why accepting advertising was necessary:

> *"Perhaps you're wondering why we're taking advertising. As you may know, I had hoped to build TWiT on donations alone, but as generous as you've been, that's just not possible. Your donations pay for our expenses, like hosting, bandwidth, rental, and equipment, but aren't sufficient to pay the podcasters themselves. All the work put into building these shows over the past year has been volunteer. None of us can keep doing that much longer. Advertising will let us pay the podcasters, and help TWiT.tv grow into a better network of shows."*[3]

Although some podcasters are *powered by passion* and aren't interested in making money from advertising and sponsorship, it is proving to be the most profitable income stream for many podcasters. Whether they have a large audience or not, many podcasters are finding that promoting a product or service to their audience is just what companies are looking for.

The advertising market overall is huge. It is estimated that companies spend over $20 billion to buy time to promote their products and services on banner ads, text ads, and other forms of online advertising.[4] Of this, PQ Media predicts that $400 million will be spent specifically on podcast advertising by the year 2011.[5]

Despite the growth of podcast advertising, otherwise known as **podvertising,** the number of companies advertising in podcasts to date is quite small. Some fear getting egg on their faces spending their advertising dollars in an unproven area. Still others believe that their target market isn't reachable through podcasts, thinking that the audience is still just geeks and tech-savvy males between 18 and 35 years old. But for those who pick up the challenge, the payoff can be worth more than the cost of the advertising or sponsorship. Companies such as GoDaddy.com and Dixie Cups report receiving favorable results from podvertising, everything from increased brand recognition to increased sales.

While convincing companies to advertise in a podcast is a big hurdle, some have developed unique ways to encourage companies to spend their money. Aside from audience numbers, some podcasters produce unique content, join a podcast network that sells advertising on their behalf or find advertising or sponsorship based on their own efforts.

Before going through some examples of advertising and sponsorship deals podcasters have arranged for their podcasts, one common question I get asked is, "What's the difference between advertising and sponsorship?" Some use the terms interchangeably, however, there are some unique differences between the two that's worth noting. What makes sponsorship and advertising in podcasts similar is that they both allow companies to pay a sum of money to access an audience. Yet, what makes them different is the relationship it forms with that audience and host.

According to *dictionary.com*, advertising is defined as:

> *...to announce or praise (a product, service, etc.) in some public medium of communication in order to induce people to buy or use it.*

Sponsorship is defined as:

> *A person who vouches or is responsible for a person or thing.*

With both advertising and sponsorship, the company, which is the customer, pays the podcaster to access its audience using a scripted message. That's where they are the same. However, what makes them different is the delivery. Most advertising in a podcast is in the form of a 30-second spot. It is a message played toward the beginning or the end of the podcast and there is a notable difference in tone from the rest of the podcast content. Some podcasters will also offer a spot on their podpage to display the advertiser's banner ad. On the other hand, sponsorship is an endorsement by the host. A scripted message is given to the host who makes his or her recommendation of the product or service. Often, the message is indistinguishable from the rest of the podcast content as the person who hosts the show is also reading the endorsement.

While there are both drawbacks and advantages to both approaches, sponsorship and advertising in your podcast comes in many forms:

- **30-Second Ad.** This is the first thing people think of when it comes to podcast monetization. A 30-second ad is run in the podcast. Depending on where it's placed in the podcast will depend on how much you charge. Typically, if the ad is placed at the beginning of the podcast, the company will pay more than if it's placed toward the end.

- **Host Recommendation.** The person who hosts the podcast will talk about the product or service for a few seconds to a few minutes. The host can read from a prewritten script or modify it so it fits his or her personality and style.

- **Product Review.** The host will give a favorable review of a product or service. Typically, the host would've used the product in some way before giving a review on their podcast.

- **Product Placement.** Most useful in video podcasts, a product is placed on screen and shows the host and guests interacting with the product. The product is typically used as a prop in the scene for a few seconds to a few minutes.

- **Logo Placement.** The company's logo is placed on the podpage or if it's a video podcast, is displayed somewhere on screen. Placing the logo of the advertising company is usually part of a package deal. For example, if the advertising company wants the host to endorse their product, the podcast producer will place the advertising company's logo on the post related to that episode.

Securing Sponsorship and Podvertising on Your Own

Many podcasters choose to find their own sponsorship and podvertising deals for a number of reasons:

- They want to keep 100 percent of the revenue.

- They know their audience the best and can then find the right company to sell advertising to.

- They stumble into it after getting many requests.

- It is the only model they know and are familiar with.

Whatever! Podcast

"I just wanted to continue buying diva things," says Beverly Mahone, host of *Whatever!,* a podcast exploring topics of interest to baby boomers.[6] Her motivation for launching the podcast wasn't money—at least, not directly. She wanted a vehicle to promote her book, and with 25 years experience in radio broadcasting, Mahone thought that podcasting was the next best thing. So, in June 2006, Mahone launched her first episode (see Figure 7.2). It didn't take long for those eager to target the baby boomer market to contact her about sponsoring the show. "I was going to do a whole month long series on women's health and a woman contacted me and said that she'll sponsor the whole month," says Mahone.

At first, Mahone was unsure what to charge. Her podcast was still in its infancy and it was difficult for her to gauge what would be too expensive and what would be acceptable. So, she asked other podcasters what would be a

Figure 7.2. *Whatever!* podcast.

good rate to charge. That's when someone recommended that she create a rate card and post it on her Web site.

> *"All of a sudden, I had women coming to me and saying, 'Can you sign me up for a week' or 'I will take a whole month.' I started out with four sponsors for the month,"* says Mahone.

She charges $250 per episode per company for sponsorship. Not only do sponsors get a mention at the beginning and at the end of each episode, but they also benefit from being mentioned in her e-mail newsletter and a link is provided to their Web site from hers. Each episode will contain up to two sponsors and they can sponsor up to a month of Mahone's shows.

Galacticast

Rudy Jahchan and Casey McKinnon didn't like each other in high school, but when they re-met years later, they fell in love with each other and discovered they had a mutual interest in B-movies, science fiction, fantasy, and comic books. They combined their interests to launch *Galacticast* in May 2006, a weekly video podcast of hilarious sketches.

Between writing the script, recording the scenes, adding the sound effects, and publishing the finished podcast, Jahchan and McKinnon spend 50 hours each week producing one episode of *Galacticast*. Much of the production work is financed out of pocket. They joined a podcast network, they sold ads to be displayed in their video podcast, and they're continuing to sell merchandise. However, Jahchan states that the sponsorship program they launched in February 2007 has proven to be a winner.

> *"Our biggest money maker is our sponsorship program. We said, 'Okay, let's start a sponsorship program, but let's not turn to big corporations to do that.' We do have plans for that, but we want something that's more immediate and more interactive."*[7]

Their strategy is to allow their friendbase (not fanbase) to purchase a sponsored credit on their show. Depending on the level purchased, people can be listed as a best boy or all the way up to producer. The person's name will appear at the end of the episode in the credits, as well as on the movie poster on the *Galacticast* home page (See Figure 7.3). In the first 30 days, *Galacticast* made $1,500 using this strategy for sponsorship.

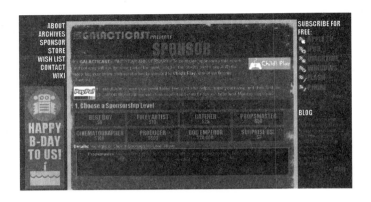

Figure 7.3.   *Galacticast* video sponsorship.

Jahchan explains why they did this as opposed to relying on a tip jar or pursuing corporate clients:

> *"Two things inspired us to do this. One was Ze Frank's duckies. He sells those duckies under his video podcast. Depending on your donation level, depends on what duckie level will show up. We couldn't put duckies, so we thought of robots and spaceships. At the end of the day, we wanted something that was uniquely us. They did this for* The Lord of the Rings. *Part of the massive budget came from fans who wanted to see a* Lord of the Rings *movie. They had a Web site and said, 'If you give us some money, your name will appear in the credits.'"*

French Maid TV

The idea for a video podcast where women dressed up as French maids and taught viewers how to do something came to Tim Street as he was snowboarding in South America one summer. "There were these French maids rescuing people on the mountain. Then I woke up and said to myself, 'Hey, that was a good idea for an online video.'"[8]

Street, who is the creator and producer of *French Maid TV,* does something a little bit different with his two- to five-minute videos (see Figure 7.4). Instead of producing the content and finding companies to advertise on it, he lets the

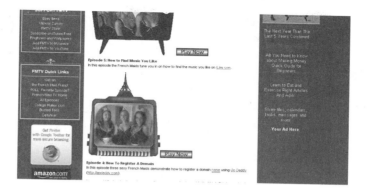

Figure 7.4. *French Maid TV* episode list.

company's product or service become the content of the episode. In one episode, the French maids are shown explaining how to register for a domain name using *GoDaddy.com*. Street explains what he charges for this type of production work:

> *"If you want to advertise on* French Maid TV, *it's $50,000 for an overall sponsored episode. There will be some different opportunities where it's just a product placement. [These opportunities] don't explain how to use your product, so they will go for $10,000 to $15,000 per episode."*

Street knows his audience well. With over 13 million downloads to date, here's how his audience breaks down:

- 95 percent are male, 5 percent are female

- 50 percent are single, 46 percent are married

- 23 percent are age 18 to 24, 35 percent are age 25 to 34

- 14 percent earn between $75,000 and $100,000

- 3 percent earn between $150,000 and $200,000

- 8 percent earn above $200,000.

Although he knows his audience really well and gears the content to his target market, Street's *French Maid TV* has been called "disgusting" by some. Street does get some strange requests of his maids, requests he has had to politely turn down. "I've had people ask for the phone numbers of the maids and ask if the maids could do appearances at parties. I even had an escort service ask if they could co-promote the maids for their service. So, it's been quite a gamut of people."

Mommycast

Paul Vogelzang knows that it pays to listen to his wife. When he first heard about podcasting in 2005, he chatted to his wife, Gretchen, about starting one called *Not Older, Better*. While Gretchen was less than enthusiastic about that show idea, she was delighted to start a podcast that would center on tips for mothers. Gretchen chatted with her close friend, Paige, about co-hosting this show and *Mommycast* was born.

Paul, who produces the show, was surprised at how quickly it took off. Not just that, but he was amazed at how connected the community of mothers really is.

> *"We get lots and lots of e-mails every single day. They point out our omissions, or the sound issues we have had. They also offer show ideas. They really give us that immediate feedback that we value.* Mommycast *has learned that women are a unique group of consumers. They are really after a third-party corroboration as opposed to just being pitched something. Speaking as a man, men need this type of community, too. It's so impressive that there are so many resources out there for women."*[9]

According to Paul, the popularity of *Mommycast* is due in part to its portability. Moms can listen to *Mommycast* while running errands, but also, they can forward the podcast to other moms who they know will be interested in the program.

> *"I'm a fan of* Oprah *and I love that program, but it's really hard for me to forward that program on to you. It's really hard for me to say, 'Hey Leesa, attached is an MP3 of the latest* Oprah *program and I think you'd really like it.' What we've heard from our audience is, they're sending those files around to one another and that is different from traditional media."*

Figure 7.5. *Mommycast* podcast.

The growing popularity caught the attention of a public relations professional who was looking for a unique way for one of her clients, Dixie Cups, to
reach out to moms. After downloading the *Mommycast* media kit, she contacted the team behind *Mommycast*. What resulted was the industry's first ever
six-figure sponsorship deal for an independent podcast. The contract has been
renewed and extended for another year.

What Dixie Cups gets is the ability to connect to a highly targeted and re-
sponsive audience through the hosts, Gretchen and Paige. Paul said that the
feedback that Dixie Cups gets is highly valuable in helping them make better
products.

> *"What our sponsors have found so interesting is that we listen to
> our listeners and our sponsors want to know what our listeners
> are saying too, particularly when it's relevant to them. We always
> share that and we always do it in a private, confidential way so
> that no one's names are exposed. Our listeners can be a great
> source of this great network where they're getting lots and lots of
> support, but also this great source of information about what
> they're interested in, in terms of entertainment or travel."*

As part of the sponsorship deal, Dixie Cups is prominently displayed in the
header, the company is mentioned in the intro of the podcast, and the name
appears in each post on the blog. Both Gretchen and Paige participate in planning meetings with Dixie Cups in regards to their outreach with moms, yet

despite building this close relationship, they're careful not to become overzealous with advertising messages.

> *"When we first did the Dixie deal, we heard a lot from people who said, 'Be careful.' So we had to be careful and once again, we listened to our listeners who said, 'Don't turn [Mommycast] into one big advertisement because we'll just tune out and we'll unsubscribe altogether.' So we've been upfront with all sponsors that this is not a 30-second ad we're putting together, this is not a commercial."*

Lab Rats TV

Andy Walker, co-host and co-producer of *Lab Rats TV* (see Figure 7.6), tried everything to make money podcasting. He tried affiliate sales, donations from his audience, and subscriptions. While some money came in, it wasn't enough to cover his rising production costs. So, Walker decided to go the traditional route and sell podvertising, although he'd never done it before in his life. Walker recounted his first attempt at approaching a possible podvertiser:

Figure 7.6. *Lab Rats TV* podcast.

"I was terrified. So I put on clean underwear, brushed my teeth, and I picked up the phone. In my stomach, I had this big knot. What if she says no? What if she says we're not good enough? What if she says 'God, I wouldn't spend 25 cents on your show.' But then she said, 'It sounds like a good idea.'"[10]

Once the conversation turned to money, Walker was unsure what to charge. Should he charge $10,000 or $100? They finally agreed to $150 per episode and Walker walked out with a six-month contract. With their first contract signed, Walker and his team were able to purchase new equipment and upgrade their hosting. From that first experience, Walker has learned a few ways to sell podvertising so you don't sell yourself short.

- **Understand your prospect's problem.** Walker recommends knowing what your prospect's needs are. You can do this by simply asking your contact, as well as doing some research by checking annual reports or reading the newspaper.

- **Demonstrate how working with your podcast can help solve their current problem.** According to Walker, it doesn't make sense to sell something if it's not going to satisfy a need. If the prospect has $7,000 that she must spend on a marketing campaign before her year end in 90 days, don't try to sell her a podcasting proposal that is 12 months in length.

- **Find out what their budget is.** Walker said that the very first sponsorship spot that he sold, he started with a very high number. The prospect brought him really low. In hindsight, Walker said he should've found out what her budget was and then met it rather than selling himself short.

- **Treat it as a limited run project.** For many companies, podcasting is brand new. Don't lock in the prospect into a lengthy contract—yet. Make the initial contract short enough so that the prospect isn't committed to something that they're still unsure about, but don't make it too short that you're not able to grab the metrics and demonstrate the return on investment.

- **Make your champion look good.** Podcast advertising is a brand-new area and the last thing your champions want is egg on their faces if it fails. So whatever you do, whoever your champion is inside that company, make them look good because if you don't, then you have lost a client. Do what you can to help she or he prove the numbers to their higher-ups, to their colleagues and peers within their workplace. Since people do business with those they like and trust, your efforts to make your champion shine will result in more advertising deals in the long run.

Walker now has ad rates that are consistent for every episode. There are two 30-second slots per episode and the standard rate is $1,500 for the first slot, which appears in the first three minutes of the show, and the second slot is $1,000 and appears toward the end of the episode. Because the content never gets stale, the ads are viewable for weeks after the episode first aired. Walker reported that each episode that sits in the archives could get 20,000 to 40,000 additional views after it's first published, so he takes that into consideration when setting the ad rates.

But Walker says that this is more than just a 30-second ad placed in their podcast—it's a relationship that's being formed. Many of the companies he works with want to have a connection with their target market in a real way. Walker feels that he provides this through *Lab Rats TV*:

> *"I consider some of my clients my friends and they love being part of the podcasting revolution. They pay for that privilege and we have that financial relationship. Sean Carruthers (Lab Rats TV co-host and co-producer) and I went to a podcast expo and staffed one of our client's booth. We're part of them now, we're part of their brand and we're part of their campaign. This becomes a true partnership."*

Producing Creative Advertisements

Many companies want to advertise in a podcast but don't have the resources to produce one on their own. Instead of passing up an opportunity, podcasters can get paid to produce the advertisement for the company, on top of the money he or she will receive for playing the ad in his or her podcast. Walker, co-host and co-producer of *Lab Rats TV*, found that his customers were eager to place ads in his video podcast, yet they didn't even have an ad in the first place.

> *"A lot of these companies don't have their own production companies. We didn't want to run a traditional 30-second ad in*

*our video podcast. So, these companies asked, 'Would you
produce it for us?' So we threw something together that was
cheap and easy to do."*

Walker put together an ad for TechSmith, which was promoting its screen
capturing software called Camtasia on *Lab Rats TV*. He remembered a comedian by the name of Jack Benny who entertained many in the 1950s. Walker
searched online and found an old Duncan Hines commercial that featured Benny.
He decided to produce something similar for Camtasia 4. Walker asked a local
musician to compose some music and then asked his ex-girlfriend to sing the
jingle. The results?

*"They loved it. The commercial was homegrown, it was designed
for our audience and it had a sense of humor. So, the idea is to get
the podcaster to make the commercial for the client because he or
she knows his or her audience the best."*

Securing Sponsorship from Your Audience

In some restaurants, it's not unusual to see a clear glass sitting on the piano
where the pianist is playing or to see one sitting near the cash register where
coffee is being served. These tip jars exist to encourage patrons to contribute
cash over and beyond the money already spent on their food. Getting money
from your listeners is another sponsorship model that many podcasters use
on their podpages. Otherwise known as tip jars or donations, many podcasters
have implemented this strategy to encourage their audience to contribute
money as a sign that they're enjoying the content (see Figure 7.7 for an example). The tip jar isn't a physical glass cup, but instead, a button that is
placed on the podcaster's podpage that says *donate*. When people click on the
donate button, they are taken to a page where they can contribute any amount
they want.

The differences between a tip jar and a donation are subtle. Podcasters call
this form of listener sponsorship a tip jar, yet the button on their page says
donate. However, there is a distinct difference between the two. Specifically:

- If you won't be issuing a tax deductible receipt for the monetary contribution, it should be called a tip jar. The button on the podpage should
  change from donate to *contribute*.

Figure 7.7. Example of a tip jar from *Gastrocast TV.*

- If you will be issuing a tax deductible receipt for the monetary contribution, it should be called a *donation*. The button on the podpage in this case can be called donate.

Tip jars were the earliest form of monetization in podcasting; however, it's also the least profitable. Many podcasters whom I chatted with reported receiving a few dollars through their tip jars, which was only enough to buy a cup of coffee. Others don't want to incorporate a tip jar on their podpages because they liken it to a homeless person begging for money. It smacks of cheapness that may ruin their brand's image. Still others don't use tip jars since it means that, like a company, those in their audience who contributed will think that he or she can tell the podcaster what products or services should or should not be profiled in future episodes.

While tips jars and donations are not a favorite tool used by podcasters to make money, some are doing a good job of pulling in some much needed cash based on the goodwill of their audience members. Here are just a few examples.

Tips Jars

One of the earliest ways Laporte raised money to offset the costs of producing a plethora of podcasts on his mammoth network called TWiT was to ask his listeners to give money on a monthly or yearly basis. Using PayPal, listeners can pay $2, $5, or $10 per month on a recurring basis to help support TWiT. While only 4 percent of his audience contributes money through the tip jars, it still brings in enough to cover his hosting and some production costs. Although the exact figures are not known, since launching it early in 2005, the only thing Laporte abandoned was the annual payments. The reason? People seemed to forget that the annual contributions would be charged automatically to their credit cards when the year turned over.[11]

Some services also offer a way for podcasters to receive contributions without adding a button on their podpage. One podcast directory, Podcast Pickle, allows its members to add a tip jar to their Podcast Pickle profile page. You can choose whether to display the tip jar or not and you collect 100 percent of the contributions through your PayPal account (see Figure 7.8). Terry Fallis, co-host of *Inside PR*, is using a service called Podio Books to raise awareness about his book called *The Best Laid Plans*, a satirical novel of Canadian politics recounting the unlikely and amusing alliance between a 30-something burnt-out, jaded political staffer, and an older, cantankerous, engineering professor. Each chapter from his unpublished novel is released in an audio format free of charge using Podio Books. Although he isn't making money as yet, there is a tip jar on Fallis's Podio Books page where people can contribute money (see Figure 7.9). For every contribution made through the Podio Books tip jar, Fallis will pocket 75 percent of it.[12]

Figure 7.8. *Cubicle Divas* tip jar on Podcast Pickle.

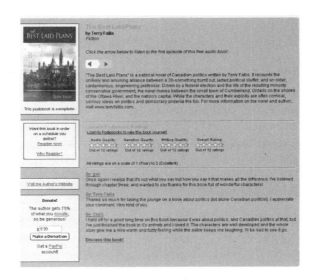

Figure 7.9. *Best Laid Plans* tip jar on Podio Books.

Donations

The award-winning video podcast *Alive in Baghdad* was created by Brian Conley, a 26-year-old U.S. journalist and writer. In starting *Alive in Baghdad*, Conley's aim is to give an insider's view of Iraq from the viewpoint of those who live there day-to-day. In a BBC article talking about his project, Conley voiced his displeasure at hearing news about a different country from journalists who were planted there for the assignment.

> *"Essentially, there's something lost when you send someone from another part of the world, or with a specific audience in mind, to tell another individual's story. We are striving to build journalism in the voice of locals, so that people in different parts of the world can communicate almost directly to their audience around the world."*[13]

While Conley has moved on to start a similar project in Mexico called *Alive in Mexico*, the number of donations received has allowed *Alive in Baghdad* to have two people working full-time on the video podcast (see Figure 7.10).

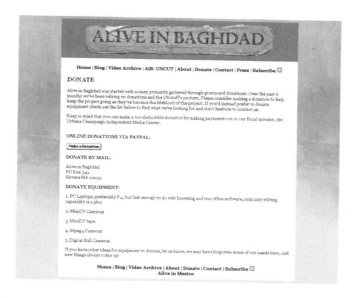

Figure 7.10. Donate page from *Alive in Baghdad*.

Securing Sponsorship and Podvertising as Part of a Podvertising Network

Many podcasters choose to add their podcast to an advertising and sponsorship network instead of seeking these types of deals on their own. For simplicity, I will use the term **podvertising network** to refer to directories that buy and sell advertising or sponsorship deals on behalf of podcasters. Podvertising networks are powerful because they make many small squeaks sound like one booming voice. Individually, the numbers that each podcast carries may not make media or buyers bat an eye. For example, my podcast audience for *Podonomics* stands at 5,000 and this may not be attractive to anyone except me. However, if there were a hundred technology podcasts, each with a podcast audience of 5,000, those numbers would cause media and ad buyers to clamour over each other for a piece of the pie.

Cali Lewis, co-producer and host of *Geek Brief TV*, and her husband who also co-produces the show, left their full-time jobs in January 2007 as a result of belonging to a podvertising network called Podshow. Lewis has no desire to seek advertising or sponsorship deals on her own:

> *"One of the reasons is that it is a full-time job in itself. That takes contacts, the know-how, and experience that I don't have. I didn't go to school for that. That would take up so much of my time that I could use instead to work on the show. So, that's one of the reasons I chose Podshow to handle that. I will handle my show and I will make it the best show I know how."*[14]

These podvertising networks represent a variety of themes, topics, and podcasters. Some will need you to sign a paper contract that's faxed or e-mailed to you after your application is approved. Most have a much looser acceptance policy. All you need to do is fill out a form asking for your contact information, podcast details, and audience information and click on the button where you accept the terms and conditions. In all cases, once you're in the network, you then wait for the opportunities to come your way. Payout is done either by check or via PayPal.

At this point, your only requirement is to ensure that you update your podcast frequently. Most podvertising networks will not police you, nor send out e-mails reminding you to update your content. The onus is on you as the producer to ensure you're delivering fresh content on a regular schedule. One of these networks, Blubrry, sends out an e-mail to its network of podcasters whenever they receive short campaigns. Blubrry will request that only those who will have new content in the next three, five, or seven days can take part in the campaign. Aside from missing out on making some quick cash, some podvertising networks will remove you from their network if you go 30, 60, or 90 days without any new content. So, it pays to update your content on a regular schedule so you don't miss out on opportunities.

Curious to know which podvertising networks you should consider joining? Whether you plan to launch a video or audio podcast, here's a sample of podvertising networks that buy and sell advertising on behalf of the podcasts that are in its network. Most of the podvertising networks listed below not only share advertising and sponsorship revenue but they also offer tools that allow podcasters to publish, promote, and listen to podcasts.

Podshow

Founded in 2004 by Adam Curry and Ron Bloom, Podshow aims to:

> *"Help people to podcast and publish their podcasts, and to help listeners to find podcasts that suit their interests. It also plans to*

use the marketing potential of podcasts by allowing advertisers to find the podcasts their target audiences will listen to and allow those podcasts to put commercials on their podcasts and receive money for it."[15]

Podshow features some of the oldest and more popular podcasts, such as *The Daily Source Code* with Adam Curry, *The Dawn and Drew Show, Managing the Gray* with C.C. Chapman, *Soccergirl* and the TWiT network. Although those signed under Podshow are sworn to secrecy and can't reveal the details of their contracts, what is known is that some owe their financial success in podcasting to Podshow. Both Cali Lewis, host of *Geek Brief TV* and Julien Smith, host of *In Over Your Head* reported that they live off the income they receive through Podshow without having to rely on being employed full-time by someone else.

Podtrac

Podtrac offers podvertising services to both podcasters and companies that want to advertise in them. Podcast producers have to fill out a lengthy form that asks for the name of the podcast and how often it's updated, among other questions. Podcast producers are encouraged to ask their audience to fill out the *Podcast Audience Survey*, a survey developed by Podtrac. The data collected through each individual podcast is used by Podtrac to tailor advertising that meets the needs of the advertiser and to help the advertiser reach the right audience. Podtrac doesn't insert ads without the podcast producer's knowledge. Instead, you can turn down any offer or ad for any reason. Podcast producers receive 35 percent commission through Podtrac.

Blubrry

Blubrry is a social podcasting community that connects podcast producers, advertisers, and anyone looking for great independently produced content.[16] Podcast producers benefit from joining a network that negotiates advertising deals on behalf of the collection of podcasts. Advertisers benefit from the wide variety of choice and new content. There are two features that set Blubrry apart. First, podcasters get 70 percent of the revenue from ads that appear in their podcast. This is the highest among all podvertising networks. Second, if you introduce Blubrry to an advertiser that eventually signs a deal with the network, you'll receive a 10 percent finder's fee.

Podango

With Podango, you can become a station director and manage a collection of podcasts that all have the same theme. Station directors earn 10 percent of all ad revenue generated by their stations, as well as a 50 percent commission on any podcasts they produce. My own podcast, *Podonomics*, belongs to a station on Podango called Podcast Mastery that is managed by Jason Van Orden, author of *Promoting Your Podcast*. Podango also offers unlimited hosting, as well as podcast production services.

Blip.tv

Called by *Fortune* magazine "media on the cutting edge," Blip.tv is a video podcasting service that offers free hosting for video podcasts. Founded by Dina Kaplan, Justin Day, and Mike Hudack, Blip.tv will meet with media buyers and negotiate sponsorship deals if you have a hit show. Revenue is split 50-50 between the content producer and Blip.tv.

Revver

Revver is a video-sharing platform where video podcasters can upload their video for free and share it with others. As people share your video with each other, you make money based on how many people view your video. Ads are placed at the end of your video and the revenue is split 50-50 between the content producer and Revver. Those who share Revver videos can make some money as well. By sharing someone else's video, Revver will pay you 20 percent and split the rest with the person who created the video.

Talkshoe

Talkshoe allows podcasters to produce and share interactive podcasts. The host creates a show, invites people to listen and interact live via a chat tool or telephone, and the recording is produced to be played back later on. Talkshoe lists a schedule of upcoming live shows on its front page to drive more listeners to individual podcasts. Podcasters make money two ways with Talkshoe—by being a host or by referring a host. As a host, every time someone listens to, downloads, or subscribes to your podcast via Talkshoe, you make money. When you refer a host, you get a 25 percent referral bonus.

This list is just a sample of the podvertising networks that exists. New ones are being added regularly to the Podcasting for Profit companion Web site, so check there regularly for updates.

Watch Out for the Fine Print

When signing up with a podcast network, it's important that you're aware of the fine print. While all podcast networks will support you and your podcast goals, you may be surprised at how much you're giving away just for the privilege of using their service to distribute your content and make some money. I'm not a lawyer and if you have any concerns about the terms and conditions, run it by a lawyer first before signing up. In most cases, however, hiring a lawyer may be overkill, so here are some things to be aware of:

1. **Owning the content you create.** Otherwise known as **exclusive rights,** whoever holds these rights owns the content. If you sign up with a podvertising network and they want exclusive rights to all content you upload to their service, go somewhere else. This is similar to a courier service telling you that they now own the vase you're sending to your great-aunt just because you're using their distribution service. Make sure the podvertising network explicitly tells you in their terms of service that you own whatever you upload to their server. If it's not spelled out, then just ask.

2. **Requiring you to only use their feed and podpage template.** On the one hand, this is a good thing considering that most podcasters want to get up and running quickly. Also, you won't have to log in to several different areas to read your stats or upload your content. The drawback is that if you decide to go on your own, the podpage and feed created by the podvertising network will be deleted or put into an inactive state. That means you'll need to create your own blog and feed, and then figure out a way to redirect your fans to your new spot so they continue to get your new episodes. What's convenient in the short term may become messy in the long term, so just double-check that you can create your own feed and podpage separate from the one created by the podvertising network.

3. **Insisting on any type of exclusivity.** If the terms state that you can't join another network or that you can't negotiate other advertising deals on your own, think long and hard before joining. There are so many in-

come possibilities in podcasting and you should have the freedom to explore other advertising deals, whether on your own or with another podvertising network. Look for podvertising networks that allow you choices.

All the podcast networks I listed here and in the companion Web site will let you review their terms before you're officially part of their network. The good news is that the people who run these networks are more than accommodating and will answer any questions you may have.

Advantages vs. Disadvantages

As we look back, there are many advantages and disadvantages to pursuing your own advertising deals or letting someone else do it for you. Whether you're like Lewis, who chooses to let Podshow bring those deals to her, or if you're like Walker who seeks them on his own, here's a snapshot of the benefits and drawbacks to each approach. As you will see in Table 7.1, an advantage with one opportunity is a disadvantage on the other side.

Other Advertising Angles

There are other advertising opportunities where you can monetize the components that support your podcast. These are advertising opportunities where you can make money off the traffic and content that support your podcast.

Independent Podvertising		Podvertising Network
Advantages:	Set your own rates. Keep 100 percent of the revenue.	Opportunities come to you.
Disadvantages:	Cold calling and relationship building to find new ad opportunities.	Rates are set by the network owners. Revenue is split between you and the network.

Table 7.1. Independent vs. network podvertising.

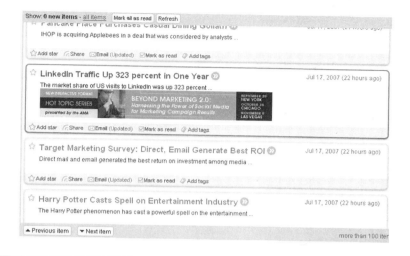

Figure 7.11. Banner ads in a feed reader.

Feedvertising

With the growing use of feed readers, many podcasters are cashing in on these eyeballs. Otherwise known as RSS advertising, or **feedvertising** for short, podcast producers can monetize their feeds by joining a feedvertising network. Banner and text ads are added to the feed and are visible only through a feed reader, such as Bloglines or Google Reader (see Figure 7.11). One such network was created by Feedburner, called the "leading provider of media distribution and audience engagement services for blogs and RSS feeds."[17] Known as the Feedburner Advertising Network (FAN), banner ads are placed in the feed. The banner ad will not appear on your podpage. Instead, the ad will be visible to the user. If you want to display the banner ads on your podpage, you'll just need to turn that option on in Feedburner, copy and paste a bit of code into your blog, and the ads appear.

On the ad buying side, companies can purchase ads according to geography, category, and content channel. Feedburner also provides demographic break-downs according to its content channel.[18, 19] For example, in the computer and technology channel, 91 percent of those serving feeds from blogs and podcasts in that category are male, while in the arts and entertainment channel, 58 percent of those serving feeds from the blogs and podcasts in that category are female. This unique information gives media and ad buyers insight as to which

Figure 7.12. *Cubicle Divas'* feedvertising statistics.

channel will fit their needs. In addition, Feedburner launched AdClimate, which is a feature that suppresses the ad if the RSS item or blog post contains key-words that an advertiser has pre-selected as inappropriate for their brand.

For podcast publishers, you won't get rich off feedvertising. In the ten months since implementing feedvertising in my *Cubicle Divas* feed, I've made $0.16 (see Figure 7.12). Yet, feedvertising is based on the long tail method, so it's important that you use feedvertising along with other podcast monetization tools.

Text Ads

Many podcasters use text ads on their podpages to earn an income. Text ads are contextual in nature, meaning that the type of ads that appear correspond with the content that the user has placed on the page (see Figure 7.13). For example, let's say the user visits a podpage to listen to an episode of how to golf effec-tively. The text ads that are displayed will list information about golfing equip-ment, golfing lessons, or golfing magazines. Podcasters are payed based on how

Figure 7.13. Text ads on *Podonomics*.

many times the ad is displayed (page views) and how many people clicked on the ad (click-throughs). However, the drawback is that podcasters are not paid based on how many people downloaded their episodes. Even if your downloads increase every month, if your page views stay consistent, that's what you'll be paid for.

To use text ads effectively as a podcaster, first you need to sign up for a service such as Google Adsense, Yahoo! Publisher Network, or Microsoft adCenter. You create a free profile by entering in the details about your podpage (not your podcast) on the sign-up form. You will then copy some code and paste it into your podpage. Once you publish your podpage, the text ads will appear. To use text ads effectively with your podcast, you will need to write up show notes or display the transcripts on your podpage. Text ads do not understand audio or video content. Text ads only understand text. So, writing show notes or publishing transcripts becomes critical if you want to use text ads.

As I said before, the drawback is that text ads rely on page views, not downloads of your audio or video podcast. Unless you have a ton of traffic coming to your Web page, text ads may provide enough money to pay for your hosting—and nothing more. This is not to say that people aren't making money with text ads. However, it may be a paltry sum. Since implementing text ads on *Podonomics* in September 2006, I've made less than $60 USD. However, during the same period, my audience kept growing. What does this mean? It means that I won't get rich off text ads, but it's another way that I derive income using the direct method.

PodcastingNews.com, operated by Elisabeth and James Lewin, is the CNN for news and information about podcasting. Not only can you find the top news of the day related to podcasting, but there's also a discussion board where people post their podcasting challenges and successes, a podcast directory, and resources on where to buy podcasting gear. In both the right- and left-side navigation bars, there are Google Ads listed (see Figure 7.14). Another directory

Figure 7.14. Text ads on *PodcastingNews.com*.

that uses Google Adsense to make money is John C. Havens's podcasting section on About.com. As its guide, Havens posts podcasting resources and audio podcasts that contain interviews with interesting podcasters. There's a large banner ad near the top and text ads that sprinkle the bottom of the page (see Figure 7.15). Havens will receive a percentage of the money generated from the text ads as compensation for updating the portal with fresh content.

Summary

The case studies discussed here all demonstrate that the rules that govern advertising in traditional media, such as radio and television, are different from those that relate to podcasting. Although there are no set rules, podcasting does allow for new ideas to take shape. Here are some things to remember when seeking and using advertising and sponsorship for your podcast:

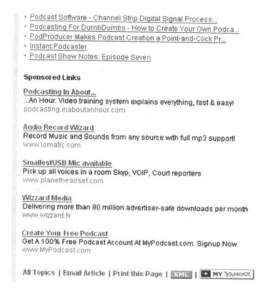

Podcast Software - Channel Strip Digital Signal Process...
Podcasting For DumbDumbs - How to Create Your Own Podca...
PodProducer Makes Podcast Creation a Point-and-Click Pr...
Instant Podcaster
Podcast Show Notes: Episode Seven

Sponsored Links

Podcasting In About...
...An Hour. Video training system explains everything, fast & easy!
podcasting.inaboutanhour.com

Audio Record Wizard
Record Music and Sounds from any source with full mp3 support!
www.iomatic.com

SmallestUSB Mic available
Pick up all voices in a room Skyp, VOIP, Court reporters
www.planetheadset.com

Wizzard Media
Delivering more than 80 million advertiser-safe downloads per month
www.wizzard.tv

Create Your Free Podcast
Get A 100% Free Podcast Account At MyPodcast.com. Signup Now.
www.MyPodcast.com

All Topics | Email Article | Print this Page | XML | MY YAHOO!

Figure 7.15. Text ads on *About.com* podcasting guide.

- **You don't have to accept every ad.** Whether you secure advertising or sponsorship deals on your own or as part of a podvertising network, you're free to refuse any advertising that isn't a right fit for your target market.

- **Think of podcast advertising and sponsorship as a partnership.** Most of the podcasters featured in this chapter have built solid relationships with the companies that pay them for access to their audience.

- **Build a long-term relationship.** Try to avoid the one-offs, the companies that come in only wanting to spend money on one episode. Instead, show the value of advertising with your podcast over a longer period of time.

- **Evergreen content means that the advertising and sponsorship will be seen or heard well after the campaign ends.** The ad deal may end in December, but the podcasts with that company's ads can still be heard or seen well into January through your archived content. Ensure that you set your ad rates accordingly.

- **Re-invent the 30-second ad spot.** It's ill advised for a company to take an ad they're running on television or radio and expect it to work in podcasting. If you plan to sell 30-second spots in your podcast, develop something that's original and clever. Educate media and ad buyers on the unique differences between radio and television spots and ones produced for podcasts.

- **Set your rates based on which companies you'd like to advertise or sponsor your show.** Mahone charges $250 to sponsor her show; however, the companies who sponsor her show are solo entrepreneurs. On the flip side, Street charges $50,000 to sponsor one of his shows because his target is larger corporations. Since there's no standard in the industry, you can charge whatever you like. Just remember who your customer will be and your customer is the person who will buy the ad spot or give you money for sponsorship.

Taking Action

Providing a venue in your podcast for other companies to promote their products and services is one of the earliest ways some podcasters made a four-, five-, and six-figure income. While advertising and sponsorship in podcasts are popular, so too are the number of tools available to help sell ads.

- Decide if you want to sell ad spots or sponsorships.

- Determine whether you'll drum up deals on your own or through a podvertising network.

- Set your rates based on who will buy ads and what their budget is.

- If you join a podvertisng network, make sure you understand the fine print before adding your podcast to its network.

- Remember that you're forming a relationship with the company that buys advertising through your podcast. Avoid the one-off deals.

8

Premium Content and Paid Subscriptions

Selling bonus or premium content is yet another way to podcast for profit (see Figure 8.1). This can be done either by selling access to the content or by allowing mainstream media to re-broadcast the podcast for a fee. In this chapter,

The 7 Steps to Podcasting for Profit

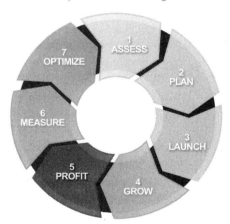

Figure 8.1. Podcasting for profit steps—profit.

you'll learn some of the unique ways podcasters are making money selling premium content and subscriptions.

Introduction

One of my favorite movies is *Total Recall*, a 1990 film starring Arnold Schwarzenegger who plays Douglas Quaid, a man who visits Mars to reclaim his past after getting clues that his memory had been erased. I didn't see the movie in theaters, but I did see it on television one night three years after its box office success. Because I'm a science fiction and action film enthusiast, *Total Recall* merged both of my loves together.

When the DVD went on sale in the late 1990s, I immediately bought myself a copy. It came in a round tin box that was designed to look like Mars. Although the round container made it difficult to store on my bookshelf, the bonus content more than made up for the awkward design of the DVD holder. I popped the DVD into my DVD player and not only watched the film again for the umpteenth time but I flipped through to the hours of bonus material.

There I learned that the script had laid around for years because no studio production company wanted to finance the film due to the amount of money that would be required to spend on special effects. I learned that Schwarzenegger wasn't the first choice to be cast as Quaid. I also learned that the producer and the writer debated on how to end the film. Should Quaid wake up in a dream? Or, should he save Mars from destruction? This premium content extended my own appreciation for the film as I got a behind-the-scenes look at how many obstacles the film went through before it was finally released to the world.

Country Club Your Podcast Content

Going behind-the-scenes and getting access to exclusive content is craved by all, but only a small few can afford it. People pay lots of money to be given the star treatment and to be treated like a VIP. These very important people get access to products and services that are not available to the general public. If you visit clubs or disco halls (my parent's wording, not mine), there's a VIP line that's shorter and moves quicker. Those who join the VIP line are checked against "the list" and if they're on it, they're quickly herded into the club and are allowed to access a private room that's above the dance floor. There is a small percentage of people who will pay lots of money for special treatment.

This special treatment can be applied to your podcast as well. A small percentage of your audience will pay a lot of money for content and services that aren't available to the rest of your audience. Premium content and paid subscriptions is the special treatment you can offer to your audience. I call this **country clubbing your podcast.** I first came across the concept of country clubbing your business while reading an ezine sent to me by Alexandria K. Brown, the Ezine Queen. In her ezine entitled, *How Starting Your Own "Country Club" Can Skyrocket Your Revenues,* Brown wrote about her recent experience shopping. While visiting a variety of stores, she was asked if she wanted to be added to the stores' mailing lists. She said no to most of them, except one. The one store she said yes to invited her to become a VIP client. Brown states:

> *"In general, [VIP] indicates a level of advantage and prestige. Suddenly, I wanted to be on that mailing list, especially when the salesman explained to me it came with certain benefits, such as early notice on new arrivals, a personal shopping service, and private trunk shows."*

Brown continued to say that people want to be part of something special and that's why country clubbing your business is important to help you skyrocket your revenues. People will pay for exclusive content and special deals that they can't find anywhere else, especially if it helps solve a problem. Brown has a Platinum Mastermind program where she charges $15,000 a year for people to work closely with her. She only accepts 15 entrepreneurs per year, which gives this small group greater access to her.

Because podcasts are offered for free, you have to be strategic about what kind of content—and how much—you offer through them. In Chapter 5, I showed you how to use a podcast to sell your products and services. Because your audience won't tolerate an endless barrage of sales pitches in your podcast, you have to be strategic about what you share and how you share it. In this chapter, I'll guide you through a number of case studies about how some podcasters are making money by offering premium content and paid subscriptions for their podcasts. This is a direct method to podcasting for profit and some podcasters have figured out how to get their audience to buy their podcast content directly. Not only are podcasters selling premium content to their own audience, they are licensing and selling content to businesses, namely media outlets and even retail stores. The whole idea of country clubbing your podcast using premium content and paid subscriptions means that you can offer special deals and a level of prestige to a portion of your audience that's willing to pay for that VIP status.

Premium Content

Premium content is when a podcaster sells access to bonus or extended content. Typically, the bonus content is offered in an area of a Web site that can only be accessed by using a user name and password. The login details are given after the podcast consumer pays for membership. Others will offer their premium content on a CD or DVD and offer them for sale in their shopping cart or online store.

As you read the examples in the following pages, you may say to yourself, "Hey, this sounds like the breadcrumb podcasting approach that I read about in Chapter 5." Well, it is—sort of. The only difference is that while the podcast in the breadcrumb podcasting approach is meant to help you turn listeners into product/service sales, with the case studies you'll read about next, their primary goal is to sell their podcast content itself as the product. This is not to say that their premium content won't spin off additional products. It will; however, the initial intent of the podcasters you'll read about in the following examples is to sell premium content.

Think of this like a television show. A show on TV is aired over 30 minutes; however, it only contains 22 minutes of content. The other eight minutes are filled in by commercials. So, there isn't a lot of room for error or for too much content. The show's producers may record 35 minutes worth of content; however, they need to edit it down to 22 minutes so it can be aired on TV. Now, what happens to those 13 minutes of outtakes that didn't make it to air? Are those minutes thrown out? No, they're added to the DVD as a bonus track. Or, the producers may add it to their Web site as premium content that can only be accessed by those who sign up for a free or fee-based membership. Get it?

Success Unwrapped

Heather Vale has a series of podcasts with the unwrapped theme. Her more popular podcast, *Success Unwrapped*, teaches people how to be more successful in their lives and businesses (see Figure 8.2). She interviews self-help gurus, authors, and experts, such as Joe Vitale, Jack Canfield, and Mark Victor Hansen, among others.

While Vale had a lengthy and successful career in traditional broadcasting, she craved the days of interviewing people and telling their stories. She describes why she chose podcasting over Internet radio when looking at ways to build her brand online while using her background in broadcasting:

Figure 8.2. *Success Unwrapped* podcast.

> *"The big talk online at the time was to host your own radio program talk show streaming live over the Internet. I liked the streaming on demand. When I looked into the different options, the people running these online radio stations were asking for crazy amounts of money to host a show. I didn't have a budget at the time. Then I discovered podcasting and I thought, 'I could put out the same exact show, I have all the parameters that I would've had on their [Internet radio] stations and either way, I'd have to promote it myself. So why not put it out as a podcast?'"[1]*

With one of her other podcasts, Vale found that affiliate marketing worked. She would interview a guest and then invite her audience to purchase the guest's book or product by clicking on her referral link. However, Vale found that with *Success Unwrapped*, the length of the content made affiliate marketing too difficult:

> *"People want to listen to shorter podcasts. My interviews are an hour long, sometimes longer than that. Previously, I would podcast the whole hour show. There was no real way to monetize the Success Unwrapped podcast with affiliate sales for the main reason that I was interviewing a lot of authors and all we were selling was their books. You make a dollar or two on Amazon. So,*

I couldn't really do the affiliate sales model. So, I said, 'This is amazing content that I'm giving away for free and I'm not really leveraging this information.'"[2]

Vale applied what she calls **selective podcasting** where she gives away about 20 minutes of the hour-long interview in her podcast for free. Once they get to the end of the interview, Vale lets listeners know that if they want to hear the complete interview, they can purchase a membership to hear the premium content. People can pay anywhere between $4.95 per month for basic access to the interviews to $19.95 per month for access to all the interviews in the archives. Vale uses a content and membership management software called Amember to manage the subscriptions to the Web site. Payments are processed through PayPal.

Anything But Monday

Frank and Mad Mike met in college back in 1985 and started a comedy radio show a year later. After just three weeks on the air, their show was cancelled for being too edgy. After an 18-year hiatus, Frank and Mad Mike reunited to launch *Anything But Monday*, a premium comedy podcast (see Figure 8.3). Frank explains why he and his co-host Mad Mike decided not to offer their podcast for free:

"All other business models are failing. So, what's the most blatant thing we could do? We could say, 'Hey, you're listening to our show, you love our show. The best thing you can do is give us

Figure 8.3. Screenshot of *Anything But Monday.*

money.' [Getting money] means we can keep doing the show and down the road, we can do this full-time. This is something that's in our blood. This is something we're passionate about."[3]

Frank and Mad Mike charge $7.99 per month for listeners to access the recordings. Users are given a user name and password after they pay and they can access the premium content in the membership area. Not only can members listen to the premium content, they can also:

- Listen to past shows in the archived section

- Submit comments on how to improve the show

- See bonus pictures of the hosts

- View videos of the hosts from their college days

- Build a community with other listeners around comedy.

The Engaging Brand

Anna Farmery believes the world is flat. Her podcast, *The Engaging Brand*, which gives tips to managers on how to motivate, inspire, and engage people at work, has helped her to connect with people all over the world (see Figure 8.4). At the end of the day, Farmery knows that whether you're in Denmark or Canada,

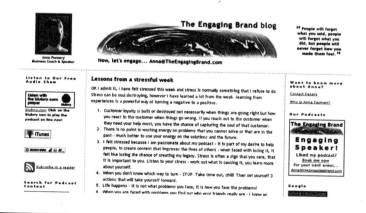

Figure 8.4.   Screenshot of *The Engaging Brand*.

China or the United States, being able to motivate employees is a common issue that all companies grapple with:

> *"There is a strong linkage between happy employees, leading to happy customers, leading to happy leaders, and therefore each week, I interview business leaders, coaches, and authors all with the intention of helping learn more about how to engage people at work."*[4]

Farmery, an organizational coach, stumbled into podcasting in 2005 after getting an iPod as a Christmas gift. She was eager to add more content to her portable device aside from music. That's when she discovered the podcast directory in iTunes and her curiosity led her to hundreds of audio and video files that she could download to her iPod. She explains her excitement about this discovery:

> *"Suddenly my whole world changed. I mean it was incredible. I could not believe there was so much great value out there, so much great content and hey, it was all for free."*[5]

Not long after, *The Engaging Brand* was launched. While Farmery admits that she's made her fair share of mistakes, what she is proud about is how she's monetized her podcast. After producing a few episodes, Farmery started to get e-mails from people asking how the tips in the podcast could be applied to their own businesses. She saw a need to develop premium content, in others words, individual audio files that featured her giving specific advice to individual listeners who expressed a need. Farmery explains what listeners get in her premium content:

> *"The individual audio files have work in them for the person to do. Either, we have a telephone conversation or e-mail conversation, depending on what they like and we address their individualized development needs."*[6]

For Farmery to create the individualized audio file, the person pays her a fee, usually a few hundred pounds. She then records her advice, posts the audio file on her blog, and sends the listener a URL. Because she uses Typepad, Farmery can password protect the post. That way, only the person she shares the password with can access the audio file. Farmery credits 50 percent of her revenue growth in 2006 to podcasting.

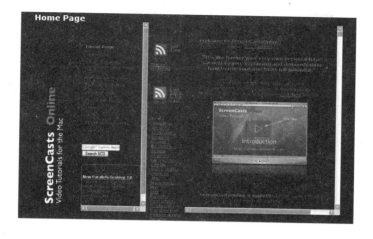

Figure 8.5. Screenshot of *Screencasts Online*.

Screencasts Online

Screencasts Online was launched in August 2005 and is the creation of Don McAllister, the host and producer of Screencasts Online (see Figure 8.5). The podcasts has a global weekly average audience of over 10,000 viewers and the show has consistently been in the Top 25 technology podcasts and in the Top 100 podcast list on iTunes.[7]

All past episodes of Screencasts Online are available in a members' area. For just $35 over six months, members receive immediate access to 80 shows from 2005 and 2006, including 10 members-only shows. In addition, members get to access and view new episodes as they are published.

McAllister shares a similar characteristic with the previous podcasters—he offers premium content on a membership Web site. The viewer sees the podcast for free on McAllister's Web page, but if the viewer wants more, he or she has to pay for a membership that will give him or her access to the archived video content. However, McAllister goes one step further and offers premium content on a DVD. The 2005 DVD, which sells for $19.99 USD, includes seven hours of tutorials, while the 2006 DVD, which sells for $39.99, includes 20 hours of tutorials. The extra tutorials, available for free to members, can be purchased individually for $3.99 if someone doesn't want to pay for membership.

Licensed Content

Allowing others to repurpose your podcast content for a fee in other distribution channels is called **licensing your content.** This model is as old as television itself and many broadcasters will pay the content creator a fee to license his or her content. The company that pays the licensing fee may want to include its branding in the broadcast of the content, plus a guarantee that the content won't appear anywhere else for a certain period of time.

Many podcasters are using this model to make money. They create the content and publish it as a podcast. The content is then sold and distributed through another channel. This typically happens through a contract that has been negotiated. The types of distribution channels podcasters have sold their content to include:

- Traditional media such as satellite or cable television, or satellite or terrestrial radio

- New media such as another Web site

- Other channels such as an in-store promotion.

Jet Set Show

Zadi Diaz and Steve Woolf, hosts of the *Jet Set Show,* got married on July 3, 2006, but they didn't videotape their wedding. Strange because they host an award-winning video podcast geared toward teenagers and they understand the value of recorded content. It took Diaz and Woolf five months to build their audience, then another two and a half months to decide how to monetize it. While selling merchandise was an option, what turned out to be the most profitable was licensing (see Figure 8.6).

They recently negotiated a low six-figure deal with Tagged.com to show the *Jet Set Show* through its Web site. With the *Jet Set Show* viewed as much as 50,000 times per day, the Tagged.com deal represents a significant portion of their income. Both Diaz and Woolf work on their video podcast full-time.[8]

Indie Feed Podcast

Chris MacDonald was a frustrated musician in law school. With graduation soon approaching, MacDonald decided that the best way to start paying back

Figure 8.6.   Screenshot of *Jet Set Show.*

his student loans was to buy a system so he could start composing music. Before he could show off his musical talent, a more lucrative career as an executive at a streaming media company popped up. As he moved from one multimedia company to another, he never quite satisfied his independent music fix until MacDonald discovered podcasting. He explains why podcasting was an exciting find:

> *"It was the first time in my life where I was like, 'Oh my gosh! I could actually take something I'm passionate about, use all my legal and organizational skills, and create something that's producing a result in the music industry.' Or, at least the potential of that."*[9]

MacDonald launched *Indie Feed*, a podcast that plays independent music from all types of genres (see Figure 8.7). Whether it's hip-hop or rock, each genre has its own feed and a select number of songs are played in each feed on the network. The network gets around a million downloads per month and MacDonald's podcast network caught the attention of Guitar Center, the largest retailer of guitars and accessories in the United States. The music played in McDonald's podcast feeds are licensed to be played in each store. MacDonald describes how he chooses the right music:

> *"At* Indie Feed, *we go through our own taste-making process. We select the music we think is appropriate for our channels. In addition, in consultation with Guitar Center, we offer up the types*

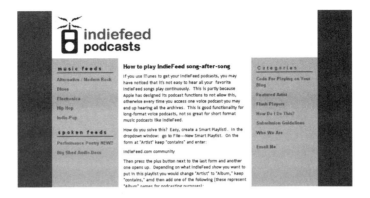

Figure 8.7. Screenshot of *Indie Feed*.

of tracks that would probably fit in a retail environment. [The songs] don't have to be fluffy, but they need to be motivational in a positive way."[10]

For Guitar Center, the retailer's goal is to demonstrate that it understands the various ways musicians can distribute their music. Although MacDonald couldn't tell me the exact numbers in the contract he negotiated, he did say that it was significant. It allows him to pay producers to put together the podcasts across the various feeds on the *Indie Feed* network. The PodJ's, a word to describe the DJs on the various channels that select what music to play, are being paid for their time and effort.

"Many of the listeners lack that friend that used to turn them on to great music. People move, they get into different areas, and they don't have access. [Indie Feed] replaces that service that they had back in college. Having a community [of independent music lovers] helps us to get the word out about independent music."

Selling the Podcast Property

A few podcasters find themselves in the position where a company wants to buy not just the content but also the logo, branding, and complete identity. In this case, selling the podcast property and relinquishing control to another company is another way podcasters are making money from their content. In May 2007, Techcrunch reported that *Wallstrip*, a video podcast that merges stock market information and pop culture, was bought by CBS for $5 million.[11]

Although the amount of money spent by CBS to purchase *Wallstrip* is significant, it was Tim Bourquin, co-producer of the Podcast and New Media Expo, who was the first podcaster to sell a podcast to a company.[12] Bourquin sold *Endurance Planet*, a podcast for runners, cyclists, triathletes, and adventure racers to USA Triathlon and another partner. According to a press release on PRWeb, *Endurance Planet* was:

> *"Launched in January 2005 and has featured interviews with triathlon greats such as Peter Reid, Chris Legh, and Barb Lindquist and running legends Dean Karnazes and Scott Jurek.* Endurance Planet *also found success interviewing 'everyday' age-group athletes who compete and train for the love of the sport. From a grandmother who is training to run 50 marathons in 50 states, to Mike Pierce, a.k.a. 'Antarctic Mike,' who trains in a giant freezer for his marathons in Antarctica, the site has featured athletes at all levels who share their stories, training tips, and racing strategies."*[13]

The financial details of the deal were not disclosed; however, what is known is that the logo, the archives, and the online property for *Endurance Planet* were all turned over to USA Triathlon and its partner.

Paid Subscriptions

In the magazine industry, paid subscriptions are more important to a magazine's profits than someone who buys a copy off the newsstands. Why? Because magazine subscribers help give a magazine consistent income for a certain period of time. For example, if I subscribe to *Sports Illustrated*, it means that I will get an issue each week for at least a year. I also get special deals and discounts for subscribing to the magazine. To me, I feel that the money spent on the subscription is worth all the extra perks. The publisher of *Sports Illustrated* will continue to offer me incentives so I will continue to subscribe for years to come.

In podcasting, paid subscriptions work the same way as magazine subscriptions. The person consumes your podcast and if they want bonus content, they pay to gain access to a special RSS feed. The RSS feed cannot be shared and each person gets his or her own unique feed. Although the feeds are different, the content they hear is the same. To date, not many podcasters are selling their content via paid subscriptions. Part of the reason is because the technology to make this happen is very complicated. You need to have advanced knowledge of certain programming languages to make paid subscriptions a reality for your podcast. Another stumbling block is that many podcasters think what they're doing is a paid subscription model, but when you dig a little deeper, what they have created is an audio or video file uploaded to a secure place on their server.

Ricky Gervais is one of the earliest examples of a podcaster who made money selling subscriptions to his podcast. Gervais, a British comedian and co-creator of the sitcom *The Office*, decided to give podcasting a go in December 2005. Season one of *The Ricky Gervais Show*, which consisted of 12 podcast episodes, were offered at no charge. Season two consisted of only six episodes; however, it was during this season that Gervais changed to a paid model. In order for listeners to get season two of *The Ricky Gervais Show*, they had to pay for a subscription through Audible or iTunes. Fans of the show paid $6.95 for a subscription to season two and season three when it was released in the fall of 2006 or to purchase an individual episode for $1.95 each.[14]

However, once Gervais moved to a paid model, his podcast was no longer syndicated. Although listeners were paying for a subscription to get new episodes of *The Ricky Gervais Show*, it had become an audio program that could only be downloaded from a store that sells audio content. Once *The Ricky Gervais Show* went from free to paid, it was technically no longer a podcast, even though *The Ricky Gervais Show* averaged 261,670 downloads a week during its first month as a paid format.[15]

This might appear to some as splitting hairs; however, a paid subscription podcast has to be a syndicated audio or video file available through an RSS feed that people pay to access. In other words, I have to pay to get the RSS feed and then I can plug that feed into a feed reader. That way, I can get new episodes without having to download them from an audio store such as Audible or iTunes. Although Gervais should be commended for pioneering a monetization strategy that wasn't based on advertising or sponsorship, Gervais's strategy should be considered under the premium content model and not the paid subscription model. Many bloggers and podcasters praised Gervais for his paid subscription strategy; however, because the files were no longer syndicated, Gervais's audio podcast had become an audio book.

I almost gave up on including paid subscriptions as a monetization strategy in this book. I had a hard time finding any podcasters who were able to sell podcast subscriptions and still call their podcast a "podcast." Some were offering what they thought was a paid subscription; however, it turned out that they weren't since their audience had to access the podcast using a user name and

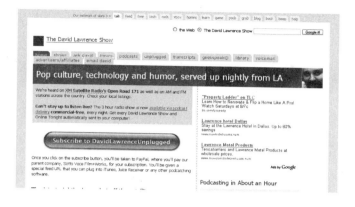

Figure 8.8. Screenshot of *The David Lawrence Show.*

password. This, again, I would call premium content rather than paid subscriptions. Then, I met David Lawrence. Lawrence, a radio broadcaster with more than 30 years of experience in the field, currently sells subscriptions to his podcast. Lawrence's show is called *The David Lawrence Show* and it is a three-hour radio broadcast heard five days per week on XM Satellite Radio, as well as on AM and FM stations across the United States (see Figure 8.8).[16]

Lawrence's show is heard live from 7 P.M. to 10 P.M. on the West Coast in the United States. While many people tune in to hear his program live, for others it's too late at night, especially for those on the East Coast. After getting many requests from his audience to make the recordings of his radio program available so they can be downloaded and listened to at their convenience, Lawrence decided to offer the recording of his radio program as a podcast. The three-hour recording of his radio show is offered commercial-free as a podcast. Despite not playing the ads, Lawrence doesn't offer the podcast for free. Instead, people are charged $7 per month to access up to two weeks worth of shows.[17]

The person is given an RSS feed that he or she can plug into his or her favorite podcatcher. Lawrence uses a service called Show Taxi that prevents people from sharing their RSS feed with anyone else. If the subscriber attempts to share the RSS feed to Lawrence's podcast, he or she is given an error message.

Lawrence reported that podcasters who are using Show Taxi are charging as little as $1 to as much as $150 a month for a subscription to their shows.[18]

Some charge a per episode fee, while others charge a monthly fee. Paid subscriptions open a variety of possibilities for content producers, as well as teachers, religious leaders, newspaper editors, and radio talk show hosts, just to name a few. In fact, here's a list from the Show Taxi Web site of a few ways people can use paid subscriptions:[19]

- **If you have a radio program, offer a commercial-free version via a paid subscription.** Be a radio talk show host without the high fees. Not every listener can hear your show at the exact time you're live on the air. Increase your income by giving listeners the opportunity to hear your show when they want, at their convenience.

- **If you're sending a text newsletter, offer the audio version for a fee.** If you're offering a printed or e-mailed text/html newsletter, record it and offer an audio version for the same subscription rate. You simply speak the same content you've already written—a whole new product for very little extra work.

- **If you're an expert, offer your advice via a paid subscription.** Take your area of expertise from the general to the specific, and make it a snap for people to pay you for any one of a series of podcasts that hones in on exactly what your audience is looking for, and gives them only that knowledge that they need. For example, if you're a home remodeling expert, consider creating a series of podcasts on just building a deck. Go in-depth, take calls and e-mails from your premium subscribers only, and superserve your constituency.

- **If you're already doing a free podcast, consider adding a premium podcast, with different content.** Give your listeners information in your free podcast, and let them know that for a small monthly subscription fee, they can get lots more information on the subject, and in greater detail. Promote the premium podcast via your free podcast and vice-versa.

- **If your podcast carries ads or sponsorships, offer your current listeners an ad-free premium version of your podcast with nothing but content—no fluff, no ads, no interruptions.** Gaming and newspaper Web sites employ this strategy all the time, upselling their visitors on a cleaner, sleeker experience for a few dollars a month. You can do the same thing, taking the existing podcast episodes you have, structuring your sponsorship messages so that they can easily be edited out, and serving up that premium version of your content only to your premium subscribers.

- **If you're a religious practitioner, create a specialty podcast on family relations or faith challenges.** Make it short and concise. Offer it to your worldwide congregation via your Web site as a way to support your ministry—not by begging for a donation, but by charging a nominal subscription fee.

- **If you're a teacher or instructor, consider a premium podcast that allows students from all over the world to take advantage of your curriculum.** Do an enhanced podcast with slides to go along with the audio, or a video podcast of lectures and labs. For distance and extension learning, podcasts are perfect, and subscription podcasts are a perfect way to collect your class fees while protecting your class materials. Add students at will, manage the class lists, and create a whole new way of learning, and a whole new audience for your teaching.

What to Use to Sell Premium Content and Subscriptions

There are several tools you can use to sell premium content and paid subscriptions:

- You can use membership or content management software to manage both payments and content you want to add to the membership area.

- You can burn your content on a CD or DVD yourself or use a fulfillment house.

- You can use a service to manage and sell subscriptions.

Content Management Software

One of the easiest ways to manage your premium content is to use a system that allows you to upload audio and video content without doing any hardcore programming. You log in to an administrator section, click a few buttons to upload your content, then it appears to your members on the membership pages. For content management software, you'll need to do a number of things to get started:

- Purchase the software

- Once purchased, download the software and then install it

- Purchase hosting that can support the software

- Sign up for a merchant account so that you can accept payments online

- Log in as an administrator, then configure it

- Upload audio and video files to the server

- Promote your membership Web site.

Amember.com

For $139 USD, you get a robust membership management system. After buying the software, you can download and install it on your own or have a member do it for you at no extra charge. You will need to buy a hosting package, as well as a domain. Once installed, you then log in to the system as an administrator, upload your premium content, and then create membership levels. You will also need to create pages in the members' area, otherwise after your audience pays and logs in, they will see nothing. I recommend using Wordpress for your member pages. It's easy to use, plus you can add audio and video files to the pages using a variety of plug-ins, namely Cool Player, Audio Player, and Podpress.

Joomla.org

Joomla is a free, open source, content and membership management system. Unless you have a programming background, it's best to get someone to install the program on your behalf. Because Joomla is open source, there are a variety of plug-ins and widgets that you can install to extend Joomla. If what you need is missing from Joomla, chances are a widget has already been written to address your problem. Like Amember, you will need to purchase a hosting account and register a domain name; however, there are options listed on the Joomla Web site. The only drawback is that there is very little documentation on how to administer the system. There are a handful of blogs and Web sites that offer tutorials, but you'll have to search for them.

CD or DVD

You can easily burn your premium content to a CD or DVD. Burning one or two copies a month from your computer to a disk won't take up too much of your time or resources. However, if you suddenly become popular and you get one or two orders an hour, you will need to find a company to help you fulfill your orders. There are companies that will burn your content to CD or DVD and ship the order directly to the customer. Otherwise known as fulfillment houses, you pay a setup fee, typically in the hundreds of dollars. You then send the fulfillment house your files in a digital format. You can also choose the type of packaging for your CD or DVD, for example, a full color or black-and-white cover, a jewel case or a sleeve, and so on. Every time an order comes through on your Web site, instead of sitting at your computer burning disk after disk, the fulfillment house will ship the CD or DVD to that person on your behalf. Check the companion Web site for a list of fulfillment houses you can choose from to make your decision.

Premium Content and Paid Subscription Services

Paid subscriptions are best managed by a service that can manage your subscriptions on your behalf. Most will require you to run a script on your own server and split the revenue with them.

Subscribecast.com

Subscribecast doesn't have any setup fees and states on its Web site that it only makes money when you do. You determine the monthly subscription fee and Subscribecast takes care of the rest. You can host your podcast on Subscribecast's servers and a fee is charged per subscriber, plus bandwidth. On their rate page, there's a calculator you can use to determine the estimated profit you can expect to pocket. If you charge a monthly subscription of $10 and you estimate that you'll have a hundred subscribers, with each file being 8 MB in size, Subscribecast estimates:

- Total podcast revenue: $1,000

- Credit card processing fee: $100

- SubscribeCast fee, including bandwidth charge: 19.04 percent of gross revenue

- Your monthly profit: $709.64.

Showtaxi.com

Showtaxi helps podcasters make money through paid subscriptions. For $75, you insert a script on your server and Showtaxi takes care of the rest. If you don't have hosting or need help putting the script on your server, Showtaxi will help. You can charge any amount for your subscription, as long as it's monthly. Showtaxi will keep 30 percent of the revenue and the remaining 70 percent is paid out through your PayPal account.

Premiumcast.com

This service allows you to create a podcast and charge people to access your feed. That way, only those who exchange money with you will get access to your premium content. You don't have to download or install any software. Just sign up for an account, choose from three monthly plans and start entering the information about your podcast.

Accepting Payments Online

Don't forget that you need a separate service to accept payments online. The most popular online payment processing system is PayPal. If you already accept credit cards, you can visit your bank and inquire about accepting credit cards online. If that is too much of a hassle, try services such as PSIGate, SecurePay, or Authorize.net. You will be required to fill out an application form, wait for approval, and then you can integrate your payment gateway into your content and membership Web site.

Taking Action

Selling access to your content through paid subscriptions and premium content is a direct method to podcasting for profit. Whether you sell your podcast content to your audience or as a license to traditional media, use these tips to take steps toward using this monetization strategy:

- Country club your podcast and offer bonus content to loyal listeners and viewers.

- Decide on how you will deliver the premium content to your audience.

- Decide how you will deliver paid subscriptions.

9

Building Your Expert Status

Self-promotion is the key to raising your profile and gaining credibility in the marketplace. There are many tools you can use to self-promote and one of these is podcasting. In this chapter, you will learn how ordinary people have used a podcast to produce extraordinary results and build their expert status. The strategies that these podcasters pursue help them to earn an income indirectly from podcasting (see Figure 9.1).

The 7 Steps to Podcasting for Profit

Figure 9.1. Podcasting for profit steps—profit.

Introduction

> *"You're going to get a call from a publisher this week. Make sure you answer your phone."*

Paul Colligan, co-author of *The Business Podcasting Bible*, said that to me over the phone toward the end of January 2007. I told everyone in my network that I wanted to write a book about podcasting, so hearing Paul say this to me was exciting. Within a period of a few days, I spoke to the publisher, signed a contract, got an advance, and started writing this book. I had about 60 days to complete the 200-page manuscript and while it was an aggressive timeline, I was pumped and ready for the challenge.

How did all this happen to a first-time author without writing a book proposal or working through a literary agent? When I tell established authors about my experience, they raise their eyebrows in disbelief. First, they question me just to make sure I'm not self-publishing. After I confirm for the umpteenth time that I do have a publisher, they start to recount all the literary agents they approached before one said yes. Then they launch into a litany of stories, telling me about the stack of rejection letters they have heaped in a pile in their office before they finally got a yes. Some authors with dozens of titles under their belts will wave me off saying that my experience getting my first book deal is a fluke, a mistake, a freak of nature.

Most people will say that this is luck, or being in the right place at the right time. I don't believe in fate, but I know that it was my podcast that helped me realize one of my professional goals. I had wanted to publish a book since 2003. I put together book proposals for a variety of book ideas and I even published an 80-page downloadable book in 2005. Yet, it was my podcast that helped me raise my platform, highlight my expertise, and put me within a circle of experts who all know and respect my knowledge. I was in the right place at the right time to receive this book deal, not because of luck, but because I used my podcast to raise my profile.

To raise your platform, you need to rely on many tools to market and promote yourself. Writing articles, speaking at events, writing a book, authoring a blog, attending industry events, and producing a podcast are just a few of the tools you should be using to raise your profile. Jay Conrad Levinson, Rick Frishman, and Jill Lublin, authors of *Guerrilla Publicity: Hundreds of Sure-Fire Tactics to Get Maximum Sales for Minimum Dollars*, call this publicity and say that it is the most overlooked marketing tool.[1] Publicity is perfect for individuals and businesses because:

- Publicity provides the widest exposure for the fewest bucks—far less than advertising.

- Publicity lets guerrillas tell their story in greater depth, which is crucial for new and unique enterprises.

- Publicity gives guerrillas credibility sooner because, unlike advertising, people believe information reported as news.

- Publicity is ideal for the Internet, which feeds on original content.[2]

Podcasts act as your personal publicity machine. Every time you publish a podcast, it showcases your talents and expertise in the most subtle way. Instead of going to the media to beg for precious airtime to tell your story, you can find an audience online on your own by publishing a podcast on a regular schedule. This is critical because in order to stand out in a market that's oversaturated with information, you need to find unique, clever, and ingenious ways to tell your story. Yet, many individuals and businesses fail to brag about themselves. If self-promotion is the way to increase your profile, then why do so many shy away from it? Peggy Klaus, author of *Brag! The Art of Tooting Your Own Horn Without Blowing It,* says that our upbringing discourages us from self-promoting.

> *"Promoting ourselves is not something we are taught to do. Even today, we still tell children, 'Don't talk about yourself; people won't like you.' So ingrained are the myths about self-promotion, so repelled are we by obnoxious braggers, many people simply avoid talking about themselves. Not only are we uncertain about what to say about ourselves, we don't know how to say it with grace and impact in a way that's inviting to others."[3]*

To move beyond our upbringing so we can toot our horn without blowing it, we need to rely on tools that can help us tell our story without being accused of bragging. Podcasting is such a tool and many podcasters have used a podcast to get jobs without sending out resumes, secure book deals without sending out a proposal, and get speaking engagements without filling out speaker request forms. What I'm describing may sound like a dream, but for many ordinary people, opportunities are falling into their laps because of their podcast. These are all the indirect ways people are making money podcasting. While their podcast helps to raise their platform, it's the after effects that help them to see an increase in their income.

Get an Award and Industry Recognition

Being recognized by your peers and colleagues is the highest compliment and an ego boost. Oscar winners typically say that they're honored to be recognized by their peers for a job well done. For many podcasters, not only are they being recognized for their use of new media, but typically, they're being nominated for these awards by people who listen to or view their podcasts.

Taylor Marek Podcast

Taylor Marek is an 18-year-old podcaster who hosts a podcast that covers finance, technology, and business (see Figure 9.2). Launched in August 2006, Marek was torn about what he should podcast about because he loves finance, technology, and business. He finally took his queue from one of his business role models, Donald Trump, and decided that he would cover all three topics in one podcast. Marek is passionate about all these topics due to his early and continuing involvement in business. He currently runs two businesses in addition to his growing podcast—a Web development company and a lawn care company. In early 2007, Marek won an award that came as a total surprise to him. Little did he know that someone who listened to his podcast was impressed with what Marek had accomplished. He remarks on how he got the referral.

Figure 9.2. Screenshot of *Taylor Marek* podcast.

"I was referred by Richard Kiyosaki's Rich Dad, Poor Dad company. I wrote some advice and someone in Arizona liked it. The person found my Web site, liked what I had, and contacted the Junior Achievement chapter where I live."[4]

As a result of the recommendation from someone who lived hundreds of miles away, Marek was interviewed by the Junior Achievement chapter where he lives and given an award for his accomplishments in business. Due to his rising popularity, Marek has also been nominated for a Podcast Peer Award and Blogger's Choice Award. Despite all these awards and nominations, Marek has not been deterred in his scholastic pursuits. College is still a reality and he's relieved that he will be able to podcast while studying at school.

"I'm thinking of college for business administration. Of course, I will have time for podcasting. I looked into it before I decided. I asked [the school's administration], 'Can I do my podcast?' They said, 'Yeah, we have WIFI and our schedule is pretty flexible, so you can do it.'"

Ripple Outdoors Podcast

Peter Wood, host of *Ripple Outdoors* podcast, is an avid outdoors journalist, photographer, and now a podcaster. Launched in September 2006, *Ripple Outdoors* is a podcast that explores issues of interest to hunters and anglers (see Figure 9.3). Wood interviews outdoor experts about a variety of topics, including how to hunt racoon, how to use peacock bask, and winterizing your boats. Wood says that his podcast has helped raise his profile in the outdoor community in Canada.

"All the outdoor writers in Canada know who I am. If they want to know about podcasting, they call me."[5]

In early 2007, Wood's wife sent in an application to place *Ripple Outdoors* in the running for a new media award. Shortly after the application was sent in, Wood received word that he won a bronze award in the new media category for his podcast. To him, it was a surprise given that he's a low-tech guy who's using a podcast to do what he loves doing—telling stories. To Wood, podcasting is just another media angle; however, he's happy to be recognized for being a leader in the outdoor community.

Figure 9.3. *Ripple Outdoors* podcast.

Wiggly Wigglers Podcast

Wiggly Wigglers is a small mail order company based on a farm in England that provides products and ideas to those passionate about gardening. In 2005, Heather Gorringe, the founder of Wiggly Wigglers, launched a podcast by the same name to connect with her customers (see Figure 9.4). Seems like it worked because *Wiggly Wigglers* draws up to 20,000 listeners per month.[6] Some of her fans describe her podcast in these ways:

> *"Funny and informative, the podcast gives down-to-earth information and promotes green living in a very positive way. The more people follow their example, the better the world will be."*

> *"Such a brilliant podcast—my own small garden patch has changed from a square of gravel to planted wildflowers, fruit bushes, and bird feeders after my listening to all their shows."*

> *"Such good quality with entertaining and interesting stuff. Not only has it introduced me to Wiggly Wigglers but it's also intro-*

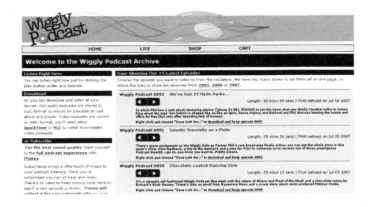

Figure 9.4. *Wiggly Wigglers* podcast.

duced me to podcasts. Absolutely brilliant on the train—beats all the depressing news and reminds you of some of the better things in life!"

"Wiggly Wigglers speaks for itself. One listen and you'll understand why I have always considered it to be the best podcast available."[7]

Early in 2007, Wiggly Wigglers was named the Best Gardening Podcast in the First Annual Mouse and Trowel Awards. This award was created by a U.S. blogger who was disappointed that garden bloggers were virtually ignored by the Bloggies.[8] As a result of this award, Gorringe reported that her team helped produce a podcast for one of the United Kingdom's highly circulated magazines, *Country Living Magazine*.[9, 10] The podcast is posted on the *Country Living* Web site and not only gives valuable information about fair trade for farmers, but helps to promote Wiggly Wigglers to a wider audience.

How to Use a Podcast to Win an Award and Gain Recognition

Being recognized by your peers can be one of the highest compliments that you can get. To be successful at using your podcast to receive awards and gain industry recognition, you have to do two things:

1. **Ask your audience for help.** Don't say that you wish you were nominated or that you hope to be nominated. Instead, ask your audience to fill out an application on your behalf. If you're one of the finalists, encourage your audience to vote. If you don't ask, you don't get.

2. **Participate in your community.** This means going to conferences, writing articles for your industry's main newsletter or Web site, and handing out promotional material that features your podcast. This type of visibility helps people to remember who you are and know that you're podcasting.

Gain Media Attention and Appear on *Oprah*

It's becoming increasingly difficult to be profiled in a magazine or newspaper. Not only are there a plethora of press releases faxed and e-mailed daily to newsrooms all around the world, but there is also a limited amount of space that the media has to profile really great stories. Podcasts are helping some podcasters get through the clutter. Many are able to use the attention they're getting in the media to catapult them to talk shows.

The Grammar Girl

The Grammar Girl's Quick and Dirty Tips for Better Writing podcast was launched in July 2006 after the host, Mignon Fogarty, got an idea to launch it while on vacation.[11] Although grammar can be a dry topic, it appears that many people wanted to learn how to use words in the English language better. Four months after launching her podcast, *The Grammar Girl* podcast was downloaded one million times. Librarians, English-as-a-second-language students, even the Average Joe wanted to learn everything he or she could about grammar (see Figure 9.5).

Pretty soon, Fogarty's success was featured on CNN, the *Wall Street Journal*, and the *New York Times*. Not only was Fogarty gaining attention in traditional media, but bloggers and podcasters were also interested in her success. In March 2007, Fogarty appeared on Oprah Winfrey's daily syndicated show seen by millions worldwide. Fogarty wasn't on Oprah's show to talk about podcasting. Instead, Fogarty gave tips on what words were used incorrectly in a title for one of Oprah's segments. In only eight months, Fogarty went from unknown to an appearance on *Oprah*. Some spend years sending press releases, e-mails, and

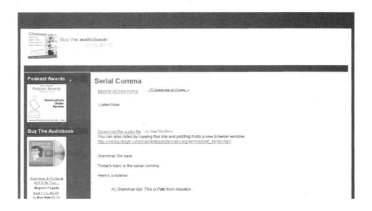

Figure 9.5. *The Grammar Girl* podcast.

product samples to Oprah's team to appear on her show with no luck and no response. Fogarty used a podcast to raise her profile and gain the attention of one of the most powerful talk show hosts worldwide. In April 2007, Fogarty left her day job as a technical writer to focus on podcasting full-time.

The American Family Podcast

Launched in early 2005, *The American Family* podcast, produced by Whirlpool, was one of the first corporate podcasts (see Figure 9.6). The host and producer of this podcast, Audrey Reed-Granger, director of public relations at Whirlpool, got the idea to launch the podcast after having a conversation with her husband one evening. He was listening to a podcast produced by a national media outlet and Reed-Granger wondered out loud if a similar thing could be done for Whirlpool. Reed-Granger presented her podcasting idea to her bosses. She indicated that Whirlpool should produce a podcast that didn't push dryers and washers, but instead, featured stories with real families going through real issues.[12]

Because Whirlpool was one of the first corporations to launch a podcast, Reed-Granger received a lot of media coverage and was invited to many conferences to share her experience. Not just that, but a search on her name in Google shows that many podcasters and bloggers interviewed Reed-Granger as well. The bulk of the results appear after the launch of the podcast.[13]

Figure 9.6. *The American Family* podcast.

Amanda Congdon

Amanda Congdon was a struggling actress when she answered an Internet ad posted by Andrew Michael Baron, the creator of *Rocketboom* in 2004.[14] When the three-minute daily video podcast starring Congdon went live in October 2004, it soon gained in popularity among viewers and the media. In its first 10 months, *Rocketboom* was featured in *Wired*, the *Associated Press*, the *CBS Evening News*, and *BusinessWeek*.[15] In January 2007, Congdon was selected by Forbes.com as one of the Top 25 online celebrities.[16] Today, Congdon is a video podcaster with ABC News (see Figure 9.7), an Internet correspondent with *Good Morning America*, and she's also producing a show for HBO.[17] Instead of waiting for casting agents to call her, Congdon used podcasting to help her create a legion of fans and a lot of media coverage.

How to Use a Podcast to Gain Media Attention and Appear on a Talk Show

Many people will tell you that the chance of appearing on *Oprah*, or any popular talk show is slim. She doesn't tape 12 months out of the year, most of her shows feature celebrities promoting their newest movie or CD, and her shows are planned weeks in advance. Despite the odds, it doesn't hurt to try, and the best way to get on Oprah's radar is to get her producers to notice you. A podcast helps you do this in an indirect way. Here are a few tips on how you can use your podcast to appear on a wildly successful talk show and gain media attention.

Figure 9.7. Amanda Congdon's video podcast on ABCNews.com.

- **Visit the talk show's Web site and look at the upcoming shows list.** You can pitch yourself as a possible guest if you know which shows are up and coming.

- **Generate a lot of buzz in national newspapers and radio.** Fogarty got a lot of coverage in a variety of newspapers that have a high circulation. Newspapers such as the *Wall Street Journal*, the *New York Times*, and *USA Today* all profiled Fogarty and her podcast. The more buzz you generate off-line in traditional media, the more this will grab the attention of talk shows.

- **Talk about your expertise, not your podcast.** Although launching a podcast was a novelty back in 2005, today it's no longer an oddity. Due to the number of podcasts launched weekly, you need to showcase your expertise, and not the fact that you just launched a podcast.

- **Be one of the first in your industry to launch a podcast.** Don't copy someone else just because their podcast strategy is successful. Instead, figure out how you can produce a podcast that's unique, then be the first in your field or industry to launch it.

- **Use bloggers and podcasters in your viral marketing campaign.** They hold a lot of weight and create much needed search engine traffic. With the right keywords used by bloggers and podcasters when reporting on your podcast, it will bring the right type of traffic to your own podcast.

Land a Major Contract Without Cold Calling

Any sales person will tell you that it takes a lot of energy to close one sale. Cold calling, attending networking events, and conducting presentations are just some of the ways salespeople generate new leads and turn prospects into clients. Often it takes many meetings to convince a prospect that you're better than the competition, then it takes many more meetings just to get a contract signed. In his ebook called *Cold Calling is a Waste of Time: Sales Success in the Information Age,* Frank J. Rumbauskas Jr. states that cold calling:

- Destroys your status as a business equal as it gives the perception that you have nothing to do but scrape up business.

- Makes timing work against you, not for you because you have to waste time sizing up whether a prospect can buy from you.

- Fails to find the prequalified, quality leads we all want because fear makes people avoid salespeople.

- Limits production and wastes valuable time since you can only make so many calls in one day.[18]

Rumbauskas Jr. encourages business people to do one thing that I mentioned in Chapter 3 which is to leverage your time using systems. Since there are only so many selling hours in each day, you need to leverage your time so that you can be in many places at once. A podcast helps you to leverage your time effectively. Since the recording can be played at any time, this frees you up to pursue other activities. Instead of cold calling prospects or visiting online job banks, you spend that time producing a podcast to showcase your skills and talents. Podcasters such as Robert Walch, host of *Podcast411*, and C.C. Chapman, host of *Managing the Gray*, both reported getting plum salaried jobs without sending out a resume or scouring online job banks. Their reputations were built as a result of their podcasts and the recruiter came searching for them with a job offer in hand.[19] Here are a few examples of individuals and companies who used their podcasts to secure a major work-related contract.

Small Cap Podcast

Agoracom, an investor relations firm, has embraced many Web 2.0 tools to convey information about the companies it represents. Discussion forums, webcasts, and podcasts are just some of the tools Agoracom uses to bring small cap companies to a vast retail audience. The financial community is quite conservative and relies heavily on the phone and faxes to communicate quarterly reports and company announcements to the media and investors through press releases. George Tsiolis, president of Agoracom, explains why his company took a different approach to investor relations.

> *"We took investor relations online. We set up these 24-hour communities where now investors, in the middle of the night, on weekends, or first thing in the morning when public companies may not be open for service yet, are able to ask questions and come back during business hours and get their answers. This makes it convenient for everybody."*[20]

In February 2007, Agoracom launched *Small Cap Podcast*, a portal that features three podcasts published weekly (see Figure 9.8). Each podcast features interviews with CEOs who lead the small cap companies that Agoracom represents. The content for the podcasts is repurposed from the interviews that are

Figure 9.8. *Small Cap* podcast.

featured on Yahoo! Finance and AOL Finance and are geared toward bringing new investors to the Agoracom portal. Because of this, Tsiolis was invited to New York to give a keynote to Wall Street investors and investment bankers on why podcasting is important in providing late-breaking investment news. It was at that conference. Tsiolis met who would become his next client. This company was so motivated by Tsiolis's keynote that they not only became an Agoracom client but launched their own bi-weekly podcast. Tsiolis said that the contract with this company has more than paid for *Small Cap Podcast.*

Amber MacArthur

How does a young woman from a small Canadian island become one of the most popular TV personalities in North America? After graduating from an eastern Canadian university, Amber MacArthur got her first taste of broadcasting in Prince Edward Island and San Francisco. After working for a couple of years at a large global technology company, MacArthur was soon starring in two technology-related podcasts—*Inside the Net* and *commandN*. On August 28, 2006, MacArthur announced that she was taking a position with a Toronto-based broadcaster to become its on air new media specialist (see Figure 9.9).

> *"Starting mid-September [2006], I'll be working at City-TV in Toronto in a new role for them as their Internet/New Media*

Figure 9.9. Amber MacArthur's podcast.

> *Reporter on City-TV News. I'll also be the host/producer of a weekly show on CP24 (which will start late October) that will cover the pop/tech culture world that I've grown to love."*[21]

The opportunity to host a segment on a television station with millions of viewers is one that couldn't be passed up by MacArthur. The best part? The television network came searching for her. They had seen her on *Inside the Net* and *commandN* and immediately knew that MacArthur was the person to fill the new role at the station.

How to Use a Podcast to Get Your Next Contract

Remember, cold calling is a lousy way to spend your time. It produces few results, plus prospects will perceive that you're desperate. Instead, follow these tips so you get your next work-related contract through your podcast.

- **Be visible.** Whether you do more speaking engagements or launch a video podcast, being seen is the key to being noticed.

- **Have a succinct message.** Develop your key message or talking points so when people ask "What do you do?" you'll know how to answer them.

- **Avoid cold calling and leverage your time.** Use your podcast as your personal sales agent. Don't treat it as an infomercial; instead use your podcast to highlight your skills and talents. This will allow you to focus on other revenue generating activities.

Taking Action

Podcasting can act as your personal publicity and sales agent so you can avoid cold calling and chasing people for opportunities. Follow these simple tips below so you can self-promote and leverage your time so you don't turn people off.

- **Use a podcast to self-promote in a subtle way.** Your podcast will show-case your talents and expertise, so avoid the temptation of talking about "me, me, me" all the time.

- **Decide on which self-promotion technique you need help with.** If you want to land a job or get more media attention, identify this as a goal, then follow the tips in that section.

- **Stick to a regular publishing schedule.** This helps to raise your credibility and helps to encourage word of mouth marketing.

10

Measure

Being able to gauge the success of your podcast will help you to understand whether you're achieving your goals, or failing. Using new media techniques to calculate the numbers produced by your podcast will help you to report more accurate results. In the sixth step of the podcasting for profit process (see Figure 10.1), you'll learn how to measure your podcast the right way.

The 7 Steps to Podcasting for Profit

Figure 10.1. Podcasting for profit steps—measure.

Introduction

During the Christmas holidays, my mother would bake something called a black cake. Every year since I could remember, I would watch my mother put together flour, butter, eggs, raisins, nutmeg, and other ingredients to make that yummy black cake. She always poured in a secret ingredient to give the black cake its dark color. She never used measuring cups. Never. She didn't even use any measuring spoons. My mother had been baking black cakes for as long as I could remember and everything was stuck in her memory.

One Christmas, I tried to surprise my mother and bake a black cake. I tried my best to remember her method and her techniques. I tried to picture how many pinches of salt she used and how many shakes of nutmeg and how many eggs she mixed in. After about three hours of mixing, shaking, and baking, I pulled the cake out of the oven. It was a complete disaster. I cut into the round, soft mold and it crumbled. As I picked up one of the crumbled pieces and put it into my mouth, it tasted funny. The worst part is that my black cake wasn't black at all. It was a deep shade of beige. I missed out on adding the secret and most important ingredient. My foray into baking a black cake was a miserable experience. I had no clue how much of anything was just enough. Without knowing how much of each ingredient needed to be included, the cake was only good enough for the trash. Had I known the exact measurement of each ingredient, I know that I would've reached my goal.

Guessing the outcome of your podcast strategy is a recipe for disaster. Just like my failed attempt at making a black cake, if you have no idea what to measure, you won't know if you've reached the results you planned for. Or worst yet, you will have to throw out your podcast and walk away from the whole new media space in embarrassment. A colleague of mine had started to podcast. After three months, she was disappointed with the results. She complained to me that she had no clue if her podcast was working. She checked her statistics and while she had a couple hundred subscribers, she couldn't tell if that was good or bad. When I asked her what her goals were when she launched the podcast, she said to raise her profile. As I grilled her some more, she finally admitted that she didn't write down clear goals. In this case, the podcast wasn't the problem. She didn't have clear goals. Because the goals were ambiguous, she had no clue whether her podcast numbers were impressive or disappointing. If you're reading this and you don't have clear goals on what you'd like to achieve with a podcast, go back to Chapter 1 and write down your S.M.A.R.T. goals. However, if you have your goals written down, read on as I will explain the best way to measure your podcast.

How *Not* to Measure Your Podcast

"What's the ROI in podcasting?"

The first time I got that question was when I presented at CaseCamp Toronto back in July 2006. I had just spent 15 minutes describing how not to put together a podcast strategy when a woman in the front row asked me about the return on investment in podcasting. I felt the heat under my shirt rising. My throat felt like it was closing up and it didn't help that there were beads of sweat on my upper lip. I speak in front of groups often, but this was the first time I felt a sense of dred wash over me. The first thing out of my mouth was:

"Well, it's difficult to measure because of all the tools available."

I stammered on, piecing together a rather inelegant answer. After scanning the room and seeing many confused faces and creased brows, I finally admitted that I really didn't know. Why was I unsure? There still isn't a strong consensus in the podcasting community on how to measure your return on podcasting investment. Some say it's the downloads that matter. Other podcasters use a combination of downloads and subscribers. Some podcasters, such as C.C. Chapman, Dave Slusher, and Robert Walch all shared with me in interviews that they really didn't care. Not because they don't want to find out more about their audience, but because podcasting gives them the ultimate freedom to voice their opinion to a wider audience.[1] The various schools of thought leave podcasters, as well as media and ad buyers, quite confused as to which method is the best to use when tracking results. If podcasters are confused, guess how everyone else feels.

The one thing that most podcasters can agree on is that using traditional media measurement tools is an antiquated approach that doesn't help podcasting. Measuring cost per thousand (CPMs), cost per action, cost per click, cost per download, or cost per subscriber does not accurately capture how successful a podcast is (or is not). Some podcasters are using CPMs and for good reason. A few who use CPMs shared with me that they have to use the language that media and ad buyers understand. Many of the companies that advertise or sponsor their podcasts are large corporations that hire agencies to buy advertising inventory. Because media and ad buyers from these agencies understand CPMs, it pays to demonstrate the numbers in a way that can be understood. No need to confuse them since a confused mind always says no.

In podcasting, each download or each subscriber in a podcast can be equated to one individual. When you look at your subscribers or downloads, each number represented means that a person took that action. This isn't true for every situation. One person, let's call her Sandy, could download a podcast episode five times because:

- Sandy lost Internet connection the first time she tried to download the episode on her home computer.

- She attempted to download it a second time on her home computer, but it was interrupted when Sandy received a Skype call from her brother who is in Hong Kong.

- Sandy downloaded it a third time after she got off Skype with her brother and this time she was successful.

- The next morning, Sandy arrives at work and downloads the episode on her laptop while waiting for a meeting to start.

- After a few busy days, Sandy downloads the episode to her home computer forgetting she did this five days earlier.

As you can see with the example of Sandy, a one-to-one measurement between a download and an individual person isn't always true. Despite this, the connection made between podcaster and audience member is much more intimate than the relationship created between broadcaster and audience member.[2] Let's just say a national car manufacturer runs a 30-second ad during the Super Bowl. Held toward the end of January every year, the Super Bowl is the most watched sports contest in the United States, pitting the two best teams in the National Football League against each other.[3] Because of the number of people watching this match, running a 30-second ad is expensive. In 2006, a half-minute ad spot during the Super Bowl cost $2.5 million USD.[4] That car manufacturer will spend millions for the ad spot, yet a car salesman at a dealership in small town Tennessee won't know if the reason Ms. Sally Montgomery bought a car from him is because she saw the splashy, high-energy ad during the Super Bowl. It's just not possible to know this unless she's asked and even if she's asked, Ms. Montgomery will most likely say she can't remember. A podcast on the other hand allows a podcaster to form that direct relationship with his or her audience. Because of this intimacy, podcast audiences can best be measured as individuals rather than in groups of thousands.

Another aspect of a podcast that's difficult to measure is whether someone consumes all of it, the first three minutes, the last three minutes, or none at all. Many people have used this as an excuse not to sponsor a podcast or to brush off podcasting as a fad. I don't see this same requirement being made of television or radio programs. I haven't heard anyone refuse to buy a 30-second spot at the midway mark of a 60-minute television drama because the station couldn't prove that their audience actually watched the entire program. A financial institution who bought a full-page color ad in the business section of a national newspaper won't get statistics to prove that every person that picked up the paper that day will see the ad. I can continue with examples from radio, outdoor advertising, and magazines to show that traditional media doesn't have the magic bullet to show how much of their media has been consumed. Hence, podcasting should not—and cannot—be held to such an unrealistic expectation. The only way you can understand how much of a podcast has been consumed is to survey your audience. Even then, the numbers won't tell the full story because not every person in your audience will choose to fill out a survey.

Podcasting may look bleak based on this evaluation. It may appear that there isn't a way to measure a podcast. This may cause you to dismiss ever knowing your return on investment. While there isn't a de facto way to measure a podcast, there are a few tools you can use to gain a clearer picture. In the following section, you will learn the three things you should use to measure your podcast so you can collect a more accurate snapshot.

What You Should Measure Instead

My clients often ask me what the numbers mean. They look at their feed requests, subscribers, and downloads and wonder if they are on their way to success or failure. For example, one of my clients had no idea if having 500 plus downloads per episode is good. Another client was disappointed that she only had 33 subscribers after six months. On the one hand, the numbers are an excellent ego boost. For example, if you were listed in the Top 25 business podcasts in iTunes, you'd be pretty impressed with this. On the other hand, the numbers can also be disappointing. If you've been publishing new episodes every week for three months or more, having just one subscriber is crushing.

First, I'm encouraging you to stop measuring your success based on someone else's landslide of listeners or viewers. Too often, the confusion and disappointment about the numbers is based entirely on comparing yours to someone else's. This isn't the prom where you eye Peggy Sue jealously from across the room because her dress has puffier shoulders than yours. Your podcast stands alone, and while you can use other podcasts as an example, it shouldn't become your rule. Podcasts such as *Rocketboom, The Daily Source Code, Keith and the Girl, Dawn and Drew, Mommycast, Ask a Ninja,* and *The American Family* all have downloads and subscribers in the thousands, even millions, because they were the first out of the gate. In other words, because these podcasts were published in late 2004 or early 2005, they have benefited from being among the first podcasts indexed by Google. For some of you, you can't beat that. Unless a device has been created that allows us to break the space/time continuum, we can't go back in time. This is not to say that you can't build an audience of millions; however, to measure your success based on podcasts that have had years to build an audience is unrealistic.

Second, you can't judge a podcast by its numbers alone. In fact, the numbers don't matter. Well, they do matter, but the number of downloads and subscribers can't be assessed on their own when determining your podcasting success. Saying that you have 3,000 subscribers and 5,000 downloads doesn't mean much. They're just a bunch of numbers. Instead, you should compliment the numbers with results. Whether you need to determine your podcast success for yourself, for a potential advertiser, or for your higher-ups, you should measure your return on investment showing the results as well as the numbers. For example:

- If you can show that 15 percent of your audience downloaded a new episode within the first 24 hours and that 65 percent downloaded the same episode 30 days later, that's much more compelling than saying you have 35 subscribers. The results show ad and media buyers that their message will be heard or seen for a long time.

- If you can show that 89 percent of your audience has bought a host-recommended product within the past six months, this positions your podcast stronger compared to saying that you have 10,000 subscribers.

- If you need to show your CEO that your podcast helped increase downloads of your white paper by 47 percent, again, that's more persuasive and will keep your podcast alive.

- If you need to show your wife that in a 48-hour period, you sold 73 copies of your band's CD to help you prove that your days of moonlighting as a rock star are actually starting to pay off, this is better than saying, "Honey, yes, I pulled a second mortgage on our house because 10 people are subscribed to our podcast."

No matter who you have to prove your podcast success to, the results will be much more impressive than the numbers. No one wants to spend money on a podcast strategy if no one in your audience will take action. I liken the uncertainty of podcast numbers to e-mail open rates—both can be skewed for many different reasons. With e-mail, whenever I hear someone brag about the number of subscribers they have on their e-mail list, I know that only 35 percent of that list will actually open the e-mail.[5] An Internet marketer with a list of 20,000 e-mails really has only 4,000 e-mails that are good. The rest of the e-mails on his list are being blocked by spam filters, are being ignored, or are no longer being checked by the recipient. This is a similar fate affecting podcasts. People will:

- Subscribe to a podcast using their favorite feed reader, then forget to check it for weeks.

- Download a podcast to their computer or portable MP3 player and never listen to or watch it.

- Subscribe to a podcast on their laptop at work, on their computer at home, and through a feed reader using their mobile phone.

All these inflate numbers and when used alone, only are good enough to show the popularity of a podcast and nothing else. Podcasters have to look beyond their egos to demonstrate the effectiveness of their podcast and media/ ad buyers have to look beyond the numbers and ask podcasters for results. When both the buyer and the seller speak the same language, it is easier for money to change hands.

Lastly, while this is a book about making money, your return on investment, or ROI, cannot be measured by money alone. I became aware of this when in a session at Podcamp Toronto, my colleague Bill Sweetman, host of *Marketing Martini,* suggested that the ROI can also be measured by the influence you have achieved in your industry. Some podcasters have interpreted ROI as the return on influence. Michael Geoghagan, president of Gigavox, as well as Audrey Reed-Granger, director of public relations for Whirlpool, have both used this term when talking about measuring your podcast. The number of press releases written, the number of blog posts, and the number of conferences you're invited to speak at all determine your return on influence. Again, the ROI isn't just the amount of money you make from your podcast. It's also the influence you've gained and the trust your target market has in your expertise.

To sum up:

- Traditional media measurements don't work for podcasting. Podcasters have to move away from using cost per thousand or cost per action to show how successful their podcast is.

- Stop hating Peggy Sue and her puffy shoulders. In other words, measure your podcast success based on the goals you set for yourself in Chapter 2, not on another podcaster's numbers.

- You can't judge a podcast by its numbers alone and that's why both podcasters and media/ad buyers need to speak the common language called results.

- You should not only measure your return on investment based on the money you make, but also the influence you have in the marketplace.

Measuring Your ROI

In the previous section, we determined that the numbers, the results, and the influence all determine your podcasting success. You'll notice that I didn't mention money. I've done that purposely only because it's rather obvious. To measure your return on investment in terms of dollars and cents the equation is rather simple. Take what you spent on your podcast (expenses) and make sure that it's less than what you bring in (revenue). The difference is your profit. See, that's simple enough. It's so simple that just focusing on the money when measuring your return on investment doesn't give the whole picture. I know, this is a book about making money with a podcast, but measuring your return on investment encompasses so much beyond money. Let's drill down to learn what to collect when reporting on the numbers, the results, and the influence and what tools you should use to analyze each in detail.

Collecting the Numbers

As mentioned earlier, the numbers are just one of the three metrics to use when measuring your ROI. There are two ways to collect the numbers:

1. Using Web site statistics, such as page views, length of visit, and referring keywords

2. Using podcast statistics, such as feed requests, downloads, and subscribers.

Web Site Statistics

You can use your Web site statistics to measure your podcast, but they don't give a full picture. Metrics such as hits, page views, and browser used will tell you who is visiting your podpage and from where, but these numbers still don't tell you how many people downloaded your podcast. Don't give up on Web site statistics just yet. You can still pull some useful information from these numbers if you focus on collecting the right information. Here are a few areas you should pinpoint in your Web site statistics:

- **Length of visit.** Measure the average number of minutes and seconds visitors spent on your podpage. This number should increase because the more episodes you have, the longer people will want to stay on your podpage to consume past episodes.

- **Number of pages visited.** These numbers will tell you how many pages people clicked through on your podpage. Again, this number should be growing. Just like length of visit, the more episodes you have on your podpage, the more pages people will click on to consume your archived content. Also, you will find people will visit the other non-podcast pages on your Web site to learn more about your company or about you as the host.

- **Referring keywords.** These are the words people type into a search engine that bring them to your podpage. In an earlier chapter, I said that referring keywords can turn into great episodes. Referring keywords can also tell you why people are coming to your podpage. This information is essential because if you approach a bank looking for sponsorship for your financial podcast, you can show that a specific keyword brought 32 percent of your traffic to a specific episode. That gives that bank added incentive to sponsor your podcast.

- **Number of visitors.** The number of people who accessed your Web page is an important metric to count. The number of visitors won't tell you how many people are downloading or subscribing to your podcast. Instead, use this number to gauge the popularity of your podpage.

The numbers from your Web site statistics are useful when measuring the direct method. Using these numbers will show potential advertisers how many people visited your podpage and how long they stayed. For the indirect and integrated method, Web site statistics won't be as important. For example, if you're trying to measure how many more speaking engagements you're getting as a result of your podcast or how many people signed up for your ezine, the number of minutes someone spent on your podpage won't matter much.

If you don't have Web site statistics that you like or are not currently using any, Google Analytics provides Web site reporting statistics. Whether you use a blog, a Web site, or a hosted solution, Google Analytics provides the statistics that will help you monitor page views, keywords, visitor and length of visit. Sign up for a free account, enter the details about your blog or Web site, then paste a line of code into the pages of your blog or Web site. Make sure that you have access to the code that powers your blog or Web site, otherwise you won't be able to use Google Analytics. After you insert the code, Google Analytics will verify that it's receiving information. Wait a few days for the information to populate, then log in again. Figure 10.2 shows you the Dashboard, a summary of all your statistics. You can then navigate to see the minute details of the statistics.

Podcast Statistics

I studied magazine publishing for about two years and publishers look at a variety of metrics to determine their circulation. Subscribers are valued the most because they take the time to purchase a subscription, but this doesn't mean that the person who buys a magazine off the newsstand is ignored. In-

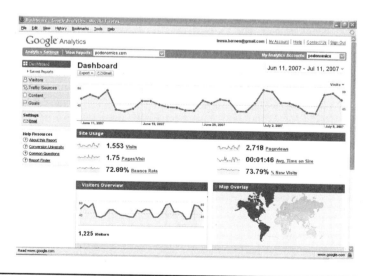

Figure 10.2. Screenshot of Google Analytics' dashboard.

stead, both the subscriber and the person who buys erratically are all considered part of a magazine's audience. Your podcasting statistics will show you the various ways your audience consumes your podcast. Information such as how many are subscribed to your feed and how many have downloaded your podcast all tell a unique story. While each tell their own story, together, all three provide you with a summary of your podcast audience. Let's take a look at each in more detail.

1. **Feed Requests**—This is the number of times that a podcast directory or some other feed service has made contact with your feed. For example, if you submit your feed information to iTunes, every time it makes a request to retrieve your feed that's considered a request.

2. **Downloads**—Every time your audio or video file is downloaded, it is counted. The act of downloading can mean several things. If you have a

Figure 10.3. *Podonomics* dashboard on *Radio Tail Ripple*.

flash player on your podpage and someone clicks on it to listen or view your podcast, that's a download. If a podcatcher displays your newest episode on its pages, that's a download. If someone right clicks on the download link and saves the audio or video file to their laptop, that's a download. As you can see, downloads can be a high number since there are so many actions that constitute a download.

3. **Subscribers**—Anyone who chooses to add your podcast feed to a feed reader, such as Google Reader or Bloglines, is a subscriber. Out of the three, your subscribers will be the smallest number. Typically, I've seen subscribers and downloads at a ratio of 1:10. In other words, if you have a hundred subscribers, you can expect a thousand downloads.[6] There is one major reason why—not everyone understands how to subscribe, but they know how to download.

If you're using an independent solution, there are a number of tools you can use to capture your podcasting statistics. Radio Tail Ripple (see Figure 10.3) and Feedburner (see Figure 10.4) provide you with statistics on number of downloads, number of subscribers, and requests for your feed. Both Radio Tail and

Figure 10.4. *Cubicle Divas'* feed statistics dashboard on *Feedburner*.

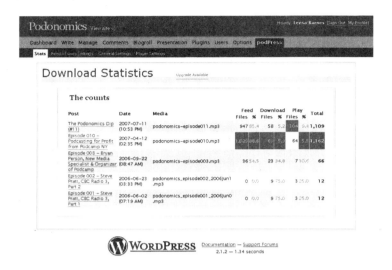

Figure 10.5. *Podonomics'* download statistics from *Podpress*.

Feedburner require that you create a free account. If you're using Wordpress as your podpage, you can use a plug-in called Podpress. Once you upload and activate the plug-in, Podpress will collect statistics and provide information on feed requests, downloads and subscribers (see Figure 10.5).

If you're using a hosted solution (see Chapter 3), you will have access to statistics provided by the hosting company. One service, Podomatic, provides information on the number of feed requests, subscribers, and downloads (see Figure 10.6). Other companies, such as Blip.tv and Libsyn, also provide podcast statistics. In Figure 10.7, you'll see the type of information Libsyn provides, such as the top podcatcher accessing your podcasts, the number of downloads, and the size of your audience.

Out of the three podcast metrics mentioned above, downloads and subscribers are what matter the most when reporting your podcasting statistics to someone else. Downloads and subscribers more likely represent an action taken by an individual. Not in all cases, but the probability that a person downloaded or subscribed to your podcast, and not a machine, is much higher than feed requests. Plus, downloads and subscribers make more sense to an advertiser, your higher-ups, or even your spouse. Until the term feed becomes more mainstream, stick to downloads and subscribers when talking about your podcast statistics.

Figure 10.6. *Podomatic* statistics page.

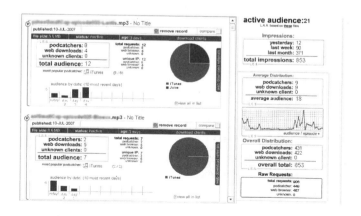

Figure 10.7. *Libsyn* statistics page.

Collecting the Results

Back in high school, I dated a really competitive guy. He was a basketball player and while he waited for the boys' season to start in November, he would come out to watch my games during the girls' season, which started in September. After every game, he'd ask me, "So, how many points did you score?" When I told him the number, he'd then respond with, "Oh, that's three more than last time. That's not enough. You won't get a scholarship if you only improve your scoring average by three points!" He didn't care about the mechanics of how I got that number, nor was he concerned about how hard I worked during the game. All he cared about was my results and whether that was a better showing than the last time. The numbers told him I showed up at the game, however, it's the results that will show whether all those numbers translate into profiles in the media or even a scholarship.

A podcast is similar to my basketball games. The numbers tell someone that the podcast was received; however, the results show that your audience took action.[7] If you have to report the metrics to your boss, colleagues, or your spouse, they really won't care that you spent a week trying to find the right voiceover artist or that you went through five microphones before you found the right one. They may not even care if you have 10, 100, or even 1,000 listeners. What people care about are the results. In other words, they want to know:

- How much money did the company save as a result of using a podcast instead of brochures to talk about an upcoming event?

- How many CDs did we sell using a podcast compared to the period when we didn't use it?

- How many more people signed up for my newsletter because I used a podcast to drive them to my Web site?

- How much more money did I make through Google Adsense now that I added a podcast to my blog?

Again, people get more excited about the money they saved or the additional income they earned, not by plain old numbers that seem to have no context. Therefore, the results are what you need to capture as well as the numbers. Results are best collected by asking your audience to fill out a survey. You don't have to be a statistician or work with a research house to put a survey together. Simply put together a list of questions, use an online tool to collect the results, then ask your audience to fill it out. Whenever I design a survey, I list a bunch of statements that I believe to be true. These statements are my hypothesis about my audience. Then, I develop questions that will help to prove or disprove my statements.

For example, before I did a survey for *Cubicle Divas*, I assumed that most of my audience was women working full-time for someone else and anxious to start their own businesses. That was my hypothesis. Given that statement, I then crafted several questions to disprove my statement, in particular:

1. What is your gender?

2. What is your employment status?

3. Do you own a business?

4. What is your number one business or career problem right now?

My survey revealed some surprising results:

- The majority of my audience was already self-employed (disproving my theory that the majority of them were working full-time for someone else).

- Although the majority of my audience was women, there was a surprisingly large number of men who listened as well (disproving my theory that my entire audience was women).

- My audience wanted tips on how to manage a business (disproving my theory that they were looking for start-up information or needed tips on how to get the most of their career).

This is just one way to create questions that won't confuse your audience. That way, you can collect results that are unbiased. You can make up questions as you go along, however, in order to collect information about your audience that ad and media buyers will find useful, you'll need to capture the demographics and downloading activities of your audience. There are two questions you have to answer when using results to measure your podcast:

1. Who's consuming my podcast?

2. How does my audience consume my podcast?

Demographic Information

The first question, "Who's consuming my podcast?" can be answered by discovering the demographic profile of your audience. Here you want to find out their age, income, gender, and education level. Here are the questions you should collect on the first page of your survey.

Age Range

Don't ask for an exact age as that's intrusive and may encourage your audience to abandon that question. Instead, ask what age range they fall in. Most statistics will list age ranges in six-year increments, for example, 18-24, 25-31, 32-38, and so on. Therefore, you should choose the age range that fits your requirements. If you have a podcast where you give tips to baby boomers on how to exit the rat race and prepare for retirement, you may want to have one age range that's under 35 and list the age ranges above 35 in six- or nine-year increments. Why? Because you want to prove that those consuming your podcast are indeed the audience you're targeting with your podcast.

Income

This question helps media and ad buyers understand whether or not your audience can spend money on the item they're promoting in your podcast. It will also help you to know what items you can and can't promote in your podcast. For example, if your podcast is targeted to college students, it doesn't make sense to promote the newest model of a Mercedes Benz no matter how much sponsorship money you will receive. Your audience will have little interest in buying the product if they can't afford it. Most surveys group income levels in increments of $20,000, for example, the first option will be under $20,000, the second option will be $20,001 to $40,000, and so on until you reach the income level where you want to stop.

Gender

Your survey should ask your audience if they identify themselves as male or female.

Location

This question is problematic. Most podcasters report that the majority of their audience isn't even in the same country where he or she lives. On the other hand, knowing which geographical area your audience lives in will prove useful if you want to sell specific items through your podcast to those who live in a specific place. I remember about a year ago, an ad buyer contacted me about a client who was interested in placing an advertisement with *Cubicle Divas*. She asked me how many of my audience lived in Canada. I had no clue, so I quickly put together a survey and asked my listeners to fill it out. On the survey, I asked: Where do you live? I gave three options: In Canada, In the U.S.A., or Outside Canada and U.S.A. If the person selected Canada, they were given an additional page asking which province they lived in. I now had the information that I could share with future media and ad buyers on where my audience lives.

Education

Knowing whether your audience went to university or graduated from high school with a diploma can give insights as to what type of jobs and salary the person may hold. Some jobs require that you have a college degree in a certain discipline. Other jobs require only a high school diploma. Education can give ad and media buyers clues as to what a person can and can't afford based on the type of education requirements needed on the job. Most surveys will ask the question, "What is the last level of education you obtained?" The options are elementary, high school, college, graduate degree, certificate, or apprentice.

Employment Status

This can tell you whether the person has money now or if they're on a fixed budget. The options I've seen on a survey are:

- Full-time

- Part-time

- Student

- Retired

- Self-employed

- Unemployed.

In all these, you can make assumptions, but it doesn't hurt if you put everything into your survey rather than leave it out. It may make your survey a bit longer, but it's better to ask than to have a survey that's incomplete because you chose not to include a question. Demographic information gives you a profile of your audience, but now it's time to take it one step further. The second question, "How does my audience consume my podcast?" is where you'll want to know how they find out about new episodes and whether or not they download it right away. Here are a few more questions you can add to your survey to report on the results.

Consumption Habits

Understanding how your audience consumes your podcast is an important factor to consider. You may be wasting time adding bling[8] to your podpage when the majority of your audience accesses your podcast through iTunes. Discovering how and when your audience accesses your podcast will help you spend time and money on the right delivery mechanism. In particular, knowing how your audience consumes your podcast will help you create a media kit that shows the results. In a media kit for the *Financial Aid Podcast*, there are two points that stick out:

1. The number of downloads in the first 24 hours after the new episode is released

2. The number of downloads 90 days after the episode was released.

The *Financial Aid Podcast* has 800 downloads in the first 24 hours. However, what's even more intriguing is that each episode gets about three times the downloads 90 days after it was released. This is important for two reasons:

1. It shows that the content is **evergreen**, meaning it doesn't expire, get stale, or grow old. The information shared in those episodes is relevant well beyond the date it was first produced.

2. More importantly, it means that a company's advertisement or sponsorship message will be heard for months beyond the original "air date," turning the company's message into evergreen advertising.

Potential Reach

All of this will help you to understand your potential reach. This is a term that those in the magazine industry use to describe the size of their audience. In most magazine readers' surveys, there's a question that asks: "How many people do you share your magazine with?"

Often, a magazine will be audited for both its number of subscribers and number of newsstand sales. For example, in 2006, *Vanity Fair* reported a circulation of 1,215,920 of which 64.7 percent were subscribers.[9] However, because *Vanity Fair* has 5.69 readers per copy, the size of its total audience is 6,238,000.[10] That means that *Vanity Fair*'s reach is five times the amount of subscribers and news sale stands combined. The reach of *Vanity Fair*'s magazine is attractive to media and ad buyers because it tells them that the person who buys the magazine is an influencer. In his book *The Tipping Point*, Malcolm Gladwell calls these people who influence others **connectors.** Connectors know a lot of people, know the right kind of people, and bring together people from unrelated worlds.[11] Ad and media buyers want to work with podcasts that are considered connectors simply because it is cheaper for them to get their message out to a wider audience.

Podcasters should also ask their audience who they share the podcast with, for example:

- If one of your viewers downloads your video podcast to their portable device and shows it to her brother, this has to be measured.

- If one of your listeners burns your audio podcast to a CD, then gives it to his mother so she can listen in the car on her way to work, this has to be measured.

- If one of your audience members shares the URL to your podcast with a discussion list he belongs to, this has to be measured.

Online Activities

Not only should you survey your audience to find out how they consume your podcast and who else they share your podcast with, but you should take the time to discover what they do online. These questions give a clue as to how comfortable your audience is with using the Internet for other purposes. Questions you should consider asking are:

- Do you shop online?

- What's the last purchase you made online?

- What do you typically purchase online?

- Do you respond to banner ads?

- Have you ever responded to a host-recommended product or service?

Some will use e-mail to send the survey questions to their database and use a spreadsheet to keep track of responses. Although this strategy may work for a small database, it can become a nightmare if lots of people respond. The manual process to copy and paste responses from e-mail into a spreadsheet will be too great a task to handle. Instead, you can collect demographic information, consumption habits, and online activities by designing the survey yourself or using one provided by a podvertising network. If you decide to design the survey yourself, you can use Survey Monkey to create the survey and analyze the results. The free version of Survey Monkey allows you to collect up to 100 responses and ask up to 10 questions. You input the questions you want to ask and choose the type of answers you want people to respond to using a variety of templates. Once you're finished, you will get a URL that you can share with people. This URL will take your audience to the survey. When you start getting responses, you log in to Survey Monkey to see the results. Figure 10.8 shows you what the results look like.

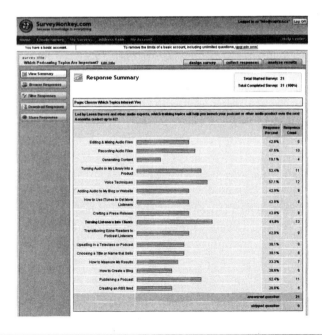

Figure 10.8. Results displayed on Survey Monkey.

Figure 10.9.   Podtrac survey welcome page.

If you don't want to craft your own survey, join a podvertising network. Some have surveys that are pre-made and contain many of the previous questions. One podvertising network, Podtrac, encourages podcasters to use the survey to gain audience information that can't be collected from downloads or subscribers. Most podcasters will add a URL to the survey in the show notes on their podpage and ask their audience to fill it out. When the URL is clicked on, the person is taken to a welcome page where the privacy information is displayed, as well as the name of the podcast (see Figure 10.9). It's a lengthy survey, however, it beats having to craft the questions and collect the results on your own.

Analyzing the Influence

Having a podcast that's good builds numbers, but having a podcast that's compelling builds a community. If you create a podcast that has the capacity or power to affect the actions, behaviors, and opinions of others, you will reap the benefits with increased rankings in search engines and more invitations to speak at events.[12] In other words, the currency here is influence. If the host is likeable and if the content is relevant, then your return on investment in this case isn't money, but influence (see Figure 10.10). In his book *The Likeability Factor*, Tim Sanders says that being likeable and being relevant are your ingredients to being recognized and praised:

likeablility + relevance = influence

Figure 10.10. The equation of influence.

"Have you ever wondered why some people seem to garner all the praise and glory, while others are overlooked? Research shows that your likeability will have a tremendous influence on your capacity to garner that respect and recognition. This vital need to be recognized may be more controllable than you think. From the classroom to the living room to the boardroom, when you are likeable, you are praised. You are acknowledged. And you know that feels great."[13]

Many podcasters are experiencing results that go beyond money due to their podcast. In Chapter 9, I detailed the many ways podcasters are raising their platform and expertise in their fields. Their investment went beyond the money and gave some of them the recognition they craved or didn't ask for. In particular, podcasters are:

- Getting book deals

- Being recruited to jobs

- Closing deals without cold calling

- Getting awards

- Being invited on talk shows

- Gaining a lot of media coverage.

Along with the numbers and the results, measuring your influence will give you a complete picture and help you understand how your business and income is changing as a result. Taking a snapshot of your rankings in search engines and social media, as well as the number of responses from your audience are just a few ways to measure influence. Let's take a look at each in detail.

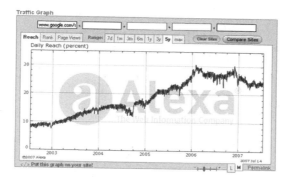

Figure 10.11.   Five-year traffic for Google search *Leesa Barnes*.

Search Engine Rankings

Search engines can tell you a lot about the growth of your influence. Right before you launch your podcast, take note of the number of search results for specific keywords, as well as what page you currently appear on. I tracked my name to see how my influence is growing. I was curious to know who was linking to me and how those links helped to increase the results for my name. About three years ago, if I searched the keywords *leesa barnes* using Google, there were only 30,000 results returned (see Figure 10.11). At the time this book was published in the fall of 2007, that number is well over 85,000. When I look at why the search results for my name have more than doubled in three years, I can see that my podcast has been a big factor. There are links created from other podcasters who interviewed me, articles that have been written about me in major newspapers, and information I have posted on my blog about podcasting.

To measure your own rankings in a search engine, use Alexa.com. Plug in any URL and Alexa will give you a history of that Web site's ranking. I used Alexa to see whether or not the traffic increased for the search term *leesa barnes* in Google. Here's how you can use Alexa to measure the traffic to your own keyword:

1. Go to Alexa.com.

2. Look for the Site Info box, then type in google.com/search?q=search+term (replace search+term with your keyword, for example, your company name, or your first name and last name).

3. When the page refreshes, change the range from daily to one year. You will then see a graph that will show whether or not searches on your keyword are increasing or decreasing.

Social Media Rankings

Millions of people around the world use a variety of Web sites to share information and have conversations. Whether someone's sharing photos using Flickr, bookmarks through del.icio.us, news through Digg, or video files through YouTube, social media is content created by people online for people online. Because the Average Jane and Joe are creating this content, monitoring these Web sites can help you to assess whether your podcast is helping your influence to grow or not. There are a number of Web sites you can check to see how you rank in social media. Let's take a look at just a few.

- **Technorati**—This directory keeps track of all the blogs, podcasts, events, videos, and photos that have been posted about you by the second. Enter your name, company name, or podcast in the search box. You will then get everything in the known universe that has been posted about your search term. In Figure 10.12, you'll see that for the search term *leesa barnes*, there are quite a number of blogs, videos, and photos posted about me.

Figure 10.12. Technorati results for *Leesa Barnes*.

We found 35 results for photos matching "leesa barnes".

View: Most relevant • Most recent • Most interesting

Show thumbnails

Sponsored Results

cameras
Shop for Brand name electronics. Only $3.99 to ship your entire order.
www.CircuitCity.com

Ritz Camera Official Site
Buy Now, Pay Nothing for 6 Months. Free Shipping & Pay No Sales Tax.
RitzCamera.com

Tripods and More on Sale with Free UPS
Find the Bushnell binoculars, Lomo cameras, tripods and more at OpticsPlanet.com - helping you...
opticsplanet.com

Nikon Repairs
V-Photo specialize in coolpix, 35mm cameras, all lenses and nikonos under water units. Free...
vphotoatlanta.com

The Olympus
Free Apartment Search at Rent.com. Report Your Lease To Us & Get $100.
www.Rent.com

Leesa Barnes introduction
Uploaded on 25 February 2007

By Bryper
See more photos, or visit his profile.

podcamp, leesabarnes, podcamptoronto, podcamptoronto2007

Leesa Barnes
Uploaded on 11 August 2006

By .gabriel
See more photos, or visit .gabriel's profile.

socialtechbrewing, womeninit, leesabarnes

Leesa Barnes
Uploaded on 11 August 2006

Figure 10.13. Photos on Flickr.

- **Photo Sharing**—Taking photos and sharing them online is another social media tool that can help increase your ranking and influence. The more photos that are snapped, the more involved you seem to be in your industry. I spoke at my first podcasting conference in 2006. After that event, I was pleasantly surprised to see photos of me uploaded to Flickr. After every conference I went to there were more photos posted of me on Flickr. Very soon, as you can see in Figure 10.13, there are pages of photos all that show me speaking or presenting. In just one year, I have amassed pages of photos without having to hire a photographer. Not just that, but because of my growing influence, people no longer ask, "Who's the gal in the picture?" The photo is now tagged with my name so I can find it easily. That's a great indicator of your influence. If people snap photos, upload them, and can tag them right away with the correct spelling of your first and last name, this is yet another way you can measure your influence.

- **Social Bookmarking**—Some Web sites allow users to bookmark their favorite URL, video file, or podcast and share it with others. The more people that bookmark the same information, the better the chances of it appearing on the front page. Some examples of these Web sites are del.icio.us, Digg, Stumble Upon, and Reddit, just to name a few. Let's just say that you recently interviewed a prominent person in your field. It takes just one person to listen or view your podcast to bookmark it. This then grabs the attention of someone else that either comments or

Figure 10.14. Results on Digg.

bookmarks your podcast. This act of bookmarking not only increases your audience but also propels your influence. In Figure 10.14, you'll notice that there is one article that received quite a number of Diggs. I didn't write it, nor is it linked to my podcast, however, it is an article written by someone else about my presentation on podcasting. It's hard to say what will become popular and what won't. As I was surfing through Digg, a news item about a 6.7 magnitude earthquake in Japan got 275 Diggs, but a question about how to respond to an Internet hacker got 705 Diggs. Just stick to your game plan. Visit these social bookmarking Web sites and search by your name, company name, and podcast. Review the results to assess how well your podcast is positioning you.

Audience Response

An actor performing on stage will know right away if the audience appreciates his or her performance. The audience will applaud or hiss or boo depending on how the actor performed his or her part. However, this isn't the only way an actor receives feedback. He or she can read the reviews in the newspaper or listen to critics on radio stations and television shows. All these give the actor clues on how well he or she did or what needs to be improved. Just like an actor, a podcaster will know how well his or her podcast is received through comments or what others are saying through their own podcasts.

You will know that your influence is growing based on the number of comments people leave on your blog. If the average number of comments you received has grown, this means your influence is growing too. People leave comments, tell their friends, who then leave comments as well. Not only should you take note of the written comments left on your podpage, but also take note of the number of podcast-related e-mails you're receiving, as well as the number of audio comments you get. The growing volume of e-mails (or lack thereof) is a good indicator of your influence.

Putting It All Together

When measuring the return on investment for your podcast, not every measuring tool will work for every situation. For example, if you're building a shed, you wouldn't use a measuring cup to measure the amount of concrete you need for the foundation. This is similar to your podcast—you'll need to use the right tools to measure the right method. In the Introduction of this book, we explored the three methods podcasters are using to make money. These methods are:

- **Direct**—Monetizing their podcast content

- **Indirect**—Selling their podcasting skills and expertise

- **Integrated**—Turning listeners into customers.

In Figure 10.15, the diagram shows how the three metrics used to determine the ROI (numbers, results, influence) and the three podcasting for profit methodologies (direct, indirect, integrated) work together. Some of you will look at Figure 10.15 and say that the numbers, the results, and the influence can be used to measure all three methods. I would agree, however, the best way to use the metrics is to select the ones that will help bolster your case. In other words, just like the construction project earlier, it's important to choose the metrics that will help prove the success of your podcast. Let's take a look at these in detail.

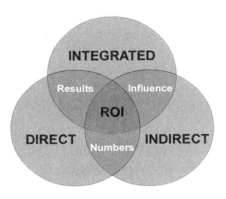

Figure 10.15. Measuring your podcast diagram.

Direct Method

In the direct method, you make money directly from your podcasting content. You sell the content itself or you use the content as a selling point to encourage others to subsidize the costs to create the content. If we take a look at the two direct methods explored in this book, the numbers and the results will be very important in helping you to measure the ROI and demonstrate value to ad and media buyers. For example:

- If you're selling advertising or sponsorship (see Chapter 7), ad and media buyers will want to know how many people are consuming your podcast (the numbers) and what action they typically take (the results).

- If you're selling premium content or paid subscriptions (see Chapter 8), you will need to show how many are accessing your podcast (the numbers) and how many of them pay for the premium content (the results).

Indirect Method

In the indirect method, you make money selling your podcasting skills and expertise. People will hire you to help them launch their podcasting strategy or tell them how to use podcasting for their business. If we review the two indirect examples used in the book, using both the numbers and the influence will help demonstrate the ROI. In particular:

- If you're consulting or teaching others how to podcast (see Chapter 6), you'll want to know how many signed up for your service or attended your workshop (the numbers) and how many launched a podcast as a result of your advice (the influence).

- If you're building your expert status (see Chapter 9), you'll want to know how many Web sites link to your podcast or how many articles have been written about you (the numbers) and how much your profile or ranking has increased (the influence).

Integrated Method

Being able to turn your audience into paying customers is a skill that's not easy to master. However, using the integrated method, you can make money from your audience using the tips in Chapter 5. In this case, the numbers don't really matter. Whether 10 people subscribed to your podcast or if 1,000 people downloaded your episode, it's the results and your influence that will give you a better indication of success. The key here is to split test. Create two separate Web pages and send prospects to two different URLs. Let's just say that your boss is insistent that you send a direct mail piece to your database. I would encourage you to do it and run a podcast in parallel to the direct mail campaign. On the direct mail pieces, send those prospects to one URL. In the podcast, send your audience to a separate URL. At the end of the campaign, compare the results. If the podcast encouraged more to download the whitepaper, sign up for your ezine or buy your book, then these are the results. The influence in this case is your ability as a host to encourage your audience to pursue a course of action. Hence, the reason both the results and the influence are what matter when measuring the integrated method.

Presenting the ROI

Compiling your ROI is one thing, but presenting it is yet another. If you don't choose the right vehicle to present the numbers, the results, and the influence, it will look like a jumbled mess. Instead of coming across as confident and self-assured, you will appear disorganized and unfocused. The best way to present your ROI is to first picture your target market. Is it your boss? Your spouse? A media buyer? Your audience will determine how formal or informal your presentation needs to be. Regardless of the audience, your presentation should flow in the following way:

- Start off with a summary about your podcast. What is it about? Who is the target?

- Next, identify the numbers. Things like subscribers and downloads will help. This is something that people understand. Leave out any language that can confuse your audience, such as feeds or feed requests.

- Then, show the results and influence. Show results from a survey, preferably a survey you conducted with your audience. Demonstrate the influence by showing how rankings improved in search engines and in social media. List all the conferences you've been invited to speak at or the awards your podcast has won. Wow your audience with the results.

- Then, list your recommendations, lessons learned, and next steps. Tell your audience what has worked, what needs to be improved, and how you see your podcast fitting into future initiatives.

- End your presentation with enough time for questions and answers. Leave the technical questions to the person who put your solution together, but answer everything having to do with strategy.

Now that you have a simple outline on how to craft your presentation, here are some tools you can use to put it together:

- **Slides**—If you plan to present the information to an audience, using presentation slides is a good idea. That way, you can include pie charts, graphics, and tables to show your podcast's success visually. *Rocketboom* has done this and makes its audience information publicly available on its wiki.[14]

- **PDF**—Otherwise known as a Fact Finder sheet or a Media Kit, you can use a Word document to create a one-pager describing your podcast. Mommycast has a media kit that shows how many listen, how many take action and what the podcast is all about.[15]

- **Buttons**—Podcasters who have won awards will post small banners or graphical buttons on their podpage, thus demonstrating their rise in influence.

- **Calendar**—A listing of the events you'll appear at is useful if you want to demonstrate your influence. You can use an online calendar system or simply list your calendar in bullet form on your podpage.

Taking Action

In this chapter, you learned how to measure your podcast using new media techniques. Knowing that your numbers, results, and influence all tell the story of your success will help you understand if you're moving ahead or falling behind. Here are a few action items:

- Measure your results based on the S.M.A.R.T. goals you identified in Chapter 1.

- The numbers, the results, and the influence all must be considered when measuring your ROI.

- Use the right tools that will help you report the right information.

- Present your ROI based on the audience you'll be presenting to.

11

Optimize Your Results

Some strategies fall short of expectations, while others exceed them. If your podcast fails to meet your initial goals, it's time to reassess where you fell short. In this chapter, you'll learn some of the common problems that contribute to a failed podcast strategy and ways to polish it up so you achieve the results you are looking for (see Figure 11.1).

The 7 Steps to Podcasting for Profit

Figure 11.1. Podcasting for profit steps—optimize.

Introduction

Since elementary school, I've had an insatiable desire to speak French. I took my first French class in eighth grade at the age of 14. My French teacher taught us pronouns, verbs, and how to pronounce words like cat, dog, and friend in French. When I got to high school, not only did I take the one required French course all high school students need to pass in order to graduate, I took it every year. While some of my friends couldn't understand why I would chose to take a French class every year, learning how to speak French and trying to make my accent sound less Anglicized became an obsession.

By the time I reached university, I was majoring in French. However, the courses had gotten harder. Instead of getting the B+ that I was used to in high school, I could barely muster a D-. While I could conjugate verbs in my sleep, my comprehension was poor. Even though I had taken French courses for close to 10 years, I could barely understand what my university professor was saying to me. Taking one French course once a day and being surrounded by an English culture for the other 23 hours did little to help my conversational skills. I could ask for the washroom, I even knew how to ask for a combo at a fast food restaurant in French, but I couldn't hold a conversation in my second language beyond "Ca Va?"

By the time I reached my second year of university, I changed my major. An embarrassing incident in my second year university course was one reason why I chose another major. When the teaching assistant asked me in French what I wanted to do in the future, I pronounced the French word *to succeed* incorrectly. As soon as I uttered the word, I regretted it. Between fits of giggles, the teaching assistant told me that I said, "I want to suck at everything I do," instead of what I meant to say which was "I want to succeed at everything I do." Not only was my confidence being eroded, but my grades were suffering as well. If I wanted to graduate and have the option of going on to do my masters or doctorate, I knew that I could no longer major in French. Despite my situation, I didn't abandon my quest to learn French. I couldn't put all those years to waste.

So, the summer before I went into my third year in university, I signed up for a government-sponsored language program. I was accepted into a program that sent those whose mother tongue is English to live with a French family for six weeks. I took the train to a rural town in Quebec, the province in Canada where French is widely spoken. The picturesque town I went to sat along the St. Lawrence River. It was definitely the hardest six weeks of my life. The French I learned in school wasn't the same as that spoken in rural Quebec. Although it was a challenge to understand my Quebec mother and father, I was forced to speak only French for almost 45 days. If I wanted to sleep, eat, or go to the washroom, I had to say everything in French.

When I returned home later that summer, I quickly enrolled in a French language school for people who want to speak conversational French. Each week for an hour, I would sit in a room with other non-native French speakers and converse in French. By the time I graduated from university in 1997, I had gone from a Grade 3 level in conversational French to a Grade 10 level. I could now watch current news programs and read newspapers in French without consulting a dictionary. Although I wasn't happy about changing my major, I didn't give up on perfecting my French skills. Instead, I took a different path toward achieving my goals.

With everything in life, you need to evaluate and make changes. In my case, I wanted to master a skill. Just because I took one path and didn't achieve my results didn't mean I gave up on my goal. Instead, I used different tools to refine my process so I could get the desired results. Your podcast is similar. If you've assessed your goals and planned your strategy, you'll find that after you launch, grow, and profit from your podcast, your numbers may not be what you hoped for. Or maybe you didn't make as much as you had planned. Or, perhaps your audience isn't growing. Just because you didn't receive your desired results doesn't mean you abandon your podcast strategy for good. It just means that you need to polish your approach and refine something along the way.

Starbucks Coffee Conversations

In the fall of 2006, Starbucks Coffee Company published an audio podcast called *Starbucks Coffee Conversations*. Many people anticipated the launch of this podcast simply because they wanted to see how a corporation as large as Starbucks was going to do it. Unfortunately, after just three episodes, Starbucks stopped podcasting and it had nothing to do with the audio production quality. Actually, the production of the podcast was top notch. However, Starbucks got the wrong type of buzz because it did a lot of things wrong. In particular:

- The podcast focused on the cultivation, manufacturing, and choosing of coffee beans.

- Both hosts were obviously reading from a script.

- The jazz music playing in the background while the hosts chatted was quite irritating.

- It was way too infomercial. Every few minutes, the hosts talked about what was for sale at their store.

- Lastly, one of the hosts sounded as if he didn't even want to be there.

Starbucks only had to change one thing in order to make its podcast right. They should've focused on the customer experience and not the coffee bean. For example:

- Get stories from those who serve coffee behind the counter on some of the weirdest requests they've received from customers. Sort of like Niles Crane from the TV show *Frasier,* when he would always ask for coffee with fat-free cream, whipped cream without the froth, and a splash of nutmeg without the spice. There must be some crazy customers like that.

- Interview customers on some of the wildest, saddest, or happiest moments that happened to them while sipping on a brew at a Starbuck's store. I know I've closed a good number of business deals at a Starbucks located in downtown Toronto, so I'd have some great stories to tell.

- Interview an expert as to why coffee is so addictive. Yes, I'd want to know.

- Do an episode simply asking customers about their first coffee sip. What was the taste like, how old were they, what did it feel like, and so on.

In this case, Starbucks should've polished their strategy and relaunched future episodes focusing on the suggestions that their audience was telling them to make. Unfortunately, Starbucks got a lot of buzz for all the wrong reasons and abandoned their strategy before it got the legs to move forward.

Common Problems and How to Fix Them

How can you determine whether your podcast requires a quick polish? What should you look for and how can you fix it? Here are some common complaints I hear from my clients and from other podcasters whom I have met and some suggested solutions on how you can address it them.

- **No one leaves comments on my blog or audio line.** This is typically an issue with your content. Here are some tips on how to polish your content.

  - Your content may not be interesting enough. Go back to Chapter 2 and plan future episodes by asking your audience what they want to hear or see.

  - Start taking a position on an issue and stop sitting on the fence. What makes Adam Curry's podcast *The Daily Source Code* so popular is that he takes a position on a topic and allows his audience to debate with him. If you're not comfortable taking a position on an issue, make sure you interview experts who are opinionated and have a very strong stand on any given topic. For example, whenever I'm invited to speak on a marketing or business podcast, I always encourage people to get rid of their Web sites and launch a blog instead. This always generates a lot of comments because I take a contrarian position on a common viewpoint.

  - Turn the comments section "on" and make it easy for people to leave their comments. Nothing discourages people from leaving their comments more than to have to jump through 20 hoops. Make it easy and double-check that you haven't closed your podpage to comments.

  - Make sure it's easy to find your audio comment line phone number. Prominently display it in the side navigation of your blog. If you can, offer a toll-free number for your audience to call.

- **My subscribers/downloads are the same for every episode.** This is generally a problem with how accessible or inaccessible your podcast is. Here are some tips on how to polish up the accessibility of your podcast.

  - Make sure people can download your podcast. Use Chapter 3 to help your technical support team double check that people can access your podcast. You can look at your site statistics or test the link yourself to make sure there are no errors.

  - Don't forget to add a flash player. This allows people to easily play your podcast right from your podpage. Review Chapter 4 and look at the various podcast directories to see if they offer a free online player. If you're using a hosted solution, double-check that there's a flash player offered through their service. If not, request this as a feature on their Web site.

- **No one seems to recognize my podcast.** Our egos need to be stroked from time to time and podcasting is no different. If you're not being selected as a Pick of the Week on anyone's list, here are some ways to polish up your podpresence.

  - Publish on a predictable schedule. Frequency is important, not only to your audience but also to those who want to bestow accolades upon you. You don't need to get it out at 8 A.M. every Monday, however, you do need to stick to one day of the week when you'll get new episodes up. *Rocketboom* publishes its video podcast every weekday morning and it's no wonder that this podcast is one of the most popular on the Web.

  - Make sure you have at least 10 episodes. People want to see that you have staying power and having more than 10 episodes helps to prove that you're in it for the long haul.

  - Don't go too long between episodes. Some podcast directories will de-list your podcast if 60 to 90 days have gone by without any newly published episodes. If you have to miss a week or two, that's okay, but don't let any more time lapse between episodes.

  - Get a swanky podcover designed. This is a big part of your podpresence. Just like people judge a book by its cover before buying it in a bookstore, your podcover will encourage someone to subscribe or give it a pass. Get a podcover designed and add the URL to the image to your feed.

  - Participate in the community. This means attending industry events (see Chapter 6), commenting on other blogs, calling other podcasters' audio comment lines, and having your own blog or podcast. There are about 20 people who regularly post to my blog. I know each of them personally because I met them at a conference or event. However, as soon as I see a new name, I immediately follow their link to their Web site or blog to learn more about this new person. Showing up makes people curious and taking part keeps your name visible.

- **I can't seem to find the time (or interest) in publishing new episodes.** Otherwise known as podfading, there comes a time when all podcasters feel that they don't want to edit or produce files. I reached that point after Episode 7 of the *Cubicle Divas* podcast. I couldn't stomach editing or mixing audio files any longer and my feelings were being transferred to my clients' podcasts. In order to stay in business and keep producing great podcasts for my clients, here's how I polished my interest so I could continue to produce new episodes:

  - Hire someone to do the production pieces for you. You can hire someone to do the interviews for you or hire someone to do the mixing and editing. I rely on three resources to do all the production work for me and I couldn't be happier. Whether it's my podcast or that of my clients, once I get the raw recordings, I forward it on to my production manager who then takes care of everything else. I've delegated everything in my Yuck Bucket—the things I don't like doing—to the people who are experts in those areas.

  - Turn long interviews into two or three episodes. If you just had a 30-minute interview with an expert in your field, you can separate the material into two or three smaller chunks. That way, you'll have enough content for three weekly episodes. That will allow you to focus on other areas of your business for a few weeks.

  - Rebrand your podcast or refine the content. Another great strategy to help renew your interest in podcasting is to launch it under a different name with a renewed focus. When I originally started the *Podonomics* podcast, it was focused on covering corporate podcasting strategies. Unfortunately, that wasn't my passion and after three episodes, I stopped podcasting. After six months, I relaunched *Podonomics* with a new tagline: "Tips on how to use a podcast to open doors and make money." Once I did that, I knew exactly what my focus was and started podcasting with much more enthusiasm.

- **I'm not making money.** This typically pops up when your expectations are unrealistic or you're using the wrong strategy. Here are some ways to polish your expectations and strategy.

  - Grow your audience. Review Chapter 4 and make sure you're doing what you can to build your audience numbers. Without the ears or the eyeballs, you won't have enough people buying from you or creating enough downloads for you to charge higher advertising rates.

- If you're using a hosted solution, review the terms to see if you're making money through the text ads placed on your podpage. Chances are, you're not. If that's the case, you may want to move to an independent solution so you can place and profit from text ads on your podpage.

- Develop a multiple streams approach. Make sure you have income coming from all three methods of podcasting for profit—direct, indirect, and integrated. Review the Introduction to this book for a definition of each method and decide on which ones you are comfortable implementing for your podcast. Like anything in life, if you put all your eggs in one basket, you'll lose everything if they fall out and smash toward the floor. You won't get rich using just text ads, however, if you combine that with speaking engagements, sponsorships, and turning listeners into clients, you'll make more money using a multiple streams approach.

Like learning a new language, you need to polish your podcast strategy and optimize the results if something isn't working. You may have to go back to Plan Your Podcast (Chapter 2), Launch Your Podcast (Chapter 3), or Grow Your Audience (Chapter 4) to tweak your assumptions and try a new plan of attack. At the end of the day, just remember that this is a cycle and by refining your approach in one area, you will be able to produce a profitable podcast that brings you the results you're looking for.

Deciding When to End It

At the end of the day, if you've built an audience and have a rapport with them, ending your podcast may be the worst decision you could make. A former client of mine hired my company to produce six audio podcasts while she took maternity leave. Her episodes were published every two weeks and after the fourth episode, with very little marketing, her podcast had 123 subscribers. After we published the sixth episode, my former client returned from maternity leave and didn't want to publish any more episodes. I was very disappointed because she now had 123 people whom she didn't have two months earlier. In her case, she should have continued podcasting, even if she could only commit to one episode per month as she built up a solid following.

On the other hand, not every podcast needs to continue. Podcasting is an excellent way to promote your products and services to a niche audience, however, there comes a point in any strategy when you just have to put your podcast to bed. You may go through all seven steps—you assess, plan, launch, grow, profit, measure, then optimize. Yet, you find that no matter what, your podcast isn't producing the results you were hoping for. Seth Godin calls this the dip and says that winners know when to quit.[1] When the project is no longer exciting and starts to drain your energy, it's time to move on. In particular, Godin says:

> *"Every new project (or job, or hobby, or company) starts out exciting and fun. Then it gets harder and less fun, until it hits a low point really hard, and is not much fun at all.*
>
> *And then you find yourself asking if the goal is even worth the hassle. What really sets superstars apart from everyone else is the ability to escape dead ends quickly, while staying focused and motivated when it really counts. Winners quit fast, quit often, and quit without guilt until they commit to beating the right dip for the right reasons. In fact, winners seek out the dip. They realize that the bigger the barrier, the bigger the reward for getting past it. If you can become number one in your niche, you'll get more than your fair share of profits, glory, and long-term security. Losers, on the other hand, fall into two basic traps. Either they fail to stick out the dip—they get to the moment of truth and then give up—or they never even find the right dip to conquer."*[2]

The podcasting dip is different for everyone. It's hard to say when to end a podcast, however, there are some basic rules. Here are some tips on when you've reached your podcasting dip:

- If you've achieved your goals. Once your targets are achieved and the numbers are crunched, your podcast has served its purpose.

- If your audience isn't ready. This rings true if you consistently receive e-mails and phone calls from your audience complaining that they have no idea how to play your podcast. Perhaps you'll just need to educate them on what to do. However, even after educating them, if you still get a ton of complaints, your audience is not the right fit.

- If you've lost interest. A tell-tale sign is when you've gone three months or more without publishing a new episode.

- If you've consistently seen a decrease in audience numbers for six months or more—even after tweaking your content over and over.

- If the amount of money you're spending to produce your podcast is increasing while the money you're taking in is nonexistent. In the first six months, this will be the case as you're busy growing your audience. However, if your production values continue to increase, yet you're not making money to offset those costs, it will be difficult to sustain your podcast.

- If you find that you're more interested in writing rather than recording audio or video content. Speaking is my strength and that's why audio podcasting works well for me. However, there are some out there who prefer to express themselves through writing and may find speaking or presenting such a chore. If you're one of those people who loves to write, you may find that podcasting is too much of a bother.

- If the champion has moved on to another race. Often, the person who was the strongest supporter of the podcast has either moved on to another project, or worst yet, another job. Without the champion, your podcast has lost its support.

- If it has become a chore. If you'd rather get an eyebrow wax than produce a new episode, it's time to put your podcast to rest.

Most podcast directories will continue to list your podcast even though you're no longer producing new episodes. There are a few that will delist your podcast after a few weeks of inactivity, although this is rare. Because of this, you may want to honor your audience and say good-bye by producing one last episode letting them know what's going on. Don't forget to remind your audience to go to your podpage to listen to past episodes in the archives. By doing this, if someone subscribes to your podcast after you've said goodbye, they'll know how to follow up with you. Just because you're no longer publishing any new episodes doesn't mean you can't benefit from the continued traffic.

And since this is a book about podcasting for profit, to save disk space and bandwidth costs, you can remove your past episodes from your server and offer them for sale on a CD or DVD. Think about it—if you end your podcast and all the episodes are still sitting on a server, that means you're still paying the monthly hosting fees, plus the extra bandwidth costs. Instead, try recouping your costs and sell your past episodes on a CD or DVD, turn your podpage into a long sales letter, then encourage people to buy using great copy.

Taking Action

Optimizing your results can help you evaluate what should be improved with your podcasting strategy so you achieve what you set out to do. Just because you didn't reach your goals doesn't mean you abandon your podcast. Here are some tips to remember before deciding to end your podcast.

- Identify what needs to be polished.

- Refine your strategy based on the suggested solutions in this chapter.

- Determine whether you've reached the end or if you've just hit a plateau.

12

Outro

In the final episode of *Star Trek: The Next Generation*, the entity called Q, who had tormented the crew of the starship *Enterprise* for seven seasons, uttered these words to Captain Jean Luc Picard as he vanished into space, "All good things must come to an end." While those words signaled the end of a great TV series, it certainly doesn't mean the end of your podcast journey. As you continue to apply the seven steps to your podcasting for profit strategy, you'll find that you'll have to tweak it and test it. A podcast is a living media that constantly grows and needs polishing.

Podcast Monetization Profile

While the number of podcasters who can comfortably live from the income generated from their podcast—without earning money on someone else's payroll—is small, those who are have income streams coming from all three methods: direct, indirect and integrated. I often get asked what percentage of my income comes from the three methods. It breaks down like this:

- 70 percent of my income is derived from the indirect method through teaching, consulting, speaking, and coaching.

- 25 percent of my income is derived from the integrated method by using the breadcrumb podcasting approach to sell my own products and services, as well as selling other people's products and services through affiliate marketing.

- 5 percent of my income comes from the direct method through Google Adsense on my podpage and through sponsorships that I get through a podvertising network.

This is what I call my Podcast Monetization Profile. As you can see, the majority of my income comes from the indirect method. This isn't by accident, it's by design. This profile works for me because my strength is inspiring and motivating people through speaking. That's what I was born to do and every skill assessment I've taken shows that my strength is using my voice to convince, persuade and motivate. Whether it's Myers-Briggs, True Colors, or some other skill assessment, my speaking and communication skills always come out on top. My Podcast Monetization Profile simply reflects where my strengths lie.

You may be tempted to follow my template for your own podcasting for profit strategy, however, this may not work for you. You may find that you're better working behind the scenes and securing sponsorship or advertising deals for your podcast. Or, you may find that you're more comfortable promoting other people's products and services. You need to discover your own strengths

Podcast Name	Direct	Indirect	Integrated
Daily technology lifestyle video podcast	80 percent	15 percent	5 percent
Podcast consultant–West Coast	10 percent	40 percent	50 percent
Weekly teen lifestyle video podcast	90 percent	10 percent	0 percent
Weekly technology how-to video podcast	60 percent	30 percent	10 percent
Podcast consultant–East Coast	5 percent	15 percent	80 percent
Conference organizer	0 percent	80 percent	20 percent
Podcast consultant and author–East Coast	5 percent	90 percent	5 percent
U.K.-based entrepreneur and coach	0 percent	50 percent	50 percent
U.S.-based podcast executive	15 percent	70 percent	15 percent
Monthly how-to video podcast	70 percent	0 percent	30 percent
Weekly dating audio podcast	10 percent	0 percent	90 percent

Table 12.1. Podcast Monetization Profile of podcasters interviewed for this book.

and exploit them in your podcast. Understanding your skill set and knowing what you're really good at will make you more successful generating a five-, six-, or seven-figure income as a podcaster.

For podcasters whom I interviewed, their Podcast Monetization Profile is much different than mine. Although they didn't provide how their income breaks down according to the three methods in my interviews with them, I can provide guestimates. Because I'm providing my interpretation of how their income breaks down across the three methods, I'm not including the name of the consultant or podcast. Instead, I'm providing a brief summary of the person or the podcast in Table 12.1.

Again, this table should only be used to give you an idea how I believe these podcasters' income breaks down according to the three methods based on the interviews I had with them. I chose these podcasters because I got a clear indication in our interview where their money comes from. Factors that influence these percentages are audience numbers, target market, frequency, format, skill set of the producers, attitudes toward the various income streams, branding, and popularity, among other factors.

Multiple Streams of Podcasting Income

At the end of the day, you need to develop a multiple streams approach to your podcast. Just focusing on advertising or sponsorship isn't enough to developing a five-, six-, or seven-figure podcasting income. Too many podcasters focus on the 30-second spot or the host recommendations as their sole income stream. Others believe that selling T-shirts or splashing text ads on their podpage is enough. It's no wonder that podcasters are struggling to figure out how to make money podcasting. In the six months that I've used text ads on my podpage, I've made $10. There's no way I could run a business, live my life, attend conferences, buy groceries and buy what Beverly Mahone of *Whatever* podcast calls "diva things" on just $10.

Instead, I made it a point to ensure that I have income coming from all three methods. In 2006, I made a high five-figure income, allowing me to replace my full-time income and rely on my own company for income. It is my hope that my podcasting income will continue to increase. This is realistic for me because I have money coming from all three methods and while the percentages in my profile will change from time to time, I'm comfortable knowing that even if one method went down to 0 percent, I could easily adjust and still make money podcasting.

This concept isn't new to podcasting. Some of the world's richest people have a multiple streams approach in their financial portfolio. Some of these include:

- Robert Allen, who wrote the book called *Multiple Streams of Income*, encourages people to buy real estate, invest in vending machines, and sell products online.

- Donald Trump, who started out as a millionaire, went bankrupt, then went on to become a billionaire, made his riches in real estate, but he also owns a television production company and a few casinos.

- Oprah Winfrey, the only African-American woman to make *Forbes* magazine list of billionaires, not only has a television production company but also produces a magazine, owns a program on satellite radio, and has produced various DVDs and stage plays.

- Tony Robbins, a peak performance coach, makes money from speaking engagements, coaching programs, as well as books, CDs, and an online membership Web site.

Developing a multiple streams approach with your podcast will help you generate a sizable income that will help you to pay off debts, leave your crummy day job, and take the trips you have always wanted to take. Kelly McCausey, host of *Work At Home Moms Internet Radio*, was lousy with money. Yet after developing a multiple streams approach with her podcast, she can now afford to send her son to college. Scot McKay, host of *DeserveWhatYouWant.com* paid off his truck lease using a multiple streams approach with his podcast.

My question to you is—what strategy will you put in place to make money podcasting? Which tools will you use in the direct, indirect, and integrated methods to make a five-, six-, or seven-figure income from your podcast? What in addition to advertising and sponsorship will help you earn the income you desire from your podcast? The only person who can stop you is you.

Afterword: Questions I'm Often Asked

I get asked a lot of questions in my presentations about podcasting for profit. I've included some of the more popular ones here. I also took the opportunity to give you my insights on what I learned after writing this book.

What percentage of podcasters are actually making money full-time from podcasting?

It's hard to tell. The interviews I did were with the podcasters who were making some sort of money from podcasting, what I could gather from our interviews, many of them were making money from one or two methods—e.g., direct, indirect, or integrated, with other sources filling up their money buckets.

I did about 50 interviews and it spanned hundreds of hours. I would guesstimate that the number of podcasters who are actually working full-time solely on their podcast would fall anywhere from 5 percent to 10 percent. Again, that's my guesstimate based on being in the industry since 2004, networking at events, publishing podcasts for many businesses, and doing the interviews for this book.

Those who aren't generating a full-time income from their podcast are supplementing their income through other means. This could include self-employment, it could include being employed by another company, and so, I would guesstimate that the number of podcasters who are actually making money full-time from podcasting is quite small.

I'm one of those individuals who is making money solely from podcasting. I'm not doing blogging consulting, I'm not doing search engine optimization, nor am I doing Web site development. What I'm doing is solely teaching people how to podcast and then I implement those podcast solutions. So for me, yes, making money full-time from podcasting is what I do. Other people such as Andrew Baron from *Rocketboom*, Cali Lewis of *GeekBrief TV*, as well as Julien Smith from *InOverYourHead.net* are just some of the podcasters who are making money full-time from podcasting.

I believe that this would probably be a natural extension of this book—to do a survey and find out how many podcasters are making money full-time. I would also let podcasters define what full-time means. Full-time could simply mean that someone has a company where they consult on blogging, podcasting, search engine optimization, and Web site development. For them, they are making money full-time from podcasting, although it's being supplemented by other new media streams. I would leave the definition of full-time to that podcaster.

If you could wave your magic wand and change just one thing about podcasting, what would it be?

Definitely, measurement. I find that the biggest hole in podcasting right now is how do we measure it.

I remember speaking to different podcasters and asking them, "How do you measure your success?" And some said, "I don't care, I don't measure it at all." Others said "We just use downloads." And others, such as Chris Penn from *Financial Aid* podcast, uses a variety of tools to report on the size of their audience. Penn does a survey, uses FeedBurner to measure subscribers, and he looks at downloads. Even hits and page views are things that he uses to generate a broad picture as to the size of his audience.

But for many podcasters who are measuring, they specifically use downloads and, well, for me, when I look at even my own podcast downloads, the number of downloads tends to be the largest number. Downloads give a fairly accurate picture as to how many people are listening because for every download, there is a person associated with it.

It also is problematic because with downloads, it can be considered like hits. Let's just say someone came to my podcast and tried to download it and they got interrupted by a phone call or maybe their Internet access went kaput at that moment. Then they came back as soon as the Internet went back up and then they tried to download again. So that would be one person downloading twice. Is that an accurate portrayal of my audience? All these questions start to pop up on how can we accurately measure a podcast.

One of the big things I hear from people is that if podcasting is more unique from television and radio, then we can't use things like CPMs (cost per thousand) or CPA (cost per action) as is done with banner ads, to measure a podcast. Those are measurement tools based on traditional media and do not apply to podcasting.

However, when I chatted with Scott Bourne in one of my interviews and I asked him about why This Week in Technology (TWiT) uses CPMs to report on audience numbers, he said,

"Quite simply, it's because that's what media and ad buyers know. You've got to speak the language that media and ad buyers are

familiar with and many of them are familiar with the term CPMs—Cost per Thousand."

At this point, if we want to tell media and ad buyers that in order to measure a podcast it has to be "this," then we have to know what "this" is and be able to use the same and consistent language. I believe that's what's confusing right now. Many podcasters use so many different things to measure a podcast that many people look at it and are surprised. Podcaster A says "It's downloads and subscribers." But Podcaster B says "It's only downloads." So even among ourselves as podcast producers, we're not even using the same language.

I remember an interview I did with Andy Walker from *Lab Rats TV* and he said that the problems we're seeing with measuring podcasts is similar to the days when banner ads first popped up. There was a lot of confusion. No one knew how to measure banners ads or how to report that so many eyeballs saw that banner ad. It took a couple of years to really come up with measurements that made sense. CPMs and CPC (cost per clicks) were finally used and podcasting needs to do that as well. So, if I could just wave a magic wand, I would want to see a more consistent language used with podcasting in terms of measurement.

What have you learned about podcasting for profit now that the book is finished?

Too many podcasters and non-podcasters still see advertising and sponsorship as the only way to make money. This was a source of frustration for me because I would approach podcasters and introduce myself saying "I'm writing a book called *Podcasting for Profit*, are any of you making money through your podcast?" And most of them would say, "No, sorry, I don't have ads in my podcast." And then I'd explain to them the three different methods—direct, indirect, integrated—and what each of them are. Then, they would still say, "No, I don't have ads or sponsorship."

I felt like throwing my head against a brick wall. It was so frustrating. I would then go through different scenarios, asking, "So is anyone paying you to produce their podcast for them?" Then some podcasters would say, "Oh, yeah, this lady down the street wanted to do a podcast and I did it for her for like, 50 bucks." So, there were many podcasters I couldn't interview because they either weren't making money or didn't have a compelling case study.

It was frustrating trying to coach and teach podcasters that there are other ways to make money podcasting beyond advertising and sponsorship, but what was equally frustrating is that many podcasters were selling their skill set very short. Instead of charging thousands of dollars to put together a podcast solution, they were casual about it. Many would say, "You know, whatever that person decides. If it's a a hundred bucks, that's fine, I can eat dinner tonight."

So, there are two things that surprised me the most while writing this book:

1. Advertising and sponsorship were seen as the only way to make money in podcasting and therefore it became almost difficult to find people to interview to present as case studies in the book.

2. Many podcasters were selling their skill set and their expertise short, either because they were in technology and just wanted to implement podcasting solutions for others just for the love of it, or because it was so easy for them to throw something together for someone else.

I want this to change. I know that this book will educate people on the various ways you can make money podcasting, but once you start to see how much other people are making from their podcasting skills and expertise, other podcasters will start to respect their craft to the point where they will raise their fees to match their experience and expertise.

What surprised you the most when writing this book?

The number of podcasters who didn't want to be interviewed for this book was the most surprising thing that I found. I thought that people would be eager to be interviewed, but that wasn't the case. For those who appear in this book as case studies, they were the most eager to share their experience. However, several declined my request.

To get interviews, I first contacted people who I knew were making money. After interviewing them, I realized I needed to talk to more podcasters since most of my early interviews were with podcasters making money from advertising and sponsorship. So, I sent out e-mails to colleagues of mine, asking them to post on their blog that I'm writing this book and I'm looking for case studies. I also posted a message on the video podcasting group on Yahoo! Groups and a few message boards where I knew podcasters congregate.

I got very few hits and I was quite surprised. At first, I couldn't figure out why. But then, it started to become clear after a few people reached out to me regarding my request for case studies. I got their e-mails saying they found my plea for case studies through other people's blogs or on a forum or elsewhere. I'd say, "Oh great. This sounds awesome. I've got to record an interview with you." And the most unbelievable thing happened—they refused to be interviewed for fear that having their name in a *Podcasting for Profit* book meant that they endorsed making money and if their audience saw that they're making money, then their audience would think that that's the only reason why they're podcasting.

I was flabbergasted at how persistent some podcasters were about not being interviewed even when I explained to them that "You are still making money podcasting. You got paid to speak about podcasting at an event, or you got a job because of your podcast and those are a couple of ways you're making money podcasting." But these podcasters would still refuse. "No, no, no, I can't." I mean, these podcasters contacted me, bragged about their podcast monetization strategy, then refused to be interviewed for this book. Now, I'm not sure if they misunderstood my plea for case studies. Maybe they did, or maybe I should've been more clear by saying, "I'm writing a book, I'm looking for case studies, and I need to interview you to include in the book." So maybe I wasn't that clear as to what I needed, but it was just shocking to me the number of podcasters who would contact me saying, "Yes, I am making money podcasting." And when I e-mailed them back saying, "I want to interview you for the book and record it," they reacted by stating, "No, no, no, no, we can't record this."

It felt as if I was doing a piece on drunk driving and I was going to interview someone who had been convicted five times of drunk driving and he requested that his name and voice be disguised so that no one would recognize who he was. That's how it felt to me in these cases. Needless to say, I did not pursue those podcasters. I figured that once the book is published and they see others who are in their shoes making money podcasting, that perhaps they'll change their minds.

If you have people willing to listen to your audio podcast or view your video podcast and are engaging with you from week to week or month to month or however often you update your podcast, it means you're doing something right. So, if you need to make a little bit of money, just to pay some of the bills, that's okay. When I chatted with Pod Chef, a farmer and chef who lives on an island and produces a podcast where he offers recipes and talks about the politics of food, he said that one day he put a tip jar on his podcast page. He was actually pretty surprised that a few episodes had gone by and he didn't get any donations. He said that he finally put together a cookbook with all the recipes that he had featured on his podcast and he didn't ask for any money for it. He placed the cookbook on his podpage and he said as soon as he did that, the donations started to pour in to his tip jar. He said that it seems as if people got value, not only from his podcast but also from the cookbook. They were willing to donate money to him. He has a wish list on Amazon.com and people send him the items on his wish list. So, for anyone out there who's afraid that their audience is going to ostracize them and flee because you're trying to make money, the opposite is going to happen. Your audience won't leave you en masse, instead they're going to appreciate that you're looking at ways to make money in order to continue podcasting and keep their favorite entertainment item online.

Which profitable strategy are you going to implement right now?

As I looked through the different possibilities of making money in podcasting, the one thing that I regretted not doing is the premium content and paid subscriptions. To be honest, when I started podcasting, paid subscriptions and premium content were not really well known and actually there wasn't a lot of technology out there to support it.

With David Lawrence's ShowTaxi, and Paul Colligan's Premiumcast the technology now exists so that if you are not a celebrity and you don't have a big name, you can actually get people to pay for a subscription to your podcast without using iTunes. If you go back to Chapter 8, Premium Content and Paid Subscriptions, you'll see that with paid subscriptions, people pay to get the RSS feed. In essence, they're paying for a subscription.

Premium content is something I was kind of doing with *Cubicle Divas*, but I wish I had done more of the membership Web site model as Heather Vale and *Anything But Monday* are doing with their podcasts. That's where you produce the interview and you offer just a portion of it as the podcast. Then, you invite people to sign up as a member in your membership Web site to hear or see the entire version, as well as past episodes in the archives area. So, I'm going to implement the paid subscriptions right away, especially since I have an idea for an instructional video podcast.

Which profitable strategy do you have the most difficulty with?

I still have difficulty with the 30-second ad. I know that a few podcasters are doing it successfully and are getting paid for it, but I'm not convinced that podcasting is the right media for the 30-second ad. The reason I'm having difficulty is because podcasting is unlike radio and TV. Well, it is a lot like radio and TV in that you're using the air waves to deliver a message, but it's unlike radio and TV because the message doesn't have to be as broad and it doesn't have to appeal to a mass market. Podcasts can be more segmented and more niche oriented.

Podcasts to me are like documentaries. Documentaries are based on real stories from real people. Although it's heavily edited, a documentary provides you with the real story. It includes the ambient sounds, they don't try to sugarcoat the story that they're trying to tell, and it's raw. It's a reason why Michael Moore's documentaries *Fahrenheit 9/11* and *Bowling for Columbine* are so popular. It's the reason why Al Gore's *Inconvenient Truth* is so popular because again, you're getting the real story, you're getting those ambient sounds, you're seeing the amateur qualities and people will find that more believable.

Does that sound like podcasting? Of course, it sounds exactly like podcasting. It has an amateur feel that really increases the credibility of a podcast, despite what the budget is behind it. There are many examples of people who use a podcast to orchestrate a story or have used a podcast to produce a very slick and polished produc,t and unfortunately people just don't believe it. I mean if we wanted an ad in a podcast, we would all just sit down and watch TV or listen to the radio.

Because podcasting is like a documentary, throwing in that 30-second ad is not a great strategy at all. A lot of people say that they don't believe ads anyway because ads always show you the pretty side. You always see the pretty side, it's just like the handsome boy you had a crush on in high school. You always saw his good side and then, one day, you finally go out on a date and as you dined on burgers and French fries, the cute boy treats the waiter very poorly. Suddenly you see the ugly side of the cute boy and you're in shock.

It's the same with ads. Ads give you the positive spin. You go out, buy that product, bring it home, and when it doesn't work exactly as the commercial said, you're disappointed. Podcasts, on the other hand, tell you the truth. It's like an old rustic cabin. What you see is what you get. How can you match the make-believe world of an ad with the reality of a podcast? Doesn't match up. On top of that, people see ads as an intrusion. There are many reports out there that show that consumers are believing ads less and less because they see them as an intrusion. They see it as an interruption and skip over them on TiVo or go to the bathroom when commercials come on. The 30-second ad in a podcast can be effective, although for a podcast, it doesn't really work. The audience doesn't want to see it. I even conducted a survey asking podcast listeners about their podcast habits and the vast majority of them would prefer a host recommendation over and above an advertisement anyday.

If you could do it over again, what would you do differently with your podcast?

There are two things I would have done differently. First, I would have stayed on a more regular schedule. I remember when I first started my flagship podcast, *Cubicle Divas*, it took me almost a year to get up and running. Although I'm tech-savvy, it was the technology that stopped me. When I first started podcasting, the people in podcasting were those with a broadcasting background and those with a technology background. Early on, the tech-savvy people were saying that you had to code your own RSS feed and do this and do that. Again, I'm comfortable with technology, but this stuff was way over my head. Then the broadcasters, mainly retired radio hosts and those with a radio background, were saying that you had to spend a minimum of $2,500 to build a home studio. So that kept me out of the podcasting picture for about 12 months, almost a year from the time I discovered it in late 2004.

When I finally got my podcast up and running, I published on a regular schedule, producing my podcast every Thursday. I did that consistently for about three months and then I started to slack off. Part of it was due to podfading. I was very exhausted updating my information weekly and getting all the pieces together. A weekly schedule turned into bi-weekly, which turned into monthly. So, if I could do it over again, I would've stayed on a more regular schedule and would've published on a weekly schedule more consistently.

The easiest way I could have stayed on that schedule was to produce a little bit less content. I had five separate segments, which meant I had to produce five different bumpers. That way when the music played, people knew that this was a new segment. I had to record five different segments that took place at all different times of the day. Sometimes I had to record first thing in the morning, sometimes last thing at night, and it was so interesting because my voice sounded different throughout the entire podcast. My voice sounded deeper when I recorded first thing in the morning, while later in the evening, the pitch of my voice was much higher. If you were to listen to the first six episodes of *Cubicle Divas*, in just the 15-minute podcast you'd hear my voice change two or three times due to the various times of the day I would record. In hindsight, I would have cut down on the number of segments to just one or two and that would have helped me stay on a more regular and consistent schedule.

If I could do it all over again, the second thing I would do differently is I would have joined a podvertising network much earlier or even formed one of my own. That way, I could have gotten a little bit more visibility and also probably would have started making money much earlier. Now this seems to be in contradiction to the question earlier, where I said that the 30-second ad is practically useless in a podcast. However, I would have benefited from joining a podvertising network and being a part of a larger community of podcasters. That way, our collective audience would help us secure more sponsorship deals. As a result of that, I probably would have made more money much faster.

I especially love the relationship that *Mommycast* has formed with Dixie Cups. Although *Mommycast* got that six-figure sponsorship deal on their own without being part of a podvertising network, it's rewarding to hear that the hosts have formed a wonderful relationship with Dixie Cups. The hosts are part of Dixie Cups' strategy team, they advise Dixie Cups on what moms want and they formed a strategic partnership. That's the type of relationship I would like to form with a company through my podcast, yet I have little time to pound the pavement looking for that type of deal. Hence, the reason being part of a podvertising network would've helped me as I'd have someone else pounding the pavement on my behalf.

Equally, I could have formed my own network and I know that Leo Laporte owns one of the more popular independent podcasting networks online called TWiT. I would have done something similar; however, because I wasn't clear on who my audience was at the time, I would have been less successful. Had I known my audience much earlier, I certainly would have formed my own podvertising network.

What gets your goat when it comes to podcasting for profit?

What really bugs me about podcasting right now is this debate as to whether or not you should be making money in podcasting. I hear this debate all the time, no matter which conference I attend. Whenever I do presentations, I always talk about podcasting for profit. When it's time for questions and answers, I would get the arguments from both sides. The hobbyists, those who are podcasting because they're passionate about their topic, are against making money. They say, "It's evil and it has no place in podcasting." On the flip side, the moneyists, those who insist that they have to make money podcasting, say, "If I can't make money right off the bat, I can't podcast."

So, the hobbyists are on one side, the moneyists on the other, and they're both knocking heads against this issue of making money podcasting. This bugs me because both need to step back and take a look and say, "Okay. How am I making money podcasting right now?" The hobbyists, surprisingly, are making money podcasting. Even though they say podcasting is their passion, if you dig down deeper and ask questions, you find out that they're getting money by consulting or teaching. A small business owner approaches the hobbyist and says, "Can you teach me how to podcast?" The hobbyist says, "Sure." The small business owner says, "I have to pay you." The hobbyist says, "Okay. Give me so much." Or, the hobbyist may have been invited to speak at an event about podcasting. The hobbyist gets an honorarium of $250 or even a speaking fee of $5,000. So, the hobbyists are saying money is evil, but they are making money indirectly. Or, the hobbyist is using the integrated method by selling T-shirts, key chains, or other merchandise. So, it's funny that when hobbyists dig down really deep, they discover, "Oh my, I am making money."

The moneyists, on the other hand, tend to come from the corporate sector and are typically people who have to prove the return on investment on just about everything they do. It comes as no surprise that the moneyists are solely focused on ads and sponsorship. They are so focused on these that they are blinded to the other ways that money can be made in podcasting. The problem is that they're not willing to wait, build an audience, and look at the long tail of podcasting. So, my message to the moneyists is wait and do it right.

There is a right way, despite what some people say. Once you understand what the right way is, then you can appreciate that there are different ways to make money. I believe that this debate between the hobbyists and the moneyists can be turned around once both sides understand that there are three methods to making money in podcasting. Suddenly, the argument becomes less of "money is evil" and "I can't podcast unless I'm making money" to "which of these income streams is the most profitable?" And once we get to that discussion, we'll have both the hobbyists and the moneyists on the same platform.

> *Is there a right way and a wrong way to do a podcast, especially if you want to podcast for profit?*

There is a right way and a wrong way, but it's not based on what you might think. When I first started podcasting, I strongly believed that your podcast shouldn't be more that 20 minutes and that you had to update your podcast with new episodes weekly. I also believed that you had to edit out all the "ums" and "ahs," but now I know that's actually the wrong way to podcast.

At the end of the day, there are two things that are going to dictate how your podcast is going to sound, how frequently you update it, and what format it's going to take. Those two things are:

1. Your goals

2. Your audience.

Frequency doesn't matter, format doesn't matter, and even the tone of your podcast doesn't matter. You can plan these things and prepare in advance and say, "Okay. This is what I believe my audience wants." But it's not until you have your podcast out there and get comments from your audience that you can know what to improve. Many podcasters I spoke to said, "In the beginning, yeah, my podcast sounded like crap." Very few podcasters are proud of their very first episode, but if you're in tune with your audience and you know what your goals are, your podcast then becomes a reflection of that.

For example, I used my podcast as a lead-generating tool. Remember the breadcrumb podcasting approach that's part of the integrated method that I explored in Chapter 5? My goal is to have people listen to my podcast, then go off and buy something from my shopping cart. With that in mind, I know that if I have a full 60-minute audio file, I'm not going to throw that into my podcast. Instead, I'm going to take the first-third, the second-third, or the last-third of that 60-minute audio file, produce a 20-minute podcast and then offer people the opportunity to listen to the full 60-minute version on my membership Web site or to buy it as a recording on CD.

My goal is to use my podcast as a lead-generating tool, so that 30-minute podcast may just be too much. My audience would also dictate whether or not they want to hear more or hear less. Kelly McCausey, whom I interviewed for this book, targets work-at-home moms with her podcast. She told me that a 20-minute podcast would not work. Her target market is work-at-home moms and once the kids are off to school, they're working on their businesses. They want to listen to a 45-minute podcast and that's okay with them. Work-at-home moms have high-speed Internet access, they've got a computer, and they want to soak it all in.

For someone like me, my audience wouldn't want this. With my podcast called *Podonomics,* I'm targeting busy professionals and busy business owners. I need to produce a podcast that will fit their busy lifestyle, so a 45- to 60-minute podcast may just be too much. So again, I believe a wrong way to do a podcast is to focus on these very rigid rules of frequency, length, and format. Instead, the right way to podcast is to let your goals, but more importantly your audience, dictate what your podcast will become.

Why is it important to understand the distinctions among the three methods to podcasting for profit?

I first heard about the three methods from Paul Colligan. He discussed two of them—direct and indirect—in his book, *The Business Podcasting Bible.* The third method—integrated—he discussed in a teleclass on the *Seven Ways to Create a Profitable Podcast.* I just love the whole concept that there are three approaches to making money in podcasting. These approaches can be applied to just about anything, whether it be blogging, Web sites, wikis, and other social media tools. Remember:

- The direct method is how you monetize your content. Advertising and sponsorship are the most known, but this also includes premium content, paid subscriptions, and tip jars.

- The indirect method is how you monetize your skills and expertise. Being hired for speaking engagements, leading workshops, consulting projects, and getting book deals are just some of the ways podcasters are making money based on what they know.

- The integrated method is how you monetize your audience. These are the ways you turn your audience into clients. So you build your list, build your database, sell merchandise, sell products, and services.

The three methods show that you're not just limited to ads and sponsorship. Many people don't like advertisements and many people don't want to sell them. But what the three methods also show is that you can develop a multiple-streams approach to your podcasting strategy. When you're making money from a variety of places, it suddenly opens up a whole new world.

For me, when I look at my own monetization profile, I can see that I have income coming in from all three methods. Being able to make money from a variety of places ensures that even if one of my income streams goes down to 0 percent, I'll have two other methods that are working for me. For example, when there's a downturn in the economy, many companies and many businesses just scale back on training. Well, I can recession-proof my business by ensuring that I've got percentages coming out of all the other methods as well.

If my indirect goes down to zero because people are scaling back on paying for training or consulting, or more companies start to add podcast production to their offerings, or new technology comes out where people can launch their podcast with one click, then I have little to worry about since I have income coming in through the two other methods—direct and integrated. All I have to do at this point is adjust. Understanding the differences among the three methods to podcasting for profit means that you have a bigger opportunity to make some serious cash in this business. I hope that all podcasters develop multiple streams of income from the three methods. Then instead of having an industry filled with brokeback podcasters, we'll have an industry filled with five- and six-figure podcasters. When the majority of podcasters are profitable, it only encourages more individuals and companies to podcast.

Which method do you think podcasters can start making money from right away—direct, indirect, or integrated?

First, I strongly suggest that any podcaster looking to make money podcasting go through the first four steps: Assess, Plan, Launch, then Grow. After that's been done, then the easiest method to make money from right away is the integrated method. The direct method really depends on numbers, while the indirect method depends on experience. Both will take some time to produce results. However, with the integrated method, you can easily upsell your audience to a product or service right away. Many podcasters have products that they sell themselves or if they don't have their own products, they become an affiliate of another product and earn commissions on every sale. That's the earliest way I earned money podcasting and it works.

Why do so many podcasters choose not to reveal their numbers?

There's a number of reasons why many of the podcasters I spoke to were not willing to share numbers:

- They couldn't because they had signed a contract stating that the details of the deal wouldn't be disclosed.

- They refused for reasons unknown to me.

- Some didn't want to reveal their numbers because they were afraid that their audience would think they're not a good person.

- And some just have general hang-ups about money.

Many podcasters operate as individuals, therefore, they are not required to reveal their numbers. Others felt comfortable enough to share their numbers. This is good because it shows that with the right strategy, anyone can duplicate their success. People at work don't sit around telling each other how much income they earn. It's a general no-no to tell others how much you're making. Some podcasters treat the income they earn from their podcast the same way—they just can't share how much they're earning. Although I could've refused to include any case studies where the podcast producer did not reveal his or her numbers, I decided against it. My goal is provide a wide range of examples of podcasters making money. Whether they reveal their numbers or not shouldn't be the focus. Instead, people should focus on whether or not they can create the same success for themselves.

Appendix A: Resource Directory

Here is a list of books, Web sites, podcasts, and other resources to help you create, launch, promote, and profit from your podcast. Although a plethora of resources are available, I included the ones that were mentioned in earlier chapters in this book or that I consult with regularly.

Books on Podcasting

How to Create a Podcast

Podcast Solutions: The Complete Guide to Podcasting by Michael Geoghegan and Dan Klass
Podcasting: Do It Yourself Guide by Todd Cochrane
Secrets of Podcasting, Second Edition: Audio Blogging for the Masses by Bart G. Farkas

How to Grow Your Audience

Promoting Your Podcast: The Ultimate Guide to Building an Audience of Raving Fans by Jason Van Orden

How to Use a Podcast in Your Business

The Business Podcasting Bible: Where My Market Is, I Am by Paul Colligan and Alex Mandossian
How to Do Everything With Podcasting by Shel Holtz and Neville Hobson
Tricks of the Podcasting Masters by Rob Walch and Mur Lafferty

Books on Creating Leveraged Income

Secrets of the Millionaire Mind: Mastering the Inner Game of Wealth
by T. Harv Eker
Multiple Streams of Coaching Income by Andrea J. Lee
Multiple Streams of Internet Income: How Ordinary People Make Extraordinary Money Online, 2nd ed., by Robert G. Allen

Books on Getting More Clients

Book Yourself Solid: The Fastest, Easiest, and Most Reliable System for Getting More Clients Than You Can Handle Even if You Hate Marketing and Selling
by Michael Port
Get Clients Now!: A 28-day Marketing Program for Professionals, Consultants, and Coaches
by C. J. Hayden
Guerrilla Publicity: Hundreds of Sure-fire Tactics to Get Maximum Sales for Minimum Dollars
by Jay Conrad Levinson, Rick Frishman, and Jill Lublin

Books on Blogging

Blog Marketing by Jeremy Wright
Blogwild!: A Guide for Small Business Blogging
by Andy Wibbels
Buzz Marketing with Blogs For Dummies by Susannah Gardner
The Corporate Blogging Book: Absolutely Everything You Need to Know to Get It Right by Debbie Weil
Naked Conversations: How Blogs are Changing the Way Businesses Talk with Customers by Robert Scoble and Shel Israel
What No One Ever Tells You About Blogging and Podcasting: Real-Life Advice from 101 People Who Successfully Leverage the Power of the Blogosphere by Ted Demopoulos

Books on Web 2.0

The Long Tail: Why the Future of Business Is Selling Less of More by Chris Anderson

Wikinomics: How Mass Collaboration Changes Everything by Don Tapscott and Anthony D. Williams

Book on Personal Success

The 4-Hour Work Week: Escape 9-5, Live Anywhere, and Join the New Rich by Tim Ferriss

Blue Ocean Strategy: How to Create Uncontested Market Space and Make the Competition Irrelevant by W. Chan Kim and Renee Mauborgne

Brag! The Art of Tooting Your Own Horn Without Blowing It by Peggy Klaus

Devil with a Briefcase: 101 Success Secrets for the Spiritual Entrepreneur by Jan Janzen

The Dip: A Little Book That Teaches You When to Quit (and When to Stick) by Seth Godin

The Likeability Factor: How to Boost Your L-Factor and Achieve Your Life's Dreams by Tim Sanders

Secrets of the Millionaire Mind: Mastering the Game of Inner Wealth by T. Harv Eker

The Tipping Point: How Little Things Can Make a Big Difference by Malcolm Gladwell

Discussion Lists/Forums

Podcast Alley Discussion Forum *(http://www.podcastalley.com/forum/index.php)*
Podcast Pickle Discussion Forum *(http://podcastpickle.com/forums)*
Videoblogging E-mail Discussion List *(http://tech.groups.yahoo.com/group/videoblogging)*

Podcasting Associations

Association of Downloadable Media *(http://www.downloadablemedia.org)*

Association of Music Podcasting (*http://musicpodcasting.org*)
Association of Poetry Podcasting (*http://www.poetrypodcasting.org*)
Hawaii Association of Podcasters (*http://www.hawaiipodcasting.com*)
Houston Podcasting (*http://www.houstonpodcasting.org*)
New England Podcasting (*http://newenglandpodcasting.wordpress.com*)
Portland Podcasting Association (*http://www.portlandpodcasting.org*)
U.K. Podcasters Association (*http://ukpodcasters.org.uk*)

Podcasts about Podcasting

Canadian Podcast Buffet (*http://www.canadianpodcastbuffet.ca*)
Daily Source Code (*http://www.podshow.com/showguide/?key_id=dailysourcecode&feed_type=pdn_show*)
Gear Media Tech (*http://gearmediatech.libsyn.com*)
Podcast411 (*http://podcast411.com*)
Podcast Brothers (*http://www.newmediaexpo.com/audio.htm*)
Podcast Mastery (*http://www.podango.com/podcast_station_home/133/Podcast_Mastery*)
Podcast Tools (*http://www.podcasttools.com*)
Podcasting for Dummies (*http://www.dummies.com/WileyCDA/DummiesTitle/productCd-0471748986,page-1.html*)
Podcasting Underground (*http://www.podcastingunderground.com*)
Profitable Podcasting (*http://www.profitablepodcasting.com*)

Legal Guides for Podcasting

Canada (*http://www.creativecommons.ca/blog/?p=225*)
United States (*http://wiki.creativecommons.org/Podcasting_Legal_Guide*)

Podcasting Conferences and Trade Shows

Podcast and New Media Expo (*http://www.newmediaexpo.com*)
International Podcasting Expo (*http://www.internationalpodcastingexpo.com*)
Podcast Academy (*http://podcastacademy.com*)
Corporate Podcasting Summit (*http://www.podcast-summit.com*)

Podcasters Across Borders (*http://www.podcastersacrossborders.com*)
Podcamp (*http://www.podcamp.org*)

Additional Resources

For additional resources, including podvertising networks, podcast hosting companies, gear recommendations, courses and podcasting directories, please visit the companion Web site.

Appendix B: Priceless Podcasting Projects and Ideas

I interviewed dozens of podcasters in preparation for this book to see how their monetization strategies differed from my own. Although all the podcasters featured in this book are making money podcasting, some have taken the time to give back in some small, yet significant ways. Whether it's a dad who has more time in his day to spend with his family, a non-profit group aimed at preserving our stories, or two men who started a free event to make everyone a rock star, these are the priceless podcasting projects that are making a huge difference in people's lives. No amount of money can pay for the joy and satisfaction that these podcasters are experiencing as a result of their priceless podcasting projects.

Eating Cereal Every Morning

When it comes to podcasting monetization, Paul Colligan is the king. Not only does he teach others how to podcast, but he's proof that you can generate a five- or six-figure income from podcasting by developing a multiple-streams approach. He's well loved at conferences and trade shows, and is sought after for his podcasting expertise. The number of projects Colligan has on the go are too many to list, however, his blog at *www.paulcolligan.com* will lead you to his many podcasting projects.

When I interviewed Colligan for this book, it was early in the afternoon during the workweek. Colligan described to me what was happening in his home while we were chatting:

> *"I'm talking to you from my basement in my home right now. My three-year-old is upstairs playing* Princess Monopoly *with my wife and my eldest daughter is in first grade. Life is good at the Colligan household because of what podcasting is enabling me to do."*

While earning an income from podcasting has helped Colligan to improve his quality of life and spend more time with his children, he recognizes that many podcasters feel that making money from their hobby is wrong. For Colligan, he knows that holding down a full-time job and trying to produce episodes on a regular schedule can be a challenge. It's for this reason that he believes earning money to cover at least your production costs makes sense:

> *"I hear podcasters saying, 'I had to work 10 hours today and then I spent 15 minutes with my kids and it's now three o'clock in the morning and I'm recording the show.' This is not going to last long."*

Colligan had a regular day job at one point, wearing a suit everyday to work, but soon grew tired of the commute and lousy pay. He shared with his wife that he would be leaving his day job to work on his Internet business full-time. Colligan said that after a few weeks working from home, he changed his perspective in a dramatic way:

> *"Being able to eat at a good restaurant is great, but being able to have cereal with my daughter in the morning is far better. The cool thing is that we still eat at good restaurants, but living and working at home has just given me this life that I could only dream about— and the pay is good too. That's why I get so passionate about podcasting because it lets me stay home with my girls."*

Giving At-Risk Kids Hope

Penny Haynes, owner of 1stpod.com, teaches virtual assistants and other solo entrepreneurs how to produce a podcast for their clients. With more than 10 years of experience in the television production industry, Haynes certainly knows the finer details about editing audio and video files. Her time is precious and she charges accordingly for her time and expertise. However, she always finds the time to work with children.

> *"I have a real soft spot or should I say a passion for kids that are in school that do not fit the school mode. Forgive me as I preach for a second, but the schools teach and not all of the students learn the way that the curriculum is presented. Because of the way public schools are, the kids that don't fit the curriculum just kind of get dumped and that really bugs me. So, my daughter fell into that area and that's why it's such a sore spot with me."*

The at-risk kids are not students who come from low-income families. At-risk kids in this case are those who are close to dropping out of school. Children who are deemed at-risk are put into a special class called Project Success. Seeing that these children needed something stimulating to motivate them to succeed, Haynes taught them how to podcast:

> *"I went and I taught podcasting to the classes in one term. I told them I was hiring a production assistant and I showed them how to do the stuff. I asked them to fill out a piece of paper saying why they wanted the job and what they would do [if they got it]. I gave them opportunities, gave them free classes on how to record and edit, and in the end, I hired someone and he was fabulous, absolutely fabulous."*

Haynes says she's not paid for this training and it doesn't matter. Her mission is not to make money at these schools, but instead to do something for these children that they're not getting anywhere else:

> *"I'm giving the school free audio and video training because I want the kids to really branch out and do whatever they want. I want them to have a sense of self-worth and a feeling of pride. I want them to be able to create and show everybody what they are doing and feel really good about it."*

Helping Everyone Become a Rock Star

At a podcasting event called Podcamp held in New York City in April 2007, Chris Brogan wore a top hat and cape. As he walked through the hallways and past the exhibitor tables, attendees stopped to point, laugh, take a picture, and get a hug from the guy who's T-shirt said: YOU ARE MY ROCK STAR. Brogan, along with Christopher Penn, founded Podcamp, an "unconference" designed to bring together podcasting enthusiasts and experts to talk about nothing but podcasting. What makes the unconference model different from a conference is that attendees don't pay to register, speakers aren't paid to speak, and expenses are covered by sponsors. Brogan explains what sparked Podcamp:

> *"I had gone to another podcasting event. It was very professionally put on, but I really didn't feel like I should be a podcaster. It felt exclusionary. Then, Chris [Penn] and I showed up at Barcamp in Boston. We sat there thinking, 'Wow, this Barcamp thing is great. It's self-organizing, people can put on their own session on*

the fly. How can we do this for podcasting?' And then an idea was spawned."

The very first Podcamp was held in Boston, Massachusetts, in September 2006. With no money spent on advertising, more than 300 people attended this event and close to $15,000 was raised in sponsorship money. It was so successful, it spawned off other PodCamps in cities around the world, including Singapore, Toronto, Munich, Copenhagen, Atlanta, San Francisco, and even a cruise.

Brogan tries to go to as many Podcamps as he can. It's not unusual to see Brogan at a Podcamp approaching people who are sitting alone in a corner and encouraging them to join others in conversations. Brogan cautions those who attend Podcamp that the energy is very different from traditional conferences:

> *"There should be a sign somewhere that says, 'Check your ego at the door.' It's definitely an unwritten rule that shows up at all the [Podcamps]. It's really hard to be elitist when everyone else around you is forcing you into the community. Forcing is probably the wrong word. The social norms [of Podcamp] are suggesting very strongly that you better be there to be a part of the team and not just a solo act."*

What's rewarding to him is that people connect and form new friendships based on just one thing—podcasting.

> *"[It's about] empowerment. It's about realizing that you are a superhero and that you have a cape and tights under your clothes. All you need to do is explore and expand your powers, then put them to use. What I find at every Podcamp I go to is that people walk away from it and say, 'Wow! This is me. I can do this. I have the control and the ability to make this thing happen'."*

Maintaining a Digital Record

Doug Kaye, executive director of The Conversation Networks was frustrated. He had attended a political debate and even though the candidates sounded well-informed, Kaye had no clue what their platforms were. As his mind wandered, Kaye imagined being able to record the speeches and debates so he could listen to them in his spare time. Not long after, *Podcorps* was born.

Podcorps is an all-volunteer team of audio and video producers who record and publish important spoken-word events anywhere in the world. Events are listed in *Eventful.com* or *Upcoming.org* and the person who posts the event needs to tag it with *Podcorps*. The *Podcorps* system will pick up the tag and locate the stringer—the name given to the podcaster who volunteers—to attend the event. Whether the event is non-profit or for-profit, if a stringer is needed and there's one who lives close by, the event will be captured. Kaye explains why having a digital record of these events is so important:

> *"Every day, there are great speeches, lectures, and meetings on this planet that disappear. They evaporate because nobody bothers to capture them. There are things that could be very interesting and exciting to a lot of people."*

Kaye started out with IT Conversations, a non-profit company that records and publishes speeches and presentations from technology events. Kaye gets a lot of feedback from people and recounts some of the most memorable:

> *"We get a lot of people who say we're helping them stay in the gym. They would give up exercising if it weren't for IT Conversations. The most inspiring are from people who are outside the United States, who are on very limited budgets who could never ever possibly get to these events. Those are the ones that really mean a lot."*

Kaye hopes that *Podcorps* will be as enriching to the non-technology community as IT Conversations has been to the technology community. By offering opportunities to event organizers to capture and publish their events, not only are these events leaving their footprint in history but Kaye believes that podcasters will enjoy the experience as well:

> *"Each podcast consultant really needs to put some percentage of his or her time in giving back to the local community. [Podcorps] is a great way to do that."*

Summary

If you podcast for profit, there's also room to podcast for passion. Although all the podcasters discussed here are making money podcasting, they have taken the time to use their podcasting skills to spend more time doing the things they love to do. Whether it's catching up with family members, giving at-risk youth a sense of belonging, building a global community of podcasters, or preserving our stories, these projects and ideas are just simply priceless.

Appendix C: How to Monetize Your Podcast in Less than 180 Days

Podcasting for Profit Timeline

Many podcasters have unrealistic views of how quickly they can expect to profit from their podcast. Without understanding what to expect, you will abandon your podcast strategy prematurely.

Although understanding the different ways to profit from your podcast strategy is a great approach, implementing that strategy will be difficult without the right plan. The *Podcasting for Profit Timeline* provides steps to help you understand how to plan and produce your podcast, as well as when and which income stream you should incorporate.

The revenue, subscribers, and timeline indicated in each phase are averages compiled from my clients' podcast strategies. You may find that you fall well below or well above these projections. I encourage you to use these numbers as a benchmark rather than the rule.

Phase 1—Plan Your Strategy

Timeline: Days 1 to 7 (One week)
Start at the beginning by understanding why you want to podcast, who you plan to target, what problems you plan to face, and how you will feed your audience through your podcast funnel. This planning is critical to understanding how you'll eventually make money from your podcast.

Tasks include:

- Plan episodes

- Define target listeners

- Fill in your podcast funnel.

Potential revenue: $0
Potential subscribers: 0
Potential downloads per episode: 0

Phase 2—Launch Your Podcast

Timeline: Days 8 to 22 (Two weeks)
After you plan your podcast, it's now time to put it together so the world can listen to or view your show. Depending on whether you do this phase on your own or if you hire someone with the technical know-how, this phase could be the longest.
Tasks include:

- Create podcast cover and podcast bumper

- Record content

- Produce podcast

- Publish podcast.

Potential revenue: $0
Potential subscribers: 0
Potential downloads per episode: 0

Phase 3—Grow Your Audience

Timeline: Days 23 to 113 (12 weeks)
At this phase, you're not only finding fans, but you're building relationships. When your audience trusts you, they will eventually buy. Plus, with increased traffic, you will start to benefit from increased page views and stuff. So, focus on building rapport and trust at this stage.
During this stage, you can add a direct income stream to your podcast. Advertising or a tip jar placed on your podcast page is a great start. Remember,

while you do want to make money, your primary focus at this stage is to build a relationship with your audience.

This stage can be accelerated by using guerilla promotional techniques; however, if it happens too quickly, you risk losing subscribers due to a lack of interest or a lack of hype. It's better to build your audience using the Long Tail approach to guarantee sales in the long run.

Tasks include:

- Enter podcast details into podcast directories

- Send out press release

- Promote podcast

- Gather feedback

- Release new episodes on a regular, predictable schedule

- Add tip jar and/or ads to your podcast page.

Potential revenue: $0 to $500
Potential subscribers: Under 100
Potential downloads per episode: 300 plus

Phase 4—Add Additional Income Streams

Timeline: Days 114 to 180 (Eight weeks)
At this point, after spending a few weeks building your audience and generating a small amount of money through ads and donations, you're ready to use the integrated method to sell your products and services through your podcast. You'll also start to realize some income through an indirect method as people contact you to teach them how to podcast or to create one for them.

Tasks include:

- Use breadcrumbs in your podcast to lead your audience to your shopping cart or Web site

- Find ways to sell your consulting services.

Potential revenue: $501 and up
Potential subscribers: 101 plus
Potential downloads per episode: 301 plus

Phase 5—Measure and Optimize

Timeline: Ongoing

- To measure your return on investment, refer to Chapter 10.

- To optimize your results, refer to Chapter 11.

Tasks include:

- Conduct split testing.

- Analyze the number of subscribers and downloads against the money spent to create and maintain your podcast.

Phases 3, 4, and 5 will continue until you decide to end your podcast. You may need to subtract and add different income-producing items depending on what works and what doesn't. Be patient in your attempt to discover the income stream that works for you and is attractive to your audience. Refine your strategy, ask your audience what they want, remove income streams that aren't working, add ones that are. At the end of the day, be disruptive by doing something other podcasters aren't doing. Your bottom line depends on it.

Appendix D: Three Methods to Monetize Your Podcast

Direct Method = Tools to use to monetize your podcast content

- Advertising

- Sponsorship

- Tip jars

- Donations

- Premium content

- Paid subscriptions

- Licensing

- Selling archived content

- Grants.

Indirect Method = Opportunities that help you monetize your podcast knowledge and skills

- Speaking engagements

- Book or music deals

- Presentations

- Consulting

- Teaching

- Job opportunities

- Movie or TV contracts.

Integrated Method = Techniques to monetize your audience by turning them into customers

- Affiliate marketing

- Selling services

- Selling products

- Selling memberships

- List building

- Contests/surveys

- Merchandise.

Appendix E: The Seven Habits of Highly Profitable Podcasters

At the end of every interview I conducted with the many podcasters for this book, I asked just one question:

> *"If someone woke up tomorrow and said, 'You know, I really like that person Leesa interviewed. I'm going to launch a podcast today and start making money,' what advice would you have for that person?"*

Based on the responses, here's a list of the seven habits that these podcasters embody that make them profitable.

1. **Be Passionate**—The money doesn't happen right away. Profitable podcasters don't start podcasting for the money. Instead, their motivation for starting a podcast is to share their passion with the world.

2. **Have Integrity**—Profitable podcasters operate from a position of transparency and honesty. They are clear about their values and understand that their morals will never be compromised.

3. **Build a Community**—Profitable podcasters understand that their audience isn't just a group of listeners or viewers, but they are people who are looking for a place to belong. Profitable podcasters integrate the tools that will encourage their audience to interact, not only with the host but with other audience members.

4. **Have a Purpose**—Planning is the cornerstone of growing a successful podcast. Profitable podcasters have a clear goal and know how their podcast will help them reach it.

5. **Be of Service**—Profitable podcasters understand that while they can't give everything away for free, they can share enough information to help their audience through their pain points and turn their challenges into triumphs.

6. **Connect with Others**—No matter how popular profitable podcasters become, they still attend industry events, share their knowledge at conferences, and speak about lessons learned at trade shows. Profitable podcasters continue to contribute to other podcasts by leaving comments or leaving feedback on an audio comment line.

7. **Be You**—Just because a formula worked for another podcast doesn't mean you have to adopt it for yourself. Profitable podcasters don't copy others. Instead, they carve their own path instead of taking the path already traveled.

As you may have noticed, none of these habits has anything to do with money. Instead, each habit highlights guiding principles to help you realize who is the ultimate focus of your podcast—your audience.

About the Author

Leesa Barnes

Leesa Barnes is president of Caprica Interactive Marketing and has helped hundreds of individuals and businesses worldwide make money podcasting using her simple seven-step process. Leesa has been featured in national and international media and is recognized as an expert in podcasting and online media. She speaks regularly about podcasting and receives rave reviews for helping audiences release their fear of technology through her use of relevant visuals, analogies, and humorous stories. For more information about Leesa, visit *www.leesabarnes.com*.

Endnotes

Introduction

1. Definition of podcasting from Wikipedia.org (*http://en.wikipedia.org/wiki/Podcasting*).
2. See *http://technology.guardian.co.uk/online/story/0,3605,1145689,00.html.*
3. See *http://news.bbc.co.uk/2/hi/technology/4504256.stm.*
4. After Leo Laporte made this suggestion at the 2006 Podcast and New Media Expo, it was the most popular story on Digg on September 22, 2006; see *http://www.digg.com/tech_news/Leo_Laporte_proposes_using_the_term_netcast_instead_of_podcast.*
5. See the presentation slides posted at *http://www.edisonresearch.com/home/archives/2007/03/the_podcast_aud.php.*
6. See *http://en.wikipedia.org/wiki/Lonleygirl15.*
7. See *http://www.time.com/time/magazine/article/0,9171,1569514,00.html.*
8. See *http://www.apple.com/pr/library/2007/04/09ipod.html.*
9. This is information that's tracked by Technorati, an online search engine that only lists blogs. See *http://www.sifry.com/alerts/archives/000436.html.*
10. See *http://nostalgia.wikipedia.org/wiki/Wikipedia_statistics/Size_of_Wikipedia.*
11. See Alexa's traffic ranks (*http://www.alexa.com*).
12. See CNN Money's Web site (*http://money.cnn.com/2006/10/09/technology/googleyoutube_deal*).
13. Don Tapscott and Anthony D. Williams, *Wikinomics*, p. 34.
14. Robert Scoble and Shel Israel, *Naked Conversations*, p. 27.
15. Chris Anderson, *The Long Tail.*
16. It's a Purl Man (*http://www.itsapurlman.com*); My Marilyn Podcast, (*http://www.marilynmonroe.ca/podcast*).
17. *The Grammar Girl* podcast (*http://grammar.qdnow.com*).
18. Paul Colligan and Alex Mandossian, *The Business Podcasting Bible*, p. 5.
19. See *http://www.kinseyinstitute.org/resources/FAQ.html#frequency.*
20. Edison Media Research, 2007 survey of podcasting among U.S. See the author's summary on his blog (*http://www.edisonresearch.com/home/archives/2007/03/2007_podcast_statistics_analysis.php*).

21. Listen to Ronald Moore's keynote on Podcast Academy's Web site (*http://pa.gigavox.com/shows/detail1569.html*).

22. Read Steve Friess' article in *Wired Magazine* (*http://www.wired.com/science/discoveries/news/2006/02/70171*).

23. Colligan and Mandossian, pp. 146 and 165.

24. Ibid, p. 283.

Chapter 1

1. The origins of the S.M.A.R.T. goal process are unknown; however, it's a popular method used by self-help gurus, coaches, and consultants to help their clients set and manage their goals.

2. See Wikipedia for details about the UCLA winning streak (*http://en.wikipedia.org/wiki/UCLA_Bruins_men's_basketball*) and (*http://www.universitysport.ca/e/story_detail.cfm?id=6430*) for the Lady Wesmen's winning streak.

3. See The Blog Squad survey (*http://www.assessmentgenerator.com/H/cRdr.patsi1136951737.html*). It is used with permission.

4. See the Canadian Podcast Listeners Survey (*http://www.canadianpodcast-listenerssurvey.ca*).

5. T. Harv Eker, *Secrets of the Millionaire Mind: Mastering the Inner Game of Wealth*, p. 9–12.

Chapter 2

1. Tara Thompson, Jay Moonah, and Tara's friend Charlotte, who traveled with us to Boston, all know that I tell this story. While I never put blame on any of them for getting lost, whenever I talk about our adventure within earshot of Moonah, he's always the first to admit it was his fault for leaving his map at home.

2. See *http://www.problogger.net/archives/2006/02/15/how-to-choose-a-niche-topic-for-your-blog* for the full text on choosing your niche on Darren Rowse's blog.

3. Ibid.

4. Quote taken from an interview the author recorded with Scott Bourne of *http://www.podangoproductions.com*.

5. See Apple's press release dated January 6, 2004 (*http://www.apple.com/pr/library/2004/jan/06ipodmomentum.html*).

6. See Apple's press release dated April 9, 2007 (*http://www.apple.com/pr/library/2007/04/09ipod.html*).

7. See *http://en.wikipedia.org/wiki/Mind_map*.

8. See the mind map process in action visually by viewing the video called *Plan a Killer Podcast* at *http://www.podcamptoronto.org in the media archives*.

9. Jan Janzen, *Devil with a Briefcase: 101 Success Secrets for the Spiritual Entrepreneur*, p. 76.

10. See CBS News coverage (*http://www.cbsnews.com/stories/2006/08/17/earlyshow/main1904502.shtml*).

11. W. Chan Kim and Renee Mauborgne, *Blue Ocean Strategy: How to Create Uncontested Market Space and Make the Competition Irrelevant*, p. 82.

12. See video archive of Bill Sweetman's presentation called *Naming Your Podcast* at *http://www.podcamptoronto.org* in the media archives.

13. Collected the 2004 numbers by plugging in the Podcast Alley URL using the Way Back Machine search field at Archive.org.

14. See Bill Sweetman's podpage (*http://www.marketingmartini.com*).

15. Read the IBM Employee Podcasting Guidelines (*http://www.ibm.com/developerworks/blogs/page/jasnell?entry=podcasting_ibm*).

16. View the disclaimer at the bottom of their podpage at *http://www.britishairways.com/travel/drsleeppodcasts/public/en_gb*.

17. See Scotiabank's example at *http://www.scotiabank.com/cda/content/0,1608,CID1136_LIDen,00.html*.

18. See the Podcasting Legal Guide (U.S.) at *http://wiki.creativecommons.org/Podcasting_Legal_Guide*.

19. See the Podcasting Legal guide (Canada) at *http://www.creativecommons.ca/blog/?p=225*.

Chapter 3

1. Source: *www.oprah.com*.

2. See *http://www.cityline.ca/showinfo/stationguide.asp*.

3. Interview with Allison McClondich of Endelman who managed the Butterball Turkey account.

4. The Podsafe Music Network (*http://music.podshow.com*).

5. Listen to Bruce Murray's presentation at the 2006 Podcasters Across Borders conference at *http://www.podcastersacrossborders.com/event-details-2006*.

6. Listen to Mark Blevis and Andrea Ross's podcast at *justonemorebook.com*.

7. See *http://en.wikipedia.org/wiki/Documentary_film*.

8. See *http://en.wikipedia.org/wiki/Lonelygirl15*.
9. See the Resource Directory at the end of this book for links to the U.S. and Canadian editions.
10. Susannah Gardner, *Buzz Marketing with Blogs for Dummies*. The comparison chart appears in the jacket of the book.
11. Ibid.
12. Charlene Li., *Social Technographics: Mapping Participation in Activities Forms the Foundation of a Social Strategy*, pp. 4–6.

Chapter 4

1. Bride Has a Massive Wig Out (*http://www.youtube.com/watch?v= _nFDnC8SSWQ*).
2. See *http://www.citynews.ca/news/news_7464.aspx* .
3. See *http://en.wikipedia.org/wiki/Bride_Has_Massive_Hair_Wig_Out*.
4. See *http://www.thestar.com/entertainment/article/176490*.
5. Survey conducted by the author's company, Caprica Interactive Marketing and Sequentia Communications in 2006 asking Canadians about their podcasting habits (*http://www.canadianpodcastlistenerssurvey.ca*).
6. Tim Sanders, *Likeability Factor: How to Boost Your L-Factor and Achieve Your Life's Dream*. pp. 98–100.
7. Ibid, p. 39.
8. Ibid, p. 40.
9. Conducted comparison of podcastalley.com using the Way Back Machine search field at archive.org.
10. Biography Channel's biography on River Phoenix.
11. See *http://www.imdb.com/name/nm0000203/bio* for the quote attributed to River Phoenix.
12. Jason Van Orden, *Promoting Your Podcast: The Ultimate to Building an Audience of Raving Fans*. p. 12.
13. Interview the author had with Peter Wood, host of *www.rippleoutdoors.com*. The full interview can be heard on the companion Web site.
14. Chiara Fox, a senior information architect with Adaptive Path, defined tags in the following article: *http://www.adaptivepath.com/publications/essays/archives/000695.php*.
15. See Podtrac press release at *http://www.podtrac.com/press/largest-demographics.stm*.
16. See *http://www.bryper.com/2006/07/18/how-not-to-pitch-a-podcaster*.
17. Ibid.

18. See *http://www.podcastasylum.com/articles/pitch.html*.

19. View Donna Papacosta's excellent use of show notes on her podpage at *http://trafcom.typepad.com/podcast*.

20. All bullet points from *http://www.how-to-podcast-tutorial.com* and reprinted with permission.

21. Listen to Andrew Michael Baron's keynote at the 2006 Podcast and New Media Expo on the Podcast Academy Web site at *http://pa.gigavox.com/shows/detail1589.html*.

22. See *http://en.wikipedia.org/wiki/Wiki*.

23. Ibid.

24. See *http://www.thenewpr.com/wiki/pmwiki.php?pagename=FIRShowNotes.HomePage*.

25. See *http://rocketboom.wikia.com/wiki/Wikiboom*.

26. See *http://pa.gigavox.com/shows/detail1589.html*.

27. David Teten and Scott Allen, *The Virtual Handshake: Opening Doors and Closing Deals Online*, p. 40.

28. See Mitch Joel's blog at *http://www.twistimage.com/blog/archives/009695.html*.

29. Ibid.

30. Ibid.

31. See the For Immediate Release twitter page (*http://twitter.com/FIR*).

Chapter 5

1. The size of the infomercial industry was gathered from a 2003 fact sheet from the Electronic Retailing Association Web site (*http://www.retailing.org*).

2. Executive summary of the 2006 Marketing Sherpa report (*http://www.marketingsherpa.com/exs/BusinessTech2006Summary.pdf*).

3. Listen to Leesa Barnes interview Kim Duke, The Sales Diva, on Episode 5 of the *Cubicle Divas* podcast *(http://www.cubicledivas.com)*.

4. My shopping cart allows me to create separate lists. I created an e-mail sign-up box specifically for *www.cubicledivas.com* and for each product sold through the site. I was then able to compare the number of people on my pre-existing list with the number of sign-ups via *www.cubicledivas.com*.

5. See *http://www.networkworld.com/news/2006/111406-online-merchants-fraud.html*.

6. See the 2006 Canadian Podcast Listeners Survey co-authored by Caprica Interactive Marketing and Sequentia Communications (*http://www.canadianpodcastlistenerssurvey.ca*).

7. From the podpage for *Marina's Podcast* (*http://www.marinaspodcast.com/index.html*).

8. All quotes from Marina of *www.marinaspodcast.com* are from an interview with the author. This interview is available in full on the companion Web site for this book

9. All quotes from Kelly McCausey of *www.wahmtalkradio.com* are from an interview with the author. This interview is available in full on the companion Web site for this book.

10. From the sales page at *http://www.mommasterminds.com*.

11. The first Mesh conference was held in March 2006. The five guys who organize Mesh every year are Mathew Ingram, Mark Evans, Stuart MacDonald, Rob Hyndman, and Mike McDerment. The author's company produced the podcasts and you can find them at *http://www.meshconference.com/blog*.

12. See the Mesh blog at *http://www.meshconference.com/blog/2007/05/22/the-dog-ate-my-homework-err-delayed-my-mesh-ticket-purchase*.

13. Michael Port, *Book Yourself Solid: The Fastest, Easiest, and Most Reliable System for Getting More Clients Than You Can Handle Even if You Hate Marketing and Selling*.

14. All quotes from Justin Hollingshead of Warner Brothers Interactive Entertainment are from an e-mail interview with the author.

15. All quotes from Mike O'Laughlin of *www.irishroots.com* are from an interview with the author. This interview is available in full on the companion Web site for this book.

16. All quotes from Dave Slusher of *www.evilgeniuschronicles.com* are from an interview with the author. This interview is available in full on the companion Web site for this book.

17. All quotes from Scot McKay of *www.deservewhatyouwant.com* are from an interview with the author. This interview is available in full on the companion Web site for this book.

18. All quotes from Christopher Penn of *www.financialaidpodcast.com* are from an interview with the author. This interview is available in full on the companion Web site for this book.

19. 2006 Canadian Podcast Listeners Survey (*http://www.canadianpodcastlistenerssurvey.ca*).

Chapter 6

1. All quotes from Jonny Goldstein of *www.jonnygoldstein.com* are from an interview conducted with the author. The interview is available on the companion Web site for this book.

2. See *http://www.iccaworld.com/npps/story.cfm?ID=1305*.

3. See *http://www.expoweb.com/headline_search.asp?id=5864*.

4. Interview with Tim Bourquin, co-producer of the *Podcast* and New Media Expo, in an interview with the author. The interview is available on the companion Web site that accompanies this book.

5. See the Podcast Academy Web site at *http://pa.gigavox.com/series/podcast-academy.html*.

6. See *http://www.podcastersacrossborders.com*.

7. The author attended the first Podcasters Across Borders in 2006 as a presenter.

8. From *Podonomics* blog post at *http://podonomics.com/a-45-minute-keynote-takes-20-hours-of-preparation-time-so-compensate-please*.

9. All quotes from Michael Geoghegan of *www.gigavox.com* are from an interview conducted with the author. The interview is available on the companion Web site that accompanies this book.

10. See *http://en.wikipedia.org/wiki/Soft_skills*.

11. See *http://www.2020insight.net/PeopleSkills.htm*.

12. See the Voices.com blog for an example of how you can use your blog to highlight your skills at *http://blogs.voices.com*.

13. Interview the author had with Geoghegan.

Chapter 7

1. A recorded conversation between Mark Blevis and Andrea Ross available from *www.PoweredByPassion.com*.

2. Ibid.

3. See Leo Laporte's blog at *http://www.twit.tv/2006/09/05/welcome_visa*.

4. See *http://www.marketingvox.com/archives/2006/06/14/online_advertising_spend_to_reach_20_billion_in_06*.

5. See the PQ Media report at *http://www.pqmedia.com/about-press-20060411-amrs1.html*.

6. All quotes from Beverly Mahone were transcribed from an interview recorded with the author. The complete interview is available on the companion Web site for this book.

7. All quotes from Rudy Jahchan and Casey McKinnon of *www.galacticast.com* were transcribed from an interview recorded with the author. The complete interview is available on the companion Web site for this book.

8. All quotes from Tim Street of *www.frenchmaidtv.com* were transcribed from an interview recorded with the author. The complete interview is available on the companion Web site for this book.

9. All quotes from Paul Vogelzang of *www.mommmycast.com* were transcribed from an interview recorded with the author. The complete interview is available on the companion Web site for this book.

10. All quotes from Andy Walker of *www.labrats.tv* were transcribed from an interview recorded with the author. The complete interview is available on the companion Web site for this book.

11. From Leo Laporte's blog at *http://www.twit.tv/2007/04/21/annual_ paypal_renewals_coming_up*.

12. This is based on an interview that Terry Fallis of *www.terryfallis.com* had with the author. The complete interview is available on the companion Web site for this book.

13. Quoted from a BBC article about *Alive in Baghdad* podcast (*http:// newsvote.bbc.co.uk/mpapps/pagetools/print/news.bbc.co.uk/2*).

14. All quotes from Cali Lewis of *www.geekbrief.tv* were transcribed from an interview recorded with the author. The complete interview is available on the companion Web site for this book

15. See *http://www.en.wikipedia.org/wiki/PodShow*

16. See *http://www.blubrry.com/about.php*.

17. See *http://www.feedburner.com/fb/a/about*.

18. See *http://www.feedburner.com/fb/a/advertising/demographics*.

19. See *http://www.feedburner.com/fb/a/advertising/adclimate*.

Chapter 8

1. All quotes from Heather Value of *www.successunwrapped.com* were transcribed from an interview recorded with the author. The complete interview is available on the companion Web site for this book.

2. Ibid.

3. All quotes from Frank and Mad Mike of *abmshow.com/blog* were transcribed from an interview recorded with the author at Podcamp New York in April 2007. The complete interview is available on the companion Web site for this book.

4. All quotes from Anna Farmery of *www.theengagingbrand.typepad.com* were transcribed from an interview recorded with the author. The complete interview is available on the companion Web site for this book.

5. Ibid.

6. Ibid.

7. All quotes from Don McAllister of *www.screencastsonline.com* were taken from an e-mail exchange with the author.

8. All quotes from Steve Woolf and Zadi Diaz of *www.jetsetshow.com* were transcribed from an interview recorded with the author. The complete interview is available on the companion Web site for this book.

9. All quotes from Chris MacDonald of *blindingflashes.blogs.com/indie_feed* were transcribed from an interview recorded with the author. The complete interview is available on the companion Web site for this book.

10. Ibid.

11. See *http://www.techcrunch.com/2007/05/13/cbs-acquires-wallstrip-for-5-million.*

12. See press release announcing sale at *http://www.prweb.com/releases/2007/1/prweb500621.htm.*

13. Ibid.

14. Pricing is listed at *www.audible.com.*

15. See *http://media.guardian.co.uk/site/story/0,1703591,00.html.*

16. See *http://www.thedavidlawrenceshow.com.*

17. See *http://www.thedavidlawrenceshow.com/unplugged.html.*

18. Interview conducted by the author with David Lawrence (*www.thedavidlawrenceshow.com*).

19. Bullet points were pulled from *http://www.showtaxi.com/examples.php* and re-printed with permission.

Chapter 9

1. Jay Conrad Levinson, Rick Frishman, and Jill Lublin, *Guerrilla Publicity: Hundreds of Sure-Fire Tactics to Get Maximum Sales for Minimum Dollars*, p. xiii.

2. Ibid, p. xiv.

3. Peggy Klaus, p. xvii.

4. All quotes from Taylor Marek of *www.taylormarek.com* are from an interview with the author. This interview is available in full on the companion Web site for this book.

5. All quotes from Peter Wood of *www.rippleoutdoors.com* are from an interview with the author. This interview is available in full on the companion Web site for this book. Wood is a client of the author's company.

6. See Trafcom News Podcast at *http://trafcom.typepad.com/podcast/2006/11/show_45_wiggle_.html.*

7. All quotes from *http://inthegardenonline.com.*

8. See *http://www.inthegardenonline.com.*

9. All quotes from Heather Gorringe of *www.wigglywigglers.co.uk* are from an e-mail interview with the author.

10. Podcast is posted at *http://www.countryliving.co.uk/index.php/landing/9076.*
11. See *http://www.cnn.com/2007/TECH/internet/01/22/grammar.girl/index.html.*
12. See *Business Week* article at *http://www.businessweek.com/magazine/content/05_46/b3959134.htm.*
13. Enter *Audrey Reed-Granger* into Google to analyze the results.
14. See *http://www.msnbc.msn.com/id/10663353/site/newsweek.*
15. See *http://en.wikipedia.org/wiki/Amanda_Congdon.*
16. David M. Ewalt, "The Web Celeb 25" at *www.forbes.com.*
17. See "Amanda Across America" at *http://amandacongdon.com/roadblog/2006/11/14/special-announcement.*
18. Frank J. Rumbauskas Jr., *Cold Calling is a Waste of Time: Sales Success in the Information Age (2nd edition)*, pp. 17–22.
19. Robert Walch and C.C. Chapmen in separate interviews with the author.
20. All quotes from George Tsiolas of *www.smallcappodcast.com* are from an interview with the author. This interview is available in full on the companion Web site for this book. *Small Cap Podcast* is a client of the author's company.
21. See Amber MacArthur's blog post (*http://ambermac.typepad.com/ambermac/2006/08/to_all_the_g4te.html*).

Chapter 10

1. C.C. Chapman of *www.accidenthash.com*, Dave Slusher of *www.evilgeniuschronicles.com*, and Rob Walch of *www.podcast411.com* in separate interviews with the author. The interviews are available on the companion Web site for this book.
2. Review the Introduction of this book for more information about a podcast being intimate.
3. According to the history timeline on *www.NFL.com*, 141.1 million people watched the Seattle Seahawks and Pittsburgh Steelers play in the Super Bowl, making it the second-most watched program in U.S. television history.
4. See *http://www.swivel.com/data_sets/show/1002826.*
5. Exact Target, a leader in providing permission based e-mail marketing strategies, reported in its 2005 Response Rate Study that e-mail open rates dropped to 35.5 percent in 2005 from 42.5 percent in the same quarter in 2004.
6. This ratio is based on my observation of my own podcast and those of my clients.
7. Mark Blevis sparked this thought through his blog post called *Rethinking the Role of Statistics*. See *http://www.markblevis.com/rethinking-the-role-of-statistics.*

8. A hip-hop term that refers to expensive jewelry worn by those in the urban community to signify wealth. In this case, I'm using *bling* to refer to ornaments, plug-ins, and widgets used to give your podpage flash and glamour.

9. Numbers pulled from *Vanity Fair*'s online media kit located at *http://www.condenastmediakit.com/vf/circulation.cfm*.

10. Ibid.

11. Malcolm Gladwell, *The Tipping Point: How Little Things Can Make a Big Difference*, pp. 38–59.

12. Definition of influence was used from *www.dictionary.com*.

13. Tim Sanders, *The Likeability Factor: How to Boost Your L-Factor and Achieve Your Life's Dreams*, pp. 54–57.

14. See *http://rocketboom.wikia.com/wiki/Demographics*.

15. See *www.mommycast.com* for a downloadable media kit.

Chapter 11

1. Seth Godin, *The Dip: A Little Book that Teaches You When to Quit (And When to Stick)*.

2. See *http://www.squidoo.com/thedipbook*.

Index

Reader Feedback Sheet

Your comments and suggestions are very important in shaping future publications. Please e-mail us at *moreinfo@maxpress.com* or photocopy this page, jot down your thoughts, and fax it to (850) 934-9981 or mail it to:

Maximum Press

Attn: Jim Hoskins

605 Silverthorn Road

Gulf Breeze, FL 32561

***101 Ways to Promote
Your Web Site,
Sixth Edition***
by Susan Sweeney, C.A.
432 pages
$29.95
ISBN: 978-1-931644-46-4

***101 Internet Businesses
You Can Start From Home
Second Edition***
by Susan Sweeney, C.A.
336 pages
$29.95
ISBN: 978-1-931644-48-8

Marketing on the Internet, Seventh Edition
by Susan Sweeney, C.A.,
Andy MacLellen & Ed
Dorey
216 pages
$34.95
ISBN: 978-1-931644-37-2

Podcasting for Profit
by Leesa Barnes
376 pages
$34.95
ISBN: 978-1-931644-57-0

To purchase a Maximum Press book, visit your local bookstore,
call (850) 934-4583 or visit *maxpress.com* for online ordering.